CELEBRITY
DIV. ST
BO
STONYBROOK, NEW YORK 11790-0344
(631) 862-8555 - F: (631) 862-0139
CELEBPRO4@AOL.COM
WWW.RICHARDGRUDENS.COM
RICHARDGRUDENSBLOG.BLOGSPOT.COM

Book Design and Editing by Madeline Grudens
ALL RIGHTS RESERVED
PRIOR PERMISSION REQUIRED FOR
REPRODUCTION IN ANY FORM
Library of Congress Control Number in Progress

ISBN: 978-0-9847878-1-4
Printed in the United States of America
King Printing Company Inc.
Lowell, MA 01852

BOOKS BY RICHARD GRUDENS

The Best Damn Trumpet Player
The Song Stars
The Music Men
Jukebox Saturday Night
Snootie Little Cutie-The Connie Haines Story
Jerry Vale-A Singer's Life
The Spirit of Bob Hope
Magic Moments - The Sally Bennett Story
Bing Crosby - Crooner of the Century
Chattanooga Choo-Choo - The Life and Times of the World
Famous Glenn Miller Orchestra
The Italian Crooners Bedside Companion
When Jolson was King
Star*Dust - The Bible of the big Bands
Sinatra Singing
Perfect Harmony

SINGING GROUPS
OF THE
20TH CENTURY

TOGETHER IN

RICHARD GRUDENS

PERFECT HARMONY
Singing Groups of the 20th Century
foreword by Patty Andrews

The Andrews Sisters
Weavers   Beach Boys
Pied Pipers   King Sisters
Modernaires   Supremes
Ink Spots   McGuire Sisters
Mills Brothers   Ames Brothers

PERFECT
HARMONY
Singing Groups
of the 20th Century

Celebrity Profiles Publishing

PERFECT HARMONY

PERFECT **H**ARMONY
Singing Groups
of the 20th Century

The Mills Brothers

2012: If you were to ask anyone under the age of 40 to identify the singing groups of the 20th Century - the Mills Brothers, Boswell's or Andrews Sisters, and you may toss in the Pied Pipers, Modernaires and Ink Spots, you would undoubtedly earn a long, blank, questionable stare of wonderment.

Needless to say, those unknowns each carved out a musical career of great stature over many years, reaching back a few generations during what was known to all as the Big Band or Swing Era, a time when the Great American Songbook was created, and developed from the 1930's through 1970 and a trifle beyond.

For those of you who were fortunate enough to have lived through a part of this era and had witnessed one or more of their performances on the stage, on film, radio and television, and for those of you who didn't, please stand by, you're ON THE AIR... this is their story.

RICHARD GRUDENS $29.95

TABLE OF CONTENTS

HARMONY ROYALTY

EXTRAORDINARY LADIES

SPECIAL FEATURE: HARMONY IN HOLLYWOOD WITH

FOLLOW THE BOYS

WHERE THEY PERFORMED

SPECIALTY MIXED GROUPS

ROYAL DUETS

A CHANCE FOR STARDOM

FINE GROUPS OF DISTINCTION

GOSPEL QUARTETS

THE TOP TEN
BEYOND THE BIG BAND ERA

SPECIALTY GROUPS

SPECIAL FEATURE

I DON'T CARE MUCH ABOUT MUSIC.
WHAT I LIKE IS SOUNDS.

DIZZY GILLESPIE

DEDICATION

THERE IS A TIME FOR DEDICATIONS TOWARDS FRIENDS OF THE PAST & PRESENT.

THE TIME IS NOW!

KATHRYN CROSBY - WHO BELIEVES

FRANKIE DEE - GREATEST PROMOTER

CAMILLE SMITH -FRIEND & PHOTOGRAPHER

GUS YOUNG - PHOTOGRAPHER

BEN GRISAFI - "BROTHER" & BANDLEADER

FRANKIE LAINE - FRIEND FOR LIFE

CHARLTON HESTON - FRIEND AND MENTOR

JERRY VALE - FRIEND AND PARTNER

PATTY ANDREWS - FRIEND AND PARTNER

MAX WIRZ - BROADCASTER AND PARTNER

SYBIL JASON - FELLOW SCRIBBLER &
 WARNERS BEST KID STAR

JOE FRANKLIN - MUSIC FROM THE BEGINNING

CONNIE HAINES - BEAUTIFUL SONGBIRD

JACK ELLSWORTH - INSPIRATION

JOE PARDEE - PROVIDER OF SONGS

VAN ALEXANDER AND LEE HALE - FRIENDS AND PARTNERS

WILL CUPPY- MENTOR OF THE EARLY DAYS

JOHN ZACHARY & LARRY MORRISON OF TOMPKINS DAYS

BOB INCAGLIATO - FRIEND FOR LIFE

ROBERT GRUDENS - RIGHT HAND MAN

ROBERT & RICHARD GRUDZINSKI -TRUE BROTHERS

MADELINE GRUDENS - MY EVERYTHING

FOREWORD

Hi, everyone! My friend of over 30 years, Richard Grudens, who has written a lot about the Andrews Sisters in books and articles over the years, and even wrote my promotional material back in the eighties when I was a single and performing in many venues in California. Richard has put together this book about the singing groups of the 30's, 40's, 50's, 60's and further up through the decades, especially about the era when we sang tunes like "Rum and Coca Cola," Apple Blossom Time," and "Boogie, Woogie Bugle Boy."

Here he lists many of these singing groups in one wonderful book. Richard has always said that his favorite Andrews recording was "Ferryboat Serenade." Well, we, of course loved it too, but there were many to choose from and I hope you, too, have a favorite.

Right now, I am no longer performing, after having lost my wonderful husband, piano accompanist and manager, Wally Wechler. I remain retired in my California home of many years, with cherished memories of him and my sisters. I have great memories of us singing live just about everywhere, and of our appearances in many motion pictures and recordings with singers like the great Bing Crosby.

We had a successful career that spanned the thirties through the nineties, and we're grateful to all the wonderful fans that helped us reach record sales of over 90 million, who attended our seventeen movies, bought tickets to our live performances and tuned in to endless radio show performances. But this book is not only about the Andrews Sisters, but all of the groups who performed before us, and after our success.

Of course our heroes and inspiration were the Boswell Sisters, whom we loved to listen to, and the Mills Brothers with "Glow Worm," and "Paper Doll." Who could forget those great performers who provided their own backup music with their voices.

Please read on about these wonderful and prolific singing groups and learn how and why we were so happy to sing our songs for all of our fans. Don't forget us. We haven't forgotten you.

Love and joy,

Patty Andrews

Northridge, California

OPENING SET

If you are not old enough to remember the original Mills Brothers singing with the Boswell Sisters, interpolated with the rich, lazy baritone voice of an early Bing Crosby on the recording of "Life is Just a Bowl of Cherries," then you missed one of the most harmonic and beautifully arranged 78s ever recorded, with three major stars of the time; the Mills, the Boswell's, and Bing Crosby himself. Or maybe you attended one of the Mills in-person shows in a theater in Chicago, New York, San Diego, or Pittsburgh, or even in your own small town somewhere in middle America. The Mills Brothers played on stages throughout America for many years.

LIFE IS JUST A BOWL OF CHERRIES

Life is Just a Bowl of Cherries
Don't take it serious
Life's too mysterious
You work,
You save
You worry so
But you can't take your dough
When you go, go, go

So keep repeating "It's the berries."
The strongest oak must fall
The sweet things in life
To you were just loaned
So how can you lose
What you've never owned

Life is just a bowl of cherries
So live and laugh
Laugh and love
Live and laugh at it all!

Maybe you recall listening to recordings of the Pied Pipers

backing a young singer named Frank Sinatra, or shoulder-to-shoulder with song star Connie Haines, on a song or two while they were the boy and girl singers with Tommy Dorsey's orchestra. Moving up a bit, you *must* have heard the wonderful harmony at one time or another, perhaps in the film, *Private Buckaroo* of

Kathryn Crosby and Richard Grudens

the greatest of all the girl-singing groups, The Andrews Sisters. Patty, Maxene, and LaVerne, still hold the record of the most charted top ten hits of all time. For the Andrews girls it became big-time for them when they recorded a Yiddish folk song added into English lyrics by Sammy Cahn "Bei Mir Bist du Shön".

Well, this book will transport you back to those fascinating days when the singing groups backed the boy and girl singers in the Big Bands, and when the big bands started to disband, the groups and some spinoff singers from the groups formed a solo act and eventually moved on to perform on their own as headliners. Patty Andrews went solo from her sisters, Andy Williams from his brothers, Jo Stafford from the Pipers, Bing Crosby from the The Rhythm Boys, Mel Tormé from the Meltones, and so on.

Meanwhile, over the years, the group singers managed to build up a mountain of great recordings that remain classics. This is their story. We will take you from the Brox Sisters right up to and including The Supremes with Diana Ross. So, don't touch that dial. Listen to the Mills Brothers, The Andrews Sisters, the McGuire's and Lennon's and all the great harmony groups of yesteryear.

Richard Grudens
Stonybrook, New York

A VOICE FROM ENGLAND

BY ALAN BROWN

The Mills Brothers were my father's favourite group. They have remained one of my favourites for one main reason-they could really harmonize. There were four members in the original group. Their version of "Up a Lazy River" with Count Basie is a classic.

The Ink Spots were another group that had an early influence on my interest in group singing. The voice of Herb Kenny was unique. In the U.K. they were very big. The recordings : "Whispering Grass," "Someone's Rocking My Dreamboat," "We Three" and "Java Jive" were a few that were very popular.

An interesting thing about the Mills and the Ink Spots was that they both recorded for Brunswick, and in those days the label on the recording was made to look like a black and white cinema screen and depicted the artist so that everyone knew what they looked like.

The first group I really thought was special was the Merry Macs, who were also featured in a couple of B movies so we got to see them performing. Their recording of "I'm Forever Blowing Bubbles" remains one of their most played recordings.

There were male groups and mixed groups and female groups, enter the Boswell Sisters, a hard act to follow, but when they disbanded, the lovely Connie Boswell, who later renamed herself Connee, went solo and produced some wonderful sides.

My favorite female group was the King Sisters, but the Andrews Sisters had the greatest impact by themselves and with just about everybody else. To name a few: there were the Clark Sisters, McGuire Sisters, De Marco Sisters, and the De Castro Sisters. Among the mixed groups were the Pied Pipers, the most popular of all the groups, who sang with the big band of the great Tommy Dorsey. They succeeded very well. The Modernaires were a superb group who fronted the Glenn Miller orchestra.

Many groups backed many of the fine solo singers that included Perry Como and Johnny Desmond. Then there were the Starlighters. Just listen to their recording of "Night and Day," just superb! Then the Meltones with Mel Tormé made some great records and when the group split, Mel went solo. Another great musical name emerged from the group, Les Baxter, a future top-notch composer and a fine arranger/conductor.

Among the specialized groups, the Four Freshmen became my favorite group. Not only were they absolutely superb, but also fine musicians. I saw the originals in person and later the New Freshmen, too. The original group could really harmonize. They appeared and sang in the MGM musical *Rich, Young and Pretty* with its stars Vic Damone and Jane Powell.

The group known as the Mary Kaye Trio, consisted of three singers, and have always interested me. They appeared on Perry Como's Kraft Music Hall, and what an accomplished group. Mary, an excellent guitarist and singer, especially on her rendition of "How Does the Wine Taste" from her *Night Life* album, and then from the album *A Night in Las Vegas*, her version of "My Funny Valentine." Mary's brother Norman, had an excellent voice, and the third member of the group was Frankie Ross, who provided good vocals and played accordion. Their sound was instantly recognizable and no group harmonized as well as them. The group unfortunately was virtually unknown in the U.K. I have six of their albums.

The harmonizing of the Hi-Lo's was considered the absolute ultimate, but when they disbanded, two from the group went to Europe and formed a group which took harmonizing to a higher, new level. Gene Puerling and Don Shelton added Bonnie Herman and Les Dresslar and named themselves The Singers Unlimited. They added multitrack recording on thirteen albums, everyone a gem. Everyone wanted to record with them leading them to record with Robert Farnon, Rob McConnell, Pat Williams, Oscar Peterson, and Art Van Damme. The sound of The Singers Unlimited can only be heard on recordings. It shows how, from the early days of the Mills Brothers to present day techniques how good voices in harmony could sound. I wonder what the Mills Brothers would have accomplished with modern technology added to their efforts.

To wrap up, a group called The Group composed of two guys and a girl made some nice albums. Listen to their version of "But Beautiful," "I Hear Music," and "The Second Time Around" --very unique, and could they harmonize. An accomplished group called the Axidentals, who like The Group, never really got the credit they deserved.

What I have listed here about vocal groups is just a personal picture of groups that have come into my life. I know there are many more good ones out there. I hope they brought as much pleasure to their fans as mine have brought to me.

I Can Dream, Can't I

Words by Irving Kahal and Music by Sammy Fain

I can see
No matter how near you'll be
You'll never belong to me
But I can dream, can't I
Can't I pretend
That I'm locked in the bend of your embrace
For dreams are just like wine
And I am drunk with mine

I'm aware
My heart is a sad affair
There's much disillusion there
But I can dream, can't I
Can't I adore you
Although we are oceans apart
I can't make you open your heart
But I can dream, can't I
-- (Reprise) --
I'm aware
My heart is a sad affair
There's much disillusion there
But I can dream, can't I
Can't I adore you
Although we are oceans apart
I can't make you open your heart
But I can dream, can't I

(Dream on, dream on, dream on)
I can dream, can't I

Professor Grudzinski on Harmony

**Richard Grudzinski
Professor, Contemporary Writing
 & Production Department
Berklee College of Music -Boston, MA
Active composer, arranger and pianist**

Harmony is a complex concept and has been discussed and argued over the centuries by musicians and music theorists. There are, in fact, several definitions. But, we will focus on two main definitions/concepts as it pertains to vocal groups.

Berklee College Syncopation Singers

1. Harmony is the simultaneous sounding of the notes or pitches that form a chord or a part thereof. A chord is the simultaneous sounding of several pitches that generally agree with the quality

of that chord. So, in this sense, a chord and harmony are synonymous In other words, the notes that make up a chord are a kind of harmony.

Harmony is derived from the Greek harmonía, meaning "joint, agreement or concord," or as a verb, "to join or fit together." Thus we have the concept of tonal agreement. That is, the constituent notes sound as if they belong together. This is, of course, a relative term.

The simplest harmony would be the simultaneous sounding of at least 2 notes or pitches. Pop singers often sing in what are called 3rds. These are usually tied to a key or tonal center and move up and down with the direction of the melody.

The most basic chord is normally considered to be the triad—three notes. Of course, chords may have more than 3 notes. When a 4th note is added to a chord it is usually called a 7th chord, 5 notes make a 9th chord, 6 would make an 11th or 13th chord.

As chords are usually built on the notes of a scale, they are named for the scale degrees that make up the chord. Chords also have qualities, usually called major or minor. There are naming conventions for types of chords based on how they relate to a given key and or scale.

Major triads are usually named with just the letter of the musical pitch that is called the root of the chord. This is the foundation of the chord and the constituent notes are generally added above the root in intervals called 3rds. Minor chords have an abbreviation of minor (min.) or a —. An interval is the distance between notes, usually measured in steps.

If we look at a piano keyboard, we can picture these intervals easily.

The interval from the first white note on the left (called "F"), to the first black note ("F#") would be called a 1st step, or a 2nd. The interval from "F to the 3rd white note ("A") would be called a 3rd, etc.

Additionally, these intervals have sub-names or qualities such as major or minor 2nds, 3rds, perfect 4ths, etc. But, this is the stuff of music theory. The more inquisitive reader can easily find out more about music theory on-line, from books, or from a teacher.

So, if the first melody note is "F", the simplest harmony note might be "A". Two singers could thus harmonize a melody in this way—singing in thirds as the melody rises and falls.

So, a triad would be the root ("F), the 3rd note of the scale ("A") and the 5th note of the scale ("C")—the 5th note from the left in our keyboard above. Thus, when we add a 4th note to the chord by adding the 7th note of the scale (and the 7th note from the left—"E" or the black note just to the left ("Eb"), we call that a 7th chord, etc.

2. A harmonic progression is a series of chords that flow from one to another according to certain musical rules that help to define a tonality or key. Chord progressions generally are related to a key and commonly involve a tension and release pattern. That is, we perceive chords as having qualities that produce tension and repose (release)—a sort of musical journey or a story that has a beginning, middle, and an end, called a resolution. Again, all of this is relative.

Keys or tonal centers usually are either major or minor and both keys will have both major and minor chords within them. Keys can be considered a kind of gravity. The notes and chords of a given key are pulled away from and towards the center much like physical gravity. What goes up, must eventually come down, or a sense of tension and release.

Popular songs usually contain a melody, chords (often called "changes" or "chord changes" because the type and quality of the chords within a song change) and, of course, lyrics.

Almost all Western music (classical and popular) have melodies and chord changes. They just handle them differently. Music from the near and far East, often only contain melodies and not much in the way of harmony—the music of Northern India, for example.

Vocal music has been around for as long as humans discovered that they could sing as well as speak. The earliest known (notated) forms of vocal singing are from the middle ages, beginning with plainchant (Gregorian Chant), organum, motets and Madrigals.

Vocal singing, in the form of choirs—both secular and religious—has continued up to the present day.

In popular vocal group type singing, we find a few different approaches or styles.

In Barbershop style singing, the group normally consists of 4 singers, called a quartet. The style of music they perform is usually simple, folk-based songs sung *a cappella*—without instrumental accompaniment. The familiar refrain "Sweet Adeline" is perhaps one of the most famous Barbershop pieces known.

The quality of the voices (assuming all men) would be a first and 2nd tenor, a baritone and bass. The 2nd tenor normally sings the melody, the first tenor harmonizes a 3rd above the melody, the bass sings the root and the baritone fills in the remaining notes of the chord (called "chord tones").

All of the singers in a Barbershop quartet sing at the same time, harmonizing the melody. This style is called homophonic. The result is that all of the melody notes become chords. The Mills Brothers started out in this fashion.

A second approach is the group that features a lead singer (who sings the lead or melody), while the others sing background parts, often oohs and aahs or a portion of the lyric. They might use this approach for an entire song, or move to a homophonic texture for the refrain. The Ink Spots often used this approach.

The 3rd and most often used approach during the 40's and into the 50's was the homophonic texture, but not in the Barbershop fashion. These groups took a lesson from the big bands (of which some of the groups were a part) and harmonized the melody like a saxophone section—the melody on top, with the supporting harmonies below. The Andrews Sisters excelled at this style.

All of these groups and approaches differed from the Barbershop style in that they had instrumental accompaniment, and featured the lead or melody on top (the highest part), either with background parts or in a homophonic (chordal) texture.

This vocal style has continued and developed to the present day in the form of groups such as: Lambert, Hendricks and Ross, The Manhattan Transfer, Take Six, as many others.

At the Berklee College of Music, where I teach, we have a resident jazz vocal group known as Syncopation. They continue the proud tradition of vocal group singing.

Professor Richard Grudzinski

MEMORIES OF HARMONY DAYS

BY FRANK E. DEE

How can any one of us who enjoyed good music recorded by the sensational singing groups of the 30's, 40's, and 50's ever forget them. We were blessed to have had The Mills Brothers, The Andrews Sisters, The McGuire Sisters, The Ink Spots, and dozens more. The list of Harmony singing groups go on ad-infinitum.

I remember them quite well. Please allow me to remind you that during that era, jukeboxes were cranking out all those great songs from harmony trios, and quartets such as The Hilltoppers, The Four Lads, The Four Aces, The Ames Brothers, The Four Freshmen, and don't forget the female groups: The Fontane Sisters (backing up Perry Como's recordings) The Andrews Sisters, charting hit after hit, The De Castro Sisters, The Chordettes, The King Sisters, and the Boswell Sisters. I recall the singing groups became very popular in the 1950's, and as a teenager, I danced to their hit songs at popular record hops hosted by local, in my case, Boston radio "disc jockeys."

INTERVIEWING PEOPLE ON THE STREETS

As director of GMMY internet radio, when I was interviewing seniors on the streets or in stores they were quick to recall. One eighty -five year old gentle-man remembers; "These talented singing groups and quartets serenaded us during those days, and even into the 1950's.

"Those singing groups brought so much comfort and joy into our lives at a time when good music was needed and appreciated."
An 80-year-old lovely lady reminisced about her youthful days growing up in Los Angeles: "As a young girl, I loved the singing groups. My brother and I would harmonize together to the those very same songs."

"I Can Dream Can't I"

While visiting a coffee shop where seniors congregated daily, I asked three mature ladies if they remembered The Andrews Sisters singing one of their hit songs, "I Can Dream Can't I." One enthused lady replied, "You've got to be kidding! How can anyone ever forget such a beautiful song, sung by my favorite Andrews girls." The Andrews Sisters and Gordon Jenkins' orchestra recorded that tune on July 15, 1949. The recordings reached the Billboard Magazine charts on September 16, 1949 and lasted 27 weeks.

One gentleman said he had the original 78 rpm Decca recording: "We had that song in our collection and it was played at our wedding in May 17, 1952. How can anyone at the age of 88 not know the work of the Andrews Sisters?"

Someone once said : "Nostalgia may be defined as a longing for the past, which can be strongly influenced by music and memory," and may I add- make no mistake, we lived in an era when good singers and big bands were a way of life, and this was the type of music we all loved.

The incredible Hilltoppers brought many a tear to younger teens with their first hit song "Trying." This song was a sure tearjerker, especially if you had been stood up by your date. This song had the unmistakable romantic power to lure couples directly to the dance floor. It was hugging set to music.

"Trying," was being played over and over on local radio stations. One of the disc jockeys sent a copy to a fledgling record label, Dot Records, that had been formed in Gallatin, Tennessee, by Randy Wood. The song took off nationally and landed in the top ten. The Hilltoppers had succeeded. They continued to record and became a very popular singing act. When appearing on the Ed Sullivan show they dressed in their signature beanies and college sweaters. The group had 18 hit songs from 1952 to 1957, the biggest of which was Gordon Jenkins and Johnny Mercer's "P.S. I Love You." Others were "Only You" (And You Alone) in 1955, and "Marianne" in 1957.

The 1950's was dominated by singing acts such as the Four

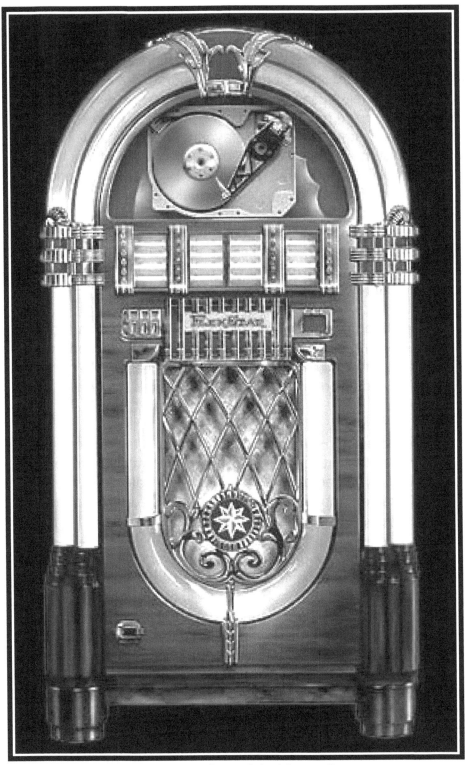

"Put another nickel in......"

Aces, The Ames Brothers, The Four Lads, The Four Freshmen, The Crew Cuts, The Hi-Lo's, and The Gaylords. And, who could forget The Chordettes who sent every teenage into a musical spin with their 1950's hits "Mr. Sandman" and "Lollipop."

The McGuire Sisters were also streaming out hit after hit, after they replaced the Chordettes on the Arthur Godfrey show. Then the fabulous De Castro Sisters came along, educating us with their big hit "Teach Me Tonight." In the latter half of the 1950's, The Four Preps took us on a sea voyage. They were sailing along with their big hit "26 Miles."

GMMY Radio Host Frank E. Dee

In those days, sales of 78's and 45's records, cassettes and 8 track tapes were selling well to both teenagers and adults. New cars featured cassette and 8 track players. When you pulled up to a light, you could hear a tune loudly playing in the car next to you. What a terrific era of great music.

Many Radio Stations would allow teens and adults to call in to dedicate their favorite song to friends, songs sung by their favorite groups or soloists. The Ames Brothers became the leading group for many dedications. The Ames Brothers were the first artists to record for Decca subsidiary, Coral Records where they scored their first hit songs "Sentimental Me" and "Rag Mop." Deejays introduced the Ames Brothers as "The Brothers Ames." They captivated the 1950's with hit after hit. Jukeboxes cranked out their records "Auf Wieder-sehn, Sweetheart," "Can Anyone Explain?" and "You, You, You." All winners.

A 1950's, fan could afford to see their favorite singing groups perform in local night clubs. For a mere $2.50 you could catch a floor show and enjoy a meal. Of course, the prices were much lower then.

Thanks to these recordings, we will always be able to hear our favorite singing groups perform for us over and over again.

HARMONY ROYALTY
THE SINGING GROUPS

The Rhythm Boys
Bing and Rinker-formerly the Musicaladers

Paul Whiteman, leader of the King of Jazz Orchestra: "I want to introduce two young fellers who have joined our great band. I picked them up in an ice cream parlor in a little town called Walla Walla, and I brought them here to perform for you. (Big jovial smile). They were too good for Walla Walla. Meet-Crosby and Rinker." (That's the way they billed themselves, back in 1926, before those two boys and a piano were singing songs their own way.)

Al Rinker's sister was America's first big band singer, Mildred Bailey. She encouraged her brother and his friend Bing to go North from Spokane, Washington, where they lived, to work their magic in Los Angeles where they met Whiteman.

L-R Bing Crosby, Al Rinker and Harry Barris

"We played anywhere we could for any price. We took whatever was offered, that's how badly we wanted bookings," said Bing," Anyway, we didn't need much money to get by in those days." They were making $150.00 a week.

Rinker and Crosby recorded what became his very first recording, Walter Donaldson's "I've Got the Girl," on October 18, 1926.

In New York ,while traveling with the Whiteman band, the two were benched because they could not be heard, while appearing at the New York Paramount. While waiting for their next gig with the band, "we ran into a feller named Harry Barris," said Bing, "a brash pianist and composer who also sang. "We convinced him to join up with us. He did and we renamed ourselves Paul Whiteman's Rhythm Boys." They were now a well balanced act, Whiteman was enthralled and accepted the freshly formed trio, featuring them in every show.

L-R, Harry Barris, Bing Crosby and Al Rinker

Some of the orchestra's stellar members were the great jazz arranger Bill Challis, whom I knew in his later years, sax player Frank [Tram] Trumbauer; trombonist and clarinetist Tommy and Jimmy Dorsey; trombonist Glenn Miller; arranger Ferde Grofe; the Teagarden brothers trombonist Jack, and trumpeter Charlie; cornetist Leon "Bix" Beiderbecke; guitarist Eddie Lang; and pianist/arranger Lenny Hayton, all future music legends to back the new trio.

One of their successful tunes was "Mississippi Mud."

MISSISSIPPI MUD
JIMMY CAVANAUGH & HARRY BARRIS

When the sun goes down, the tide goes out
The people gather 'round and they all begin to shout,
Hey! Hey! Uncle Dud,
It's a treat to beat your feet on the Mississippi mud
What a dance do they do
Lordy how I'm tellin' you
They don't need no band
They keep time by clappin' their hand
Just as happy as a cow chewin' on a cud
When the people beat their feet on the Mississippi mud.

Bing appeared in the film *The King of Jazz* with the Rhythm Boys and a pre-Andrews Sisters singing group, the Brox Sisters, performing Barris' bright and tuneful ditty "A Bench in the Park."

After the appearance in the film with Whiteman, the boys embarked on their own. Harry Barris had written "I Surrender, Dear," a song perfectly suited for Crosby that would catapult him into the big time as he interspersed his solo ballads with the bright, jazzy patter of the trio. Barris also composed "So the Bluebirds and the Blackbirds Got Together," a ditty that left audiences fractured.

After some work at the Montmartre Café in Los Angeles, their new agent Leonard Goldstein booked them into the famous Cocoanut Grove, where the creme-de-la-creme of celebrities gathered. The house bandleader, Gus Arnheim, signed the boys to perform. The shows from the Grove would broadcast two hours each night, spreading the boys musical fame north to radio outlets from Tacoma and Portland, Washington, and were able to stretch into some Midwest cities. The band's personnel included Shirley Ross, who would later sing a duet with Bob Hope entitled "Thanks for the Memory" in

L-R Harry Barris, Bing Crosby, Al Rinker

the film *The Big Broadcast of 1938*, and singers Andy Russell, Russ Columbo, and the lovely Loyce Whiteman, who later married Harry Barris.

Besides "I Surrender, Dear," Barris composed another of Bing's most successful songs, "Wrap Your Troubles in Dreams," when they performed at the Grove. Both songs were pivotal to Bing's career. Singers who appeared at the famous Cocoanut Grove were, in those days, a sure stepping stone to success while Arnheim managed the very popular nightclub.

Bing met his first wife, Dixie Lee, one night at the Grove. Dixie was an film actress and Bing fell head-over-heels in love with her and they married on September 29, 1930.

Bing: "I know her family thought I was just marrying Dixie to attach myself to her career, because of who she was. But I was just a crooner working down there at the Grove in L.A. with the Rhythm Boys and had no hope or aspirations other than that."

A momentous reunion - Bing Crosby (L) with the Rhythm Boys and Paul Whiteman at the piano

The rest, as they say, is history.

THE HOBOKEN FOUR

Once known as The Three Flashes, America's Best Known and most formidable singing artist, Frank Sinatra and his three singing partners, James Petrozelli, Pat Principle, and Frank Tamburro, auditioned for the famous radio show *The Major Bowes Original Amateur Hour* in 1935. That's where their name was changed to The Hoboken Four by the Major. The boys went on to win the contest and toured with Bowes. Sinatra was nineteen years old. The song they chose was "Shine," after the Bing Crosby version that achieved so much success recording it with the famed singing group, The Mills Brothers. Frank was featured on the Bing Crosby part of the song.

So how did it all start?

Sinatra's first radio appearance in 1935 on the
Major Bowes Amateur Hour with the Hoboken Four

SHINE

W. Cecil Mack, L. Lou Brown, M. Ford Dabney

Just because my hair is curly
Just because my teeth are pearly
just because I always wear a smile
Like to dress up
In the latest style
Cause I'm glad I'm livin'
I take my trouble all with a smile
Just because my color's shady
That the difference maybe
Why they call me Shine

Shine away your bluesies
Why don't you shine
Start with your shoesies
Shine the place up
Make it look like new
Shine your face up
I wanna see you wear a smile or two
Why don't you shine
your these and thosies
You'll find everything will turn out fine
Folks will shine up to you
Everybody's gonna howdy, howdy do ya
You'll make the whole world shine.

The Three Flashes were performing at the Rustic Cabin in New Jersey. Frank invited himself into the singing group. They took him in because he had a car and they didn't. Frank and his Chrysler were the wheels they needed to get them around the town of Hoboken, New Jersey.

When they performed on the *Major Bowes Hour* he introduced them as "singing and dancing fools," and when someone offstage asked why he called them by that sobriquet, he replied,"I guess because they seem so happy all the time whether singing or just sitting, especially Sinatra."

During the six month tour the other members became jealous of Sinatra because he was receiving most of the attention. The group broke up after the tour during which time the others would taunt him mercilessly.

Frank sang with the Pied Pipers when he was with Tommy Dorsey and fellow band singer Connie Haines. But only Frank Sinatra went on to great singing success. But, I think you knew that was coming.

THE MILLS BROTHERS AND I

BY DANIEL R. CLEMSON

Most musicologists will agree: The internationally acclaimed Mills Brothers were the greatest vocal group of the 20th Century. These family singers set the style and pattern in their field through much of the 1900s.

I had the good fortune of knowing the Mills boys from a different perspective. My family and theirs shared the same ancestral home in Central Pennsylvania: Historic Bellefonte, where I grew up with their uncles, aunts and cousins. Their father who later became a member of the vocal group, was born there.

John H. Mills and his wife moved to Piqua in Western Ohio, where the famed quartet of brothers was born. Because of the aboli-

Herbert , Don, Harry and John - 1932 Columbia Records

tionist tendencies of the local Quakers, most of the Bellefonte citizenry had a different mindset on racial understanding. Granted it was not perfect, but the town was among the nation's integration leaders in public education, public burial grounds, U. S. Colored Troops recognition, among other initiatives.

John Mills' father, William H. Mills, owned the longest operated family business at that time-the town's most popular barbershop for sixty years. It also gave William Mills the opportunity to "bend the ears" of the community's leading white fathers. In that position, he soon became the leader of the town's black community. And he was the genesis of the family's musical gift, singing as basso for the local Jubilee Singers.

It is important to present some of Bellefonte's African American history in order to more fully appreciate the interracial attitude of many of its citizens. This allowed John H. Mills and other black pupils to attend integrated classes, be a member of the school's first football team and play in

Dan Clemson

Brouse's barn with the white boys in the neighborhood. It was in that barn that John earned his lifelong nickname. He had lost his hat in a hay stack. When found, it was bent out of shape. His brother Quinn suggested it looked like Pike's Peak. Thus John was called Pike. In later life when singing with his world-traveling sons and someone in the audience yelled "Pike," John knew it was a Bellefonte voice.

The brothers' favorite aunt was Harriet Mills. When they came to town in the 1930s, the quartet always visited Aunt Hat. There they rehearsed, using her "Cabinet Grand" from Weser Bros. in New York. A decade later I served as Aunt Hat's paper boy. In the 1980s, the family "adopted" me as a cousin. They eventually would present me with the treasured family piano. It proudly stands in my entertainment room-missing ivories and all.

The brothers: John C., Herbert, Harry and Donald, gained an audience at Radio Station WLW, Cincinnati, in 1925. The brothers were hired and soon had their own program. They immediately told their dad, who had returned to Bellefonte to operate the barbershop for his ailing father. Having no radio, John H. visited the nearby Hood's Billiards Hall and asked the owner if he could listen to his sons' first radio broadcast.

Mr. Hood readily complied. I never had the opportunity to see the first two compositions of the Mills quartet in concert. The only professional appearance in Bellefonte by the father and sons was at the Plaza Theatre in 1938-a two-day performance, plus a parade through town in their honor and a special banquet at a local hostelry. The family performers as a group last visited relatives there in 1949. My only opportunity to see Bellefonte's pride and joy sing with his sons was in 1952. I was at Ogden Air Force Base in Utah for a Force wrestling tournament. (I won my weight class!) While there paid a visit to downtown Salt Lake City, and walked past a theater featuring The Mills Brothers that night. This was a chance in a lifetime! I dug deep into my wallet, but could not come up with enough money to cover the price of admission-let alone dinner. I considered groveling before the theater manager in my Air Force blues, but just couldn't bring myself to do that.

Finally, I had an chance to see The Mills Brothers trio (Herb, Harry and Don) up front and personal in 1978. They were appearing at the Holiday House in Monroeville, near Pittsburgh, Western Pennsylvania's last supper club. A member of my staff in the PA Auditor General Department had arranged for a table down front. Finally, I got to hear the world's greatest singers in person. At intermission,

PRESENTS NEXT WEEK

AMERICA'S
MOST SENSATIONAL
SINGING ATTRACTION

THE MILLS BROS.

the staffer took me backstage to meet the guys. He introduced me as "Dan Clemson of Bellefonte, PA." Not one word from the trio. Taken aback, the staffer once again presented me to the group. This time, Don replied, "We're not from Bellefonte!"

This was a defensive retort the brothers had developed after their father joined them in 1936. When reporters learned he was from Bellefonte, they assumed the boys were born there, too. So it got to be a distraction. I assured them that I knew they were born in Piqua,

wn up with their relatives, including Aunt Hat. Things
and we had a nice conversation.

blind and ailing, recalled the trout stream there where
ne nad fished. I told him that was Spring Creek. Don's son Alan was
traveling with the group. He offered to take my photo with the famed
family. It has been a cherished part of my Mills memorabilia ever
since.

Don and I became good friends over the final years of his life.
The slot of historian was an unfilled post. Probably because they
were quiet, unassuming and gracious-not braggadocio. And also perfect gentleman. I gradually assumed the role of artists' historian and
family genealogist. Charlie Horner of New Jersey, a leading expert on
black vocal group harmony, once tabbed me as "The world's leading
authority on The Mills Brothers." I can only hope that he is correct.

A reprise of The Mills Brothers harmony still survives. John H.
Mills II and his father continued to perform after the original brothers
finally hung it up in 1982, after 57 years of close harmony. Donald
and son John entertained as a duo until Don's death in 1999. John
II-a fourth-generation family performer-still offers the Mills sounds,
now with Elmer Hopper, former 20-year singer with the popular Platters.

John made several return performances in his ancestral home,
with his father as well as Elmer. On two visits they were the high-
light of International Mills Brothers Society conventions. The society,
which functioned for ten years, was a major force in the vocal group
gaining a 1998 Grammy Award from the National Academy of Recording Arts and Sciences. It took two years of letter-writing to finally
convince NARAS that The Mills Brothers truly were the greatest vocal
group of the 20th Century.

Young John is gradually falling in love with Bellefonte. Regarding his last performance there in April 2011, he wrote, "The trip back
to Bellefonte was joyful beyond words, as it meant so much more
than just a job." The crowds are getting older-and smaller-but the duo
persists in the challenge to preserve the beautiful music of the past.
God bless them.

Richard Grudens' Report on the Mills Brothers

On April 29, 1998, Donald Mills had celebrated his 83rd birthday and his 74th year as an entertainer. For the previous three years he had served as patriarch of the Mills family in America. In February, 1998 The Mills Brothers were honored with a Grammy Lifetime Achievement Award. What a deserved, uplifting honor for this amazing man and his wonderful brothers!

In January of 1998, I received an encouraging word from Donald Mills' son, John: "I have received your request to interview my father with regards to your book. He will be happy to talk to you next week. Best Wishes." signed: John H. Mills,II. This was a break and a privilege for me since Donald Mills had avoided personal interviews in the past few years. The Four Boys and a Kazoo (a popular tinny, musical toy) started their career at the Mays Opera House in Piqua, Ohio, an event that would alter their musical style and catapult them to fame as a quartet. Stage fright before a large audience and the fact that young John had forgotten the all-important kazoo, the desperate trouper cupped his hands over his mouth and to the surprise of everyone produced sounds far better than that of the tinny kazoo, causing a sensation. What a revelation- what a sound! What an idea!

By now the boys, John-bass, Herbert- tenor, Harry - baritone, and Donald- lead -- added realistic imitations of various musical instruments to their barbershop harmonies. Mastery of the sounds of first, second, and third trumpet, combined with the accompaniment of a $6.25 mail-order guitar played by John, would soon earn them the title of the "human orchestra."

The boys, now with matured voices, impressed programmers at radio station WLW, Cincinnati, and they were subsequently hired. Within a year, they left and with the help of Duke Ellington and Seger Ellis (the Mills longtime manager), made their way to New York City in 1929, auditioned for CBS radio, and signed a three-year contract with a young, fledging radio executive named William S. Paley. They went from $140.00 a week to $3,250.00 thanks to their radio show and a 14 week engagement at the Palace Theater, where they shared the bill with Bing Crosby, establishing one of the fastest climbs in show business.

Their first recording with Brunswick, "Tiger Rag" and "Nobody's Sweetheart," reached the top of the charts, becoming the first million-selling record ever by a vocal group. Their unique sound caught the attention of the movie studios, and in 1932 they appeared with Bing Crosby in his first starring film,

Herbert, Harry and Don - 1960

The Big Broadcast, singing "Hold That Tiger." The film also featured a now legendary cast of greats: George Burns and Gracie Allen, Kate Smith, Cab Calloway, The Boswell Sisters, and The Street Singer-- Arthur Tracy. It was the first of their 14 feature film appearances: "We did a lot of cartoons too, you know, the bouncing ball films where we sang the lyrics and everybody in the audience sang along," Donald explained, "It was wonderful going from cartoon to The Mills Brothers."

The boys vocalized their way through Twenty Million Sweethearts in 1934, Broadway Gondolier in 1935 (with Gary Cooper), Reveille with Beverly in 1943, and When You're Smiling in 1950. Interesting sidelight: Brunswick printed a disclaimer on every Mills Brothers recording: "No musical instruments or mechanical devices were used on this recording other than the guitar," because their special sounds were often mistaken for the real thing.

"Shine," with Bing, reached number one in January 1932, the first of a string of Top 10 tunes that year. "'Good-bye Blues,' our theme from the start, was finally recorded in 1932," said Don, "The flipside was "Rockin Chair" with Harry doing a talking bass bridge and me repeating the lyrics on the afterbeat." In 1933, the Mills and Bing Crosby recorded "My Honey's Lovin'

Charting The Mills Brothers

Recordings by The Mills Brothers have appeared on nearly every major chart over a forty-year period, from 1931 through 1970. The group's most popular hits include

1931 "Tiger Rag," "Nobody's Sweetheart"
1932 "Dinah" and "Shine" with Bing Crosby, "You Rascal, You," "I Heard," "Good-Bye, Blues," "Rockin' Chair," "St. Louis Blues," "Bugle Call Rag," "Sweet Sue, Just You"
1934 "Swing It, Sister," "Sleepy Head"
1937 "Darling Nelly Gray"
1938 "Sixty Seconds Got Together," "Sweet Adeline"
1939 "You Tell Me Your Dream, I'll Tell You Mine," "Basin Street Blues"
1940 "Old Black Joe"
1943 "Paper Doll," "I'll Be Around"
1944 "You Always Hurt The One You Love," "Till Then"
1945 "I Wish," "Put Another Chair At The Table"
1946 "I Don't Know Enough About You," "I Guess I'll Get The Papers (And Go Home)"
1947 "Across The Alley From The Alamo," "When You Were Sweet Sixteen"
1948 "Gloria," "Manana"
1949 "I Love You So Much It Hurts," "Someday You'll Want Me To Want You"
1950 "Daddy's Little Girl"
1951 "Nevertheless"
1952 "Be My Life's Companion," "The Glow-Worm," "Lazy River"
1953 "Say 'Si Si'"
1954 "The Jones Boy"
1955 "Suddenly There's A Valley," "Opus One"
1956 "Standing On The Corner"
1957 "Queen Of The Senior Prom"
1958 "Get A Job"
1959 "Yellow Bird"
1968 "Cab Driver," "My Shy Violet"
1970 "It Ain't No Big Thing"

Arms" on January 26th. The musical sounds reproduced by those wonderful guys are astounding. It is my preferred Mills Brothers/Bing Crosby recording, also featuring Bunny Berigan on trumpet, Tommy Dorsey on trombone, and Eddie Lang on guitar at the beginning and close of the record. What a collection of talent on one recording.

The Mills Brothers performed with many big bands: "Diga Diga Do" with the great Duke Ellington, "Doin the Low-Down" with the wild Cab Calloway, and "In the Shade of the Old Apple Tree" with jazz master Louis Armstrong. "We exhibited our drive and even dared to emulate instruments." Don recalled.

"In 1934, we played London's Palladium and were even invited to appear before King George V and Queen Mary, the first Command Performance ever by black artists. I guess we were the Beatles of the 1930s. Harry later loved to tell our audiences that anecdote."

After the death of young John from a lung ailment, the boy's father took his place, literally saving the group from disbanding. He remained rhythmic bass for the next twenty years. The Mills Brothers' career spanned the world, and in 1942 they unearthed an old, unknown song called "Paper Doll."

"When we first heard the song, we didn't like it. So, we worked on it, came up with a new concept and recorded it," Donald remembered, "It was a turning point for us." The recording remained number one for 30 weeks, including 12 weeks on Your Hit Parade radio program.

Other great hits during this period include "Up a Lazy River," "You Always Hurt the One You Love," "Till Then" and with new lyrics by Johnny Mercer, "Glow-Worm." When their father retired in 1956, they carried on as a trio, continuing on the club circuit and recording sessions. On Dot Records, they recorded "Get a Job" and "Cab Driver" in 1968.

"By 1981, the boys disbanded after 56 fruitful years. Harry passed away in 1982 and Herbert in 1989. Don and his son, John Hutchinson II, continued on after a brief respite, becoming the fourth generation of Mills family performers. The duo's sounds have always featured a repertory of old Mills Brothers favorites, and are strikingly similar to that of the former trio. But, they would never add a non-family member. We considered that way back in 1936 when our brother passed away," Don added, "We tried different guys and it never worked. So, we decided against it, and our father ended up joining us. There are natural harmonies in family groups, a special blend. There are only two of us now, but young John and I are accorded the same standing ovations that the full group received throughout the decades. We flip-flop the harmony parts, just as we used to do, and take turns singing lead."

Henry Miller, then president of General Artists Corporation, has been faithfully booking Mills engagements all over the world for over 50 years. "It's remarkable how the two men achieve the same harmony and beat the original group had," he told me. So, how do they do it? "The simplicity of the songs that we sing makes the audience tap their feet and clap their hands," said Don, "Lyrics you can understand, melodies that are melodic, does it just fine." Of course, you have to add the inimitable Mills' skills. No one knows how long Donald will continue to sing: "It's been a long, long road. I thought I would be retired by now. But, I enjoy singing; this is my life," Don said to me then, "And I have my son to work with, so everything's going to be just fine."

"The Mills Brothers were the genesis of modern-day black close harmony singing," said Dan Clemson, "They were preceded by a handful of black groups in the style of the traditional camp meeting shouts. The Mills raised the black vocal group from one of novelty status to a commercially accepted form. This singularly unique family fed the dreams of younger black artists and showed them they could reach for the stars.....and touch them. The later accession of Motown groups proves that to be true.

As I write this piece John and Elmer utilize the original, priceless charts of the Mills discography in their performances with such tunes as "Cab Driver," "Glow Worm." "Lazy River." "Yellow Bird." "Basin Street Blues," "Opus One," and "Paper Doll," my own favorite. The mystique remains.

"Paper Doll," their signature song, sold over six million copies in its first release and was just one of more than 2000 recordings, including 36 hits.

The Mills Brothers are certainly the King of all the male singing groups by any measure. The amount of records sold are uncountable.

PAPER DOLL
JOHNNY MACK

I'm gonna buy a Paper Doll that I can call my own
A doll that other fellows cannot steal
And then the flirty, flirty guys with their flirty, flirty eyes
Will have to flirt with dollies that are real
When I come home at night she will be waiting
She'll be the truest doll in all this world
I'd rather have a Paper Doll to call my own
Than have a fickle-minded real live girl
I guess I had a million dolls or more
I guess I've played the doll game o'er and o'er
I just quarrelled with Sue, that's why I'm blue
She's gone away and left me just like all dolls do
I'll tell you boys, it's tough to be alone
And it's tough to love a doll that's not your own
I'm through with all of them
I'll never ball again
Say boy, whatcha gonna do?
I'm gonna buy a Paper Doll that I can call my own
A doll that other fellows cannot steal
And then the flirty, flirty guys with their flirty, flirty eyes
Will have to flirt with dollies that are real
When I come home at night she will be waiting
She'll be the truest doll in all this world
I'd rather have a Paper Doll to call my own
Than have a fickle-minded real live girl

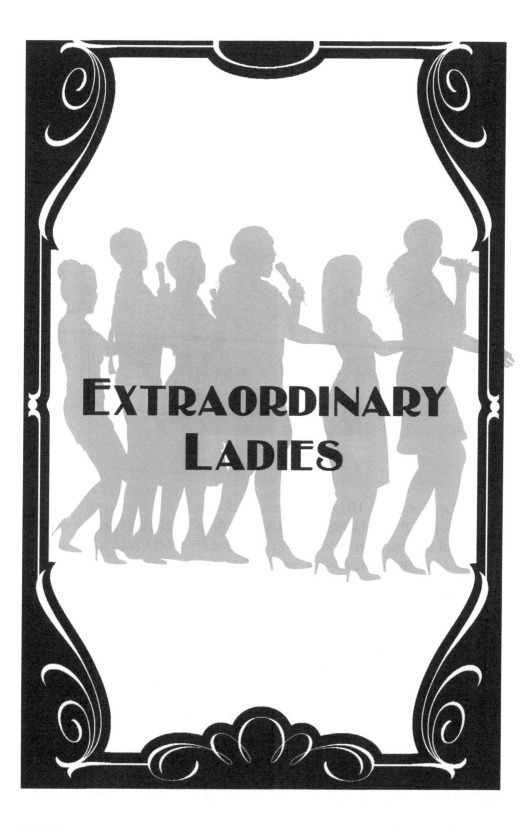

EXTRAORDINARY LADIES

THE ANDREWS SISTERS

IT'S APPLE BLOSSOM TIME IN MINNEAPOLIS

LaVerne, Patty, Maxene

On February 16, 2012, Patty Andrews, a truly great girl singer of the 1940s, the girl who helped shape American music at the end of the Great Depression, and during the second World War with her two sisters, Maxine and LaVerne, will be 94 years young.

Patty and I have been friends for many years ever since our first interview in the early eighties which led to a magazine article about Patty and her sisters, the ultra-famed Andrews Sisters. She utilized the article for presenting her then single act in and around Los Angeles, California.

I have always been in love with the Andrews Sisters. Ever since I first heard heard Patty and her sisters vocalize "Bei Mir Bist Du Schoen" (It Means That You're Grand or Pretty). The song is an old Yiddish song with English words added by songwriters Sammy Cahn and Saul Chaplin. It became the beginning of my long-running affection for the three singing and swinging gals from Minneapolis. The Andrews girls from Minneapolis became personal entertainers for many a serviceman during the war years with their mega-hits "Rumors are Flying," "I'll Be with You in Apple Blossom Time," and "Rum and Coca Cola."

By her own description, Patty is a very happy and contented retired vocalist living in a beautiful, Tudor-style house near Encino, California with her husband and manager Wally Weschler. After many happy years together, Patty lost her beloved Wally in the fall of 2010. Patty had just completed writing the foreword for this book. Looking back a few years: I had dialed the telephone to a number given to me by my friend, musical director and songwriter, Lee Hale: "Hello, who is this?

"Hi, said I," and I identified myself, then inquired "is this the office of Wally Weschler, manager of the Andrews Sisters? "Why, Yes!" "Well, I'm actually looking for Patty Andrews," I inquired. "It's me...it's Patty!" was the bubbling reply. "Patty Andrews?" I repeated in disbelief and relief.

Maxene, Patty, LaVerne

"Yeah!" she shouted gleefully over the phone wires spanning three-thousand miles from her home in Northridge, California, to me in New York.

Well, it just was too easy. I had found one of my musical heroes. Patty and I talked for two hours about her then current appearances with the Big Bands of Tex Beneke (once Glenn Miller's favorite sax player who doubled as band vocalist on songs like "Chattanooga Choo Choo"), Larry Elgart's band and the Harry James orchestra, at

Patty, Maxene, Frank Sinatra and LaVerne

venues like the Hollywood Palladium. Her concerts consisted of new and refreshing popular songs of the day, but she always closed appearances with some of the vintage, sensational Andrews Sisters' tunes of earlier days.

Speaking of those early days, when they were kids attending dancing school, the three girls began mimicking the popular Boswell Sisters. They entered the Kiddy Reviews during the summer months on the Orpheum Theater Circuit in Minneapolis. One of the headliners on the show invited the girls to become a permanent part of his touring show. They performed five shows a day sandwiched between movie showings. They gleefully copied the Boswell's charts but added some extra zest.

LaVerne, Bing Crosby, Patty, and Maxene

"When you are young, there is always someone you look up to," Patty told me, "so we did what they did and it helped launch our career." The girls sang tunes like "Shuffle Off to Buffalo," "When I Take My Sugar to Tea," and "I Found a Million Dollar Baby in a Five and Ten Cents Store."

Patty, Glenn Miller, LaVerne, Maxene

Patty sang the lead and solos, Maxene the high harmony, and LaVerne took the third part, even though they had no formal training. "It wasn't until many years later-after serious problems with laryngitis --I finally had to take singing lessons to learn how to properly breathe in order to prevent damage to my vocal chords," Patty explained.

"We would work all day until we perfected new songs in our own bouncier style. It was then we realized we had something special to offer." And offer it they did, joining up with a big band, they began singing on the radio in New York City with Billy Swanson's band from the popular Hotel Edison. It was to be their big break, as Dave Kapp, Vice President of Decca Records, heard them on his car radio and rushed to the hotel to meet them. Contracts were signed the following day.

Decca had them record consistently with all the greats that included Bing Crosby, Al Jolson, Dick Haymes, Bob Crosby, Woody Herman, Jimmy Dorsey, and every known big band, over a seventeen year triumphant run. Jack Kapp, President of Decca, took them in hand and guided them to great success as he did for Bing Crosby and many others.

Jack Kapp was the creative genius behind the Decca label: "He was young and aggressive and like a father to us young girls. He was Dave's older brother and President of the company. He also helped us get into the movies with the Ritz Brothers, Abbott and Costello, and with Bob Hope and Bing Crosby."

The movies were *The Road to Utopia*, *Buck Privates*, *Argentine Nights*, *Follow the Boys*, *Stage Door Canteen*, and *In the Navy*, and nine others. Dave Kapp would select their movie songs: "Aurora," " Yes, My Darling Daughter," and "Daddy," became ours to sing in the movie and on records."

Patty, Lou Costello, LaVerne, Bud Abbott, Maxene

It was a constant barrage of wonderful recordings that were rhythmic, bouncy,and gutsy--- including that '40s expression ---jivey. "I'll Be with You in Apple Blossom Time," a 1938 Decca Record with Vic Schoen and his Orchestra and a cornet solo by Bobby Hackett, "The Boogie, Woogie, Bugle Boy from Company 'B'," "Don't Sit Under the Apple Tree," "Beer Barrel Polka," "Pistol Packin' Mama," (the later two with Bing.) "Joseph, Joseph," "Hold Tight," "South America, Take It Away" and "Ciribiribin," "Billy Boy," Well, All Right,"and "Ferryboat Serenade." I reminded Patty that Ferryboat was my personal Andrews Sisters favorite. It just clicked with me, but all their songs are great and you can purchase them anywhere today in CD form.

"We loved recording with Bing. It was always so exciting. He used to do a little something unexpected, like the time he sneaked in that line at the end of 'Pistol Packin' Momma' -- 'Lay that thing down before it goes off and hurts someone.' He broke us up. He would always record at eight in the morning," she revealed, "I guess he used to vocalize in the car on the way to the studio---and he always wore his golf outfit. He claimed his voice had a husky quality in the morning.

"We had such fun with Bob and Bing when we did the Road picture," Patty recalled, "Bob and Bing would each have their own gag writers on the set and would sneak in special gags and lines and throw them at each other in front of the cameras. And they were kept in too--you can tell--if you look closely--they always surprised each other."

However, it was "Rum and Coca-Cola" that sold a whopping seven million records in a time when a million records were hard to sell. It was a favorite of tens of thousands of G.I.'s during the war, considering the shortage of shellac, the raw material that made the 78s. The demand for that recording was so great that both RCA and Columbia Records gave up their shellac allotment to allow Decca to meet the demand.

The girls also sang some of those songs at the Stage Door Canteen and Hollywood Canteen, which were sort of night clubs where armed forces personnel could go cost-free and meet movie stars and famous celebrities when on liberty or leave. They also performed regularly at Armed Forces camps, and USO shows.
In 1942 came the memorable "Don't Sit Under the Apple Tree," the bubbly "Pennsylvania Polka," and one of most stirring songs of World War II, "When Johnny Comes Marching Home." The very recall of that tune reminds me, as an eleven year old kid living in Brooklyn, New York, of the lines at the butcher shop and grocery stores where you had to turn in your limited supply of ration stamps or tokens, part

Patty Andrews Weschler

Dear, Richard

I'm lousy at writing but I have to tell you how much I love everything you write — its always so good to hear from you and what you're doing with your Books.

You don't need me for any Info. I felt Bad about Peggy Lee — she had such a creative mind for everything and then Rose mary Clooney and so many more — I guess I'm the only old girl Singer around — For a long time I hope — I send love to you and I hope your well and making lots of Money

Patty Andrews

of the wartime food rationing program, and of the frightening wail of the 'blackout' sirens, even though it was just practice drills. Patty remembered rationing too: "Especially when you couldn't get nylons---so we had to beg our friends. You didn't wear slacks then so you needed those stockings."

The girls also toured with the most famous of all the Big Bands, Glenn Miller's fine orchestra. In June, 1944, the girls went on a USO tour. They had to endure passing the required physical and receive inoculations when they went on secret destinations to entertain the troops. Overall they performed for over 150 million members of our armed forces over the four traveling years. They actually had to wear army uniforms in Italy to North America where the daily temperature reached over 100 degrees.

On VJ Day, the sisters were performing in the South Pacific when the Commanding Officer allowed them to read to the troops they were entertaining, that the Japanese had surrendered. The place went crazy with joy.

In 1950's, the Andrews Sisters capped their career when they performed at the London Palladium. As a singing group the girls broke up a few years later. Afterwards, Patty went on to perform as a single in the 1980s with bands like Tex Beneke, who was fronting the Glenn Miller Orchestra, before he too went out on his own after Glenn Miller became lost over the English Channel in 1944. She recorded two great hits with arranger and orchestrator Gordon Jenkins, "I Want to Be Loved" and "It Never Entered My Mind," Patty performing at her melodic best. It's so pure, and performed so perfectly. "I Can Dream. Can't I?" rose to number one on Billboard's chart and remained in the Top Ten for 25 weeks, Patty was indeed the leader of the girls and all the sounds must be channeled through the leader. The Andrews Sisters succeeded because of Patty's leadership and soloing.

The trio's last recording with Decca was "In the Good Old Summer Time" and "Take Me Out to the Ball Game." Their last three top-ten hits were in 1951 including two with Bing, "Sparrow in the Treetop," and "A Bushel and a Peck." The other was "Too Young," that was also a big hit for Nat "King" Cole.

To effectively write about the Andrews Sisters career alone, it would take a book. It would take another book to write about Patty Andrews own single career.

With Maxene and LaVerne gone, Patty has virtually retired, although she used to regularly attend local jazz festivals where she and husband Wally would meet with old musician friends including trombonist Milt Bernhart to live music, music she has always enjoyed both listening to and singing.

Patty sidestepped the inevitable inquiry about naming her favorite recording: "It's like a mother with ten children. You can't say which one is the favorite."

In the early nineties Maxene became active in night clubs. Her last performance was in Honolulu at the 50th Anniversary of the end of World War II. She passed away in October of 1995. La Verne, due to illness, passed on in 1967, and was replaced for a while by Joyce (Murray) De Young. Lee Hale, who directed the music on Dean Martin's Television Variety Show, recently told me Joyce fit in very well when appearing and singing with Maxene and Patty. Patty thought Joyce's voice was close to her sister LaVerne's. You have to realize that the Andrews Sisters had 46 top-ten, hit songs in their career. Neither Elvis nor the Beatles never reached that plateau. During the 1980's Patty successfully used my articles and promotional material to sell her one-woman act and would always call when she landed a gig. Patty is truly grateful for an abundant and fruitful career and acknowledges her debt to all the fans, young and old alike. We are fortunate to have the recordings of the Andrews Sisters, which will probably be used by female group singers as a measure of their own abilities for many years to come. Happy Birthday a little early Patty Andrews of 2012. We love the music you three girls sang. Those songs will always captivate all of us. So, thanks for all that beautiful music.

In 2005, Tom Rockvan wrote a neat little book about The Andrews Sisters and the summers they spent in Mound, Minnesota. The town named The Andrews Sisters Trail after the girls. Their Uncle Pete and Ed Solie had a grocery store in Mound. Maxene told Tom, "The summers spent in Mound created a wonderful childhood and a major sense of normalcy for us girls in contrast to the very pressured and busy life we led performing in show business."

Tom's book is charming and acknowledges the girls connection to Lake Minnetonka and Mound, Minnesota. Tom Rockvan can be reached at 2670 Commerce Blvd in Mound, MN 55364 or on line at hurl2rock@aol.com if you want to buy a copy of the book.

SINGLES OVER THE YEARS
1938
"Bei Mir Bist Du Schön"
"Nice Work If You Can Get It"
"Joseph, Joseph"
"Tip-Pi-Tin"
"Shortenin' Bread"
"Says My Heart"
"Tulip Time"
"Sha-Sha"
"Lullaby To a Jitterbug"

1939
"Pross-Tchai (Goodbye)"
"Hold Tight, Hold Tight"
"You Don't Know How Much You Can Suffer"
"Beer Barrel Polka (Roll Out the Barrel)"
"Well All Right (Tonight's the Night)"
"Ciribiribin (They're So In Love)" (with Bing Crosby)
"Yodelin' Jive" (with Bing Crosby)
"Chico's Love Song"

The Andrews Sisters Clean Dad's Car

1940
"Say Si Si (Para Vigo Me Voy)"
"The Woodpecker Song"

"Down By the O-Hi-O"
"Rhumboogie"
"Ferryboat Serenade"
"Hit the Road"
"Beat Me, Daddy, Eight To the Bar"

1941
"Scrub Me, Mama, With a Boogie Beat"
"Boogie Woogie Bugle Boy"
"I Yi, Yi, Yi, Yi (I Like You Very Much)"
"(I'll Be With You) In Apple Blossom Time"
"Aurora"
"Sonny Boy"
"The Nickel Serenade"
"Sleepy Serenade"
"I Wish I Had a Dime (For Every Time I Missed You)"
"Jealous"

1942
"The Shrine of St. Cecilia"
"I'll Pray For You"
"Three Little Sisters"
"Don't Sit Under the Apple Tree"
"Pennsylvania Polka"
"That's the Moon, My Son"
"Mister Five By Five"
"Strip Polka"
"Here Comes the Navy"

A personal message to Richard from Patty

1943
"East of the Rockies"
"Pistol Packin' Mama" (with Bing Crosby)
"Victory Polka" (with Bing Crosby)
"Jingle Bells" (with Bing Crosby)
"Shoo-Shoo Baby"

1944
"Down In the Valley"

"Straighten Up and Fly Right"
"Tico Tico"
"Sing a Tropical Song"
"Is You Is Or Is You Ain't My Baby" (with Bing Crosby)
"A Hot Time In the Town of Berlin" (with Bing Crosby)
"Don't Fence Me In" (with Bing Crosby)

1945
"Rum and Coca Cola"
"Accentuate the Positive" (with Bing Crosby)
"The Three Caballeros" (with Bing Crosby)
"One Meat Ball"
"Corns For My Country"
"Along the Navajo Trail" (with Bing Crosby)
"The Blond Sailor"

1946
"Money Is the Root of All Evil"
"Patience and Fortitude"
"Coax Me a Little Bit"
"South America, Take It Away" (with Bing Crosby)
"Get Your Kicks On Route 66" (with Bing Crosby
"I Don't Know Why"
"House of Blue Lights"
"Rumors Are Flying" (with Les Paul)
"Winter Wonderland" (with Guy Lombardo)
"Christmas Island" (with Guy Lombardo)

1947
"Tallahassee" (with Bing Crosby)
"There's No Business Like Show Business" (with Bing Crosby and Dick Haymes
"On the Avenue"
"Near You"
"The Lady From 29 Palms"
"The Freedom Train" (with Bing Crosby)
"Civilization" (Bongo, Bongo, Bongo)" (with Danny Kaye)
"Jingle Bells" (with Bing Crosby)
"Santa Claus Is Comin' To Town" (with Bing Crosby)
"Christmas Island" (with Guy Lombardo)

"Your Red Wagon"
"How Lucky You Are"

1948
"You Don't Have To Know the Language" (with Bing Crosby)
"Teresa" (with Dick Haymes)
"Toolie Oolie Doolie" (The Yodel Polka)
"I Hate To Lose You"
"Heartbreaker"
"Sabre Dance"
"Woody Woodpecker" (with Danny Kaye)
"Blue Tail Fly" (with Burl Ives)
"Underneath the Arches"
"You Call Everybody Darling"
"Cuanto La Gusta" (with Carmen Miranda)
"160 Acres" (with Bing Crosby)
"Bella Bella Marie"

1949
"Christmas Island" (with Guy Lombardo)
"The Pussy Cat Song (Nyow! Nyot! Nyow!)" (Patty Andrews w/Bob Crosby)
"More Beer!"
"I'm Bitin' My Fingernails and Thinking of You" (with Ernest Tubb)
"Don't Rob Another Man's Castle" (with Ernest Tubb)
"I Can Dream, Can't I?"
"The Wedding of Lili Marlene"
"She Wore a Yellow Ribbon" (with Russ Morgan Orchestra)
"Charley, My Boy" (with Russ Morgan) - 1950
"Merry Christmas Polka" (with Guy Lombardo)
"Have I Told You Lately That I Love You" (with Bing Crosby)
"Quicksilver" (with Bing Crosby)
"The Wedding Samba" (with Carmen Miranda)
" I Wanna Be Loved"
"Can't We Talk It Over"
"A Bushel and a Peck"

1951
"A Penny a Kiss, a Penny a Hug"
"Sparrow In the Tree Top" (with Bing Crosby)

"Too Young" (Patty Andrews)

1955
"Suddenly There's a Valley" (Patty Andrews)

THE ANDREWS GIRLS GOLD RECORDS
Showing "A" side and "B" Side.
1937 "Nice Work if You Can Get It"; and "Bei Mir Bist Du Schön"
1939 "Beer Barrel Polka" - "Well All Right!"
1943 "Pistol Packin' Mama" (with Bing Crosby) - "The Vict'ry Polka"
1943 " Jingle Bells" (with Bing Crosby) - "Santa Claus is Coming to Town"
1944 "Don't Fence Me In" (with Bing Crosby) - "TheThree Caballeros"
1944 "Rum and Coca Cola" - "One Meat Ball"
1946 " South America, Take It Away" (with Bing Crosby) -"Get Your Kicks on Route 66"
1946 "Christmas Island" - "Winter Wonderland"
1949 "I Can Dream, Can't I? - "The Wedding of Lili Marlene"
1974 "Over Here!" - from the play at the Shubert Theater

FILMOGRAPHY

FILMOGRAPHY

Argentine Nights (Universal Pictures, 1940)

Buck Privates (Universal Pictures, 1941)

In the Navy (Universal Pictures, 1941)

Hold That Ghost (Universal Pictures, 1941)

What's Cookin'? (Universal Pictures, 1942)

Private Buckaroo (Universal Pictures, 1942)

Give Out, Sisters (Universal Pictures, 1942)

How's About It (Universal Pictures, 1943)

Always a Bridesmaid (Universal Pictures, 1943)

Swingtime Johnny (Universal Pictures, 1943)

Moonlight and Cactus (Universal Pictures, 1944)

Follow the Boys (Universal Pictures, 1944)

Hollywood Canteen (Warner Brothers, 1944)

Her Lucky Night (Universal Pictures, 1945)

Make Mine Music (Walt Disney Studios, 1946)

Road to Rio (Paramount Pictures, 1947)

Melody Time (Walt Disney Studios, 1948)

Brother, Can You Spare a Dime? (1975)

THE ANDREWS SISTERS - MAXENE, PATTY, LAVERNE

PATTY PASSES
THEIR LEGACY TO...

SALLY, ANNEKA, ISABELLE

Don't Sit Under the Apple Tree (with Anyone Else but Me)

Words and Music by LEW BROWN, CHARLIE TOBIAS
and SAM H. STEPT

THE THREE BELLES FROM ENGLAND
A TRIBUTE TO THE ANDREWS SISTERS

Isabelle, Anneka, Sally

I'll Be With You In Apple Blossom Time
w. Neville Fleeson, m. Albert Von Tilzer

I'll be with you in apple blossom time
I'll be with you to change your name to mine
One day in May, I'll come and say
Happy the bride that the sun shines on today
What a wonderful wedding there will be
What a wonderful day for you and me
Church bells will chime,
You will be mine,
In apple blossom time

I'll be with you
(When?)
In Apple blossom time
(Then what will you do?)
Then, I'll be with you to change your name to mine.
(When will that be?)
One day maybe in May,
(Then what will you do?)
I'll come and say to you dear
Happy the bride that the sun shines on today
Then what a wonderful wedding there will be
(One day in May)
What a very, very wonderful day for you and me dear.
Church bells will chime,
You will be mine
(When?)
in apple,
in apple blossom time

There are times you can find them performing in front of a mike, outfitted in polka-dot house dresses, directly aligning themselves with the ladies of the 1940s, while matching their clothing with songs from that era, at places in England, like the Station Theater in Hayling Island.

Well, my friends, these girls are the upcoming stars of a new and popular British singing group known as The Three Belles, followers of the singing style of the world famous and the most popular American singing group, Patty, Maxene, and LaVerne- The Andrews Sisters.

The Three Belles are Anneka Wass, Isabelle Moore, and Sally Taylor -known as Betty, Dorothy, and Gail, names they have chosen to match their singing personalities. They developed a genuine 1940's style to fit their new experience show they named "In the Mood," after Glenn Miller's runaway song hit of World War II.

Talking to Anneka (Betty) who is 22: "I'm always smiling and happy. Gail (Sally) who is 21, is the cheeky and flirtatious one. Dorothy (Isabelle) who is also 21, is the sensible Belle who sings about love and scolds us when we get carried away."

The girls got started working as part of their University project in their final school year by organizing a 1940s evening of entertainment to help earn a degree for their Creative and Performing Arts Course. The songs were typically the tunes made famous by the Andrews Sisters. Like "Beat Me Daddy, Eight to the Bar," "Don't Sit Under the Apple Tree," and the great "Bei Mir Bist Du Schön," and the list of great tunes goes on and on. These girls have the sound and enthusiasm, and if you watch their performances on You Tube you will simply have to agree that the Andrews Sisters, who have been imitated by dozens of tribute singers, have been duplicated in these three girls.

One Sunday in October 2011, I talked with the girls just before a scheduled gig . "We haven't as yet made any records, but they are in the works soon." Right now they are on the road doing local gigs ala The Andrews Sisters, and they are performing on Youtube quite nicely.

"We are working on a couple of things other than just singing. We have created a theater show we call "In the Mood." The show is a 1940s style that we hope to take on the road this summer, and we will be going to France on tour in Normandy in honor of the "D" Day Landings Celebration," said Anneka.

The girls claim they never get the jitters before shows when they are local, but when they are larger shows they tend to get edgy, but we will get used to it as we go along," said Sally. Remember, these girls are just out of their teens.

"The name The Three Belles came from a picture of a pack of cigarettes in a 1940s scrapbook. The cigarettes were named the Three Bells, as in chiming bells. We just added an "es," Sally added. The girls accompanying backup varies from recorded music backgrounds to a three piece swing band. Sally and Isabelle usually share the lead, as Patty Andrews always did in their work. The girls really are great fans of the Andrews Sisters and watch them every day on Youtube. They get the chance to polish their tribute to them and learn to sing from them as well.

"We had a band in Portsmouth called the Tomcats" Anneka said, "who were a swing band and now we have a new band in London when we perform there.

"We will stick to our current way of performing for a while. We are not exactly sure what we will be doing but you can be sure we will be doing our thing every chance we get and change and grow as we go along." Right now the girls act as their own bookers, provide all the mailing and e-mails, and plan their own schedules, "When we are not giging," said Sally. The girls hope one day to come to the United States. Anneka: "As soon as we are ready and earn enough money to get there. We will have our agent set it up for us and we'll see you there!" Keep your eyes and ears on The Three Belles.

THE THREE BELLES AT GRADUATION IN ENGLAND

THE BROX SISTERS

The Southern born Brox Sisters, Bobbe, Patricia, and Lorayne became very popular in the first Music Box Revue at the New York Theater that ran from 1921 to 1924, then appeared all over the U.S. in various productions, and in the London version of the same show in 1923. They appeared in the film *The King of Jazz* in 1930 with the Paul Whiteman Orchestra and Bing Crosby's Rhythm Boys singing "A Bench in the Park" backed by famed guitarist Eddie Lang and jazz violinist Joe Venuti. Their original names were Josephine, Kathleen, and Eunice. And their original last name was Brock. The names were summarily and totally changed. Their singing evoked Southern inspired sounds. Irving Berlin wrote a special song for the girls entitled "Everybody Step."

Bobbe, Patricia and Lorrayne

The sisters performed in vaudeville and in the musical comedy *The Cocoanuts* with the crazy and zany Marx Brothers and later in the Ziegfeld Follies of 1927 with vaudeville favorite Eddie Cantor. Before Gene Kelly performed the song "Singing in the Rain," the Brox Sisters sang it twenty years earlier in the film *The Hollywood Revue* in 1929 with Cliff Edwards.

One of the girls favorite recording was "Down Among the Sleepy Hills of Ten-Ten Tennessee," recorded with the Bennie Krueger Band in 1923. When the girls decided to marry, they broke up the act. Interesting thing. Some report the girls went by the names of Kathlyn, Dagmar and Lorraine.) Will we ever know the real names of the Brox Sisters?

The Boswell Sisters

Connee Boswell (lead singer of the Boswell Sisters), who shored up the bands of both Dorsey's, Red Nichols, and Don Redman, too, was also the arranger for the singing Boswell's. She was Bing Crosby's favorite female partner on radio's *Kraft Music Hall*, and an early role model for Ella Fitzgerald on "scat" singing. A brave girl confined to a wheelchair most of her career due to an early bout with polio, Connee excelled on piano, sax, and trombone, too.

The three Boswell Sisters, Connee (earlier Connie), Martha, and Vet (for Helvetia), who sang earlier as a pre -Andrews Sisters group, were far ahead of their time. Born in Los Angeles (not in New Orleans), the girls won a radio contest while in their early teens and began recording, went on tour to California, and performed on Los Angeles radio station KFWB in 1930. They moved to New York and had great success on radio and in theaters. Then on to London in 1933 thru 1935 and back they traveled to New York.

The girls originally arrived on the music scene in 1925 and became nationally prominent and acclaimed by 1931. Their own family members were the girls mentors as they all sang together in quartets. The sisters could play many different instruments and performed earlier as an instrumental group, then graduated to vocalizing after experimenting with their creative, special voices. They worked so long and hard together developing their vocal capacity that they were always instantly in tune with one another.

Connee Boswell

Bing Crosby sings with the Boswells

The prolific Boswell's recorded with the premium bands of The Dorsey Brothers, Victor Young, Jimmy Grier, Ambrose's Orchestra from England, and later by Connee alone singing with Bob Crosby, Ben Pollack, John Scott Trotter, and Woody Herman Orchestras.
My favorite all-time Boswell Sisters recording was with Bing Crosby and the Mills Brothers with Victor Young's orchestra featuring Bing's favorite guitarist Eddie Lang and Tommy Dorsey on trombone, in

1931. The song was "Life is Just a Bowl of Cherries." What a wonderful recording. The girls best seller was, however "Tiger Rag/Nobody's Sweetheart" and was the first million seller by any vocal group.

After her sisters left the act, Connee continued as a single, setting early styles of jazz-oriented "scat" singing. Her best recordings were "They Can't Take That Away from Me" "The Loveliness of You," "That Old Feeling," "Bob White," and "An Apple for the Teacher," (the last two with Bing Crosby) and "Stormy Weather." Connee passed away on October 12, 1976 at the age of 69. A childhood victim of polio, Connee performed from a wheelchair throughout her career. I'm thankful the Andrews Sisters came along and continued the great tradition of the excellent Boswell's, aren't you?

The Pied Pipers

Of course, the Pipers were around even before Jo Stafford joined the once all-male singing group back in the California movie studio days. The original members were John Huddleston, Chuck Lowry, Hal Hopper, Woody Newbury, Whit Whittinghill, Bud Hervey, and John Tait. It became an octet with the addition of the soulful voice of Jo Stafford.

Jo Stafford with The Pied Pipers

The group came to the attention of the public while performing on the Raleigh-Kool (cigarettes) radio show in 1938, when Tommy Dorsey hired the group to sing with his band. Because he could not afford to pay eight singers, Tommy let them go after the show. When the group reemerged as a quartet - three guys and a gal, Tommy reconsidered and re-hired them. The group was now composed of

Jo Stafford, Chuck Lowry, Clark Yocum, and John Huddleston.

While with Tommy Dorsey, the Pipers also backed singers Connie Haines, Frank Sinatra, and later Dick Haymes, especially on specialty songs and recordings. Frank would always do his best to work harmonically with the group. Jo was a very cool and calm sing-

Coming of Age...

Today's Pied Pipers™

Top to Bottom: Michael Jackson, Roland Michaud, Nancy Knorr, Scott Whitfield

Tommy Dorsey, John Huddleston, Jo Stafford, Frank Sinatra, Chuck Lowry, Clark Yocum

er, but always considered herself simply the distaff member although she sang lead, and as her husband, musician and bandleader Paul Weston observed, "Jo's voice is in perfect pitch every time." Their first and biggest hit "I'll Never Smile Again," was written by Ruth Lowe who, while mourning the loss of her husband, was inspired to compose the song.

"Oh! Look At Me Now" was another big hit, written by pianist Joe Bushkin and included my lovely and close friend Connie Haines, and her singing partner Frank Sinatra.

During that time the Pipers and Dorsey were featured in the movies *Ship Ahoy* and *DuBarry Was Lady* for MGM with Frank Sinatra, Jo Stafford, Buddy Rich and Ziggy Elman as stars. The Pipers remained with Dorsey for two years: 1940 to 1942.

The Pipers began working with Johnny Mercer, becoming the first artists to sign with his newly-formed Capitol Records. That recording and now Piper theme song "Dream" won the first Gold Record for Capitol and the Pipers were featured on their own *Chesterfield Music Shop* radio show.

They performed with Frank Sinatra on the Lucky Strike program *Your Hit Parade*. In 1944 June Hutton, bandleader Ina Ray Hutton's younger sister and wife of arranger Axel Stordahl, replaced Jo Stafford, who left the Pipers to go out on her own at the urging of

Johnny Mercer who wanted her to record solo for Capitol. She had just married Capitol arranger and leader Paul Weston.

Warren Covington told me an amazing story: "The Pipers with June, who remained for four years, appeared in the film *Make Mine Music* in 1946. When Tommy Dorsey suddenly died

Richard Grudens and
Bandleader Warren Covington of the Pied Pipers

in his sleep on November 26, 1956, Willard Alexander, head of the booking agency, called upon me to front the Tommy Dorsey Band, which I did until 1962. At that time the Pipers were simply composed of various studio singers.

Warren Covington's Pied Pipers with Nancy Knorr

"In the Seventies, because of my association with Tommy Dorsey's great band, I was asked to organize a "salute" to Tommy and include a vocal group like the Pipers. Researching ownership of the Pied Pipers, I learned that no one had retained rights so I was able to obtain ownership through properly registering copyrights and trademarks. The smooth sounds of the Pied Pipers were alive once again.

"At one time Lillian Clark Oliver, one of the Clark Sisters and Sy Oliver's wife, performed with the Pipers for a while, as did lead singer Lynn Roberts, Tommy's former soloist, and the last of the big band singers.

During the Eighties and right up to today, the Pipers still play "gigs" at showcases everywhere with Big Tribute Bands like Tommy Dorsey under Buddy Morrow's direction. (We lost Buddy in 2010) Of course, personnel in the Pipers has revolved throughout the years. The group today is composed of singers Nancy Knorr, Chris Sanders, Don Lucas, and Kevin Kennard. Some of their best performances have been what they've always been, "I'll Never Smile Again," "Sunny Side of the Street," "At Last," "Dream," "There are Such Things," "Street of Dreams," and "Oh, Look at Me Now," all perennial Pied Piper favorites and all performed in the original arrangements. The Pipers still have millions of fans. They wrote the book on singing groups. Their timeless songs and the nostalgia evoked by those memories keep the Pied Pipers music going and going.

Nancy Knorr, a Song Star in her own right with her own unique style, has been a classical musician, once playing viola with the St. Louis Philharmonic Orchestra and within many chamber groups. As a vocalist Nancy has performed over the years with the Tommy Dorsey Orchestra, Les Brown's Band of Renown, Tex Beneke's band, as well as the Warren Covington and Jimmy Dorsey bands. As Pied Piper proprietor and lead singer, Nancy continues to tour and also solos with the Pipers, to recreate the elegance and sound of America's greatest music.

THE INK SPOTS

Bill Kenny, Orville "Happy" Jones, Charlie Fuqua, and Ivory "Deek" Watson were the original Ink Spots, one of the best singing quartets during the Big Band Era. Throughout the forties they produced the numbers "We Three," "I Don't Want to Set the World On Fire," "I'm Making Believe," and, with Ella Fitzgerald, "Cow-Cow-Boogie" and "Into Each Life Some Rain Must Fall."

Their songs began with a guitar riff, then the song by the tenor, who sang the entire song through. Then the bass would either recite the first half, or the bridge of the song, or would speak the words in a free form, adding phrases like "Honey Child," or "Honey Babe," or "Honey lamb," expressing his love for a lover in the song. This was followed by the tenor, who closed by singing the last refrain or the last half of the song.

The Ink Spots began with the name The Four Riff Brothers, but changed it after a 1934 appearance at the famed Apollo Theater in New York, when they were supporting Tiny Bradshaw's appearances, and at the request of bandleader Paul Whiteman to avoid confusion with his vocal group "The King's Jesters." Later that year, The Ink Spots achieved international success touring England with

Jack Hylton's Orchestra.

I liked the Ink Spots when performing my late friend Jack Lawrence's "If I Didn't Care." Al Rivers, a later Ink Spot from 1949 to 1958, recorded all the famous numbers and even started another Ink Spots in 1985.

Past members were Jerry Daniels, Bernie Mackay, Huey Long, Billy Bowen, Cliff Bowen, Cliff Givens, and Herb Kenny.

"The Gypsy" was their biggest chart success, remaining at the #1 position for 13 weeks. They also recorded for Grand Award Records (two records in 1955, one in 1956-1957 and one in 1958). Their 1941 song, "I Don't Want to Set the World on Fire" is a song played on the in-game radio station Galaxy News Radio in the 2008 video game Fallout 3. I first heard the Ink Spots sing "I Don't Want to Set the World on Fire" when I was 9 years old. I was in a hospital where they removed my tonsils and they played that song in the children's ward and hallways, especially during visiting hours. I'll never forget it.

The Best of the Ink Spots, according to me, recorded from 1939-1952:
"If I Didn't Care"
"Address Unknown"
"My Prayer"
"Bless You"
"We Three"
"Do I Worry"
" I Don't Want to Set the World on Fire"
"Someone's Rocking My Dreamboat"
"Cow, Cow Boogie"
"Into Each Life Some Rain Must Fall"
"The Gypsy"

THE GYPSY
BILLY REID

In a quaint caravan
There's a lady they call the Gypsy
She can look in the future
And drive away all your fears
Everything will come right
If you only believe the Gypsy
She could tell at a glance
That my heart was so full of tears
She looked at my hand and told me
My lover was always true
And yet in my heart I knew, dear
Somebody else was kissing you
But I'll go there again
'Cause I want to believe the Gypsy
That my lover is true
And will come back to me some day

THE MODERNAIRES

When Glenn Miller was adding more musicians to his band he extended it even further by experimenting with a singing group known as the Modernaires, whose spokesman was Hal Dickenson. Earlier in 1936 through 1939 the Modernaires recorded a number of tunes with Paul Whiteman's Orchestra before joining up with Miller.

"The first time we did anything with Glenn was recording a theme for the great WNEW disc jockey Martin Block. It was entitled "It's Make Believe Ballroom Time," and was recorded on October 11, 1940. That's where Glenn first got the idea that he wanted to have a quartet singing with his band. Just a few recording sessions later, we became an official part of the Glenn Miller organization for good."

On Christmas day of 1940, the Modernaires stepped into New

Tex Beneke, Marion Hutton singing together with the Modernaires on WNEW in New York with Martin Block on the left and Glenn Miller behind him.

York's Pennsylvania Hotel's beautiful Cafe Rouge, and sat down at a table in their raggedy clothes. Observing the Miller band in rehearsal, they were awe stricken by the hearty, twangy vocals of sax man Tex Beneke, and were mesmerized by the musical excellence of the number one band in the world, a band who had just won the coveted Billboard listener's poll.

"The fact that we were going to appear with the band was almost breathtaking. Glenn bought us dinner. If we'd have known that in advance, we would have ordered something more expensive to eat. We officially joined with the band in 1941. At the first session we performed a Jimmy Van Heusen song, 'You Stepped Out of a Dream.'"

The Modernaires were a group of four musical guys from Buffalo, New York, with diverse backgrounds. Hal Dickenson was the lead singer and a Presbyterian; Ralph Brewster, a Christian Scientist who played trumpet; Chuck Goldstein was Jewish, and Bill Conway was Catholic, who also played guitar. None of them read music. They sang and played, as they say, strictly by ear.

Chuck Goldstein: "Hal was the lead singer, but could only sing the melody. I could sing both upper and lower harmony. Bill would sit with his guitar and we would learn our songs working together in our own special harmony. And we made pretty good money, getting a hundred and twenty-five bucks each, plus a bonus."

The Modernaires with Paula Kelly

As I mentioned earlier, the "Mods" had been working with Paul "Pops" Whiteman, who graciously allowed them to tear up their contract with him in order for them to join up with Glenn. Glenn, a former Whiteman band member himself, felt the presence of a vocal group would attract customers around the bandstand enabling people to stand eye-to-eye with both players and vocalists. At the time Glenn's orchestra was number one in America, and still is 60 years later.

Aside from the great hits "Chattanooga Choo Choo," (with Tex Beneke) "Don't Sit Under the Apple Tree" and "Kalamazoo," (also with Tex Beneke), the Mods also produced the beautiful ballad "Perfidia," with Dorothy Claire, "You Stepped Out of a Dream," with Ray Eberle, "Sweeter Than the Sweetest," with Paula Kelly, "Booglie Wooglie Piggy," also with Paula Kelly and Tex Beneke, as well as "I Know Why," one of Glenn's greatest hits, also with Paula Kelly. Of course, the hits came through the years until the disbanding of Glenn's civilian band in September of 1942 when he formed the Army Air Force Band, named The American Band of the Allied Expeditionary Force Trumpeter. Later, bandleader Billy May arranged specifically for the Modernaires from time to time.

"When the Mods wanted to do something other than backing up the featured singers, they came up with their solo 'Sweeter Than The Sweetest,' so I made a special arrangement for them. Chuck Goldstein and Hal Dickinson and I were never really happy with that arrangement, but Glenn was in a hurry to get it to the recording studio. I think it could have been even better. With Glenn, you know, the band was always very well rehearsed and everything was marked. There was no need to conduct the band. So with great arrangements and strong rehearsals, the band didn't need anyone standing up there waving a baton." One of the Mods best was backing the vocal on "Serenade in Blue" whose opening orchestral introduction was arranged by May.

Today's Modernaires are known as the *Moonlight Serenaders*, made up of members of the orchestra and the band's girl singer. Julia Rich is the most recent female singer with the Mods today, and perhaps the longest running female Mod, combined with playing members of the band doubling up as vocalists. You could close your eyes and appreciate each interpretation of the original charts with full orchestral backing, transporting you back a few years evoking the sounds of the original Modernaires. Julia had something to say about her assocation with the Serenaders:

THE MOONLIGHT SERENADERS AND ME

Vocalist Julia Rich

I love singing harmony; I learned it from the Beatles and the Methodist hymnal In fifth grade, I argued with classmate (and fellow Beatles tribute band member) Judy Bennett over the exact harmony notes in "All My Loving" and where in the song they occurred. My sisters and I sang "In the Garden" and "Whispering Hope" from the time we were sprouts. On the secular side, we still turn out a mean "Winter Wonderland" and "Some of Shelley's Blues." It's hereditary: my father, the Right Reverend H. Fred Blankenship, had several brothers (more ministers among them) who sang the old hymns at every family reunion. They were handsome and had slicked back hair

Julia Rich

like Glenn Miller vocalist of the 40s, Ray Eberle. Mother couldn't sing, but she was a good critic.

As an adolescent, The Girl Scouts taught me rounds like "White Coral Bells" and "Make New Friends." In junior high glee club, I learned "Dona Nobis Pacem." As a teacher, I watched students discover the joy of holding one part against another. We did everything from "Chapel of Love" to (of course) "Dona Nobis Pacem." The art of blending voices sends good medicine through body and soul.

At Middle Tennessee State University, I was a member of Margaret Wright's Sacred Harp Singers. She introduced me to shaped note singing and those wonderful Appalachian folk songs, like "My Shepherd Will Supply My Need." My sisters and I even sang "I'll Fly Away" and my own arrangement of "Be Thou My Vision" at sister Martha's funeral, in her honor and with a nod to the Blankenship boys.

In 1985, I joined the World Famous Glenn Miller Orchestra and became vocal group leader of the Moonlight Serenaders. I adored listening to the original recordings and hearing the laid-back sound and diction of the Modernaires. They sang "zoo," we sing "zoo;" but it's not the same. Theirs had no diphthong—and I'm not talking southern here. Theirs was a little bit lazy and a whole lot swinging. Reproducing the exact sound of the Modernaires is as difficult as reproducing the exact look of women in the '40s. Attitudes have changed, and style is all about attitude. I do love the old style and hold it as the standard. But we give it our best and the folks are generous with their response.

As the Moonlight Serenaders' group leader I learned all the harmony parts to each song so I could best assess prospective new singers for the group. I wanted us to be spot on for performances and recordings. I still thrill to hear someone nail a part and rejoice in a good lead voice. Nick Hilscher sang with the group like a lead player in a horn section. That was heaven. The girl part tends to double the lead, but every now and then I've gotten to sing a harmony part (if someone is sick). I've especially enjoyed singing a duet with the boy singer, be it "White Christmas" with Nick or "Our Love Is Here to Stay" with Matt Johns or "Don't Sit Under the Apple Tree" with Bryan Anthony. I love singing harmony!

{Author's Note: - I just learned that Julia has rejoined the Glenn Miller Organization performing the very same things. And are we glad she's back! Nick Hilscher is now Musical Director in place of retired Larry O'Brien}

The King Sisters-America's First Family of Song

Donna, Yvonne, Luise, and Alyce King gained prominence during the Big Band Era with a number of hits: "In the Mood," "San Fernando Valley," "I'll Get By," "Rose O'Day," "Jersey Bounce," a World War II song "Milkman! Keep Those Bottles Quiet," "Saturday Night is the Loneliest Night of the Week," and "Six Lessons from Madame La Zonga." The girls were from Salt Lake City, Utah.

Donna: "We never really had any big, big hit records because we never had very good management and that really held us back. Also we were too smart. We thought we knew everything. We had our own ideas about how our career should go, and I think that also stood in our way. If we had been able to place ourselves in someone else's capable hands, one who had a real career plan, I think we would have been a lot more successful."

The girls soon became regulars on the Ozzie Nelson and Harriet Hilliard Show, (Ozzie and Harriet were married), and then on Kay Kyser's radio show where they got into minor scrapes with a sponsor's wife, and somewhat adverse relations with Horace Heidt that became strained, causing them to leave the show. They disbanded to become soloists with various bands of the day including Artie Shaw and Charlie Barnet, separately and sometimes together, and then joined a new band formed by Luise's husband, the man who invented the talking steel guitar, legendary guitarist and bandleader Alvino Rey. They made the "Hut Sut Song" and "I'll Get By" hits for the band. Luise and Rey married and kept the union going for 60 years. At 95 Luise passed before Rey, who was also 95 when he died in February 2004.

Donna, Yvonne, Alyce and Luise

Following an appearance on the Hollywood Palace in the early sixties, ABC Television launched the *King Family Television Show* which ran from the mid-1960's until 1969 as the girls eased into retirement. An additional thirty-seven members of the extended family also appeared on the show. They ranged in age from seven months old to 79 years old.

The girls appeared in the films *Nobody's Fool*, *Crash Donovan* (they sang "Devoted to You"), *King of Burlesque* with Alice Faye and Jack Oakie, singing "One, Two, Button My Shoe," (another Crosby favorite and three 10 minute Columbia Pictures shorts: Community

The Four King Sisters with Alvino Rey, in 1942

Yvonne, Alyce, Luise, Donna with Alvino Rey

Sing No.1, 7, and 10, and Irving Berlin's *Second Fiddle* with Tyrone Power & Sonja Henie (they sang "I'm Sorry for Myself") Snow Follies, and Swingin' In the Barn, a 20 minute western style short wherein they sang the old standard "I Like Mountain Music."

In 1942 they performed in *Sing Your Worries Away* with comedian Bert Lahr, Buddy Ebson, June Haver, and Alvino Rey with the Orchestra; *Follow the Band* in 1943 with Frances Langford, one of my personal friends and one of Bob Hope's favorite singers, wherein they sang "My Devotion" (in this film Peggy Brosen had replaced Alyce during her pregnancy).

The girls also performed in a handful of films starring themselves with Alvino Rey. Other films were *Meet the People*, *Cuban Pete*, *On Stage Everybody*, *Larceny* with Music starring Allan Jones (Father of Jack Jones), and Kitty Carlisle, (who sang with Bing Crosby in films over the years.)

When they were asked why, as a quality singing group, they had never caught on like the Andrews Sisters and the McGuire Sisters:

"I think our harmonies were a little too complex for the average listener," said Donna King. "The musicians who heard us, I think were impressed with us. But our harmonies were voiced like a horn section. I think the public could understand the simpler, three-part groups like the Andrews Sisters and the McGuire Sisters a little easier."

The King Sisters

Celebrating the 45th Anniversary of their television debut, the family debuted on Public Television in 2009 with their *King Family Christmas Special* and again in 2010. Marilyn King performed a live, one-night special in 2009 upstairs at Vitello's in Studio City, California.

The standard and extended talented King Family moves on with plans in the future for even more appearances in honoring the original and fabulous King Sisters.

The McGuire Sisters

From singing at a small church in Middletown, Ohio, to five White House appearances (and you may add a command performance for the Queen of England), the McGuire Sisters - Christine, Dorothy and Phyllis - actual sisters, sang their heart out throughout

Phyllis, Dorothy, Christine

an amazing career that has lasted forty-six years. Generations of Americans, and other fans around the world, enjoyed listening to the definitive successors to the greatest girl singing of all time, the Andrews Sisters. The McGuires built up a string of billboard hits with their lovely close harmony - as enjoyable today as it was when they began back in 1952. Through their recordings, those terrific, beautiful girls have established forever the immortal tunes "Sugartime," "Sincerely," "Picnic," "Something's Gotta Give," and "Goodnight, Sweetheart, Goodnight." Everyone a winner. Everyone a million seller.

These girls, who truly love to sing, began it all in that church in Middletown. Ohio. Phyllis was but four. By 1949, they were performing at military bases and other worthy functions which built up their confidence and garnered important and needed experience through practice. In 1952, Arthur Godfrey and his radio and television talent show placed them high

in the public eye, as he did for my friends Julius La Rosa, Carmel Quinn, and other singers when they warbled for the old maestro of talent presenters. They became resident singers on the show for six years, replacing the Chordettes.

PREMIER VOCALISTS

Back Row: The McGuire Sisters with
Front Row L-R: Theresa Brewer, Margaret Whiting, Patti Page and Fran Warren

Over the years the girls performed before Presidents Richard Nixon, Jimmy Carter, Gerald Ford, Ronald Reagan and George Bush, Sr. They signed an unprecedented, lucrative contract with the Coca-Cola Company and appeared on the highest rated TV shows, and played on stages from Las Vegas to the Empire Room in the famed Waldorf Astoria in New York City.

By 1968, The McGuires decided to put a hold on their careers, with Phyllis breaking away and performing as a single. Dorothy and Christine began devoting time to their growing families. For the following seventeen years, the girls performed only at personal family events. Then a unique twist of fate changed everything. When Chris-

The McGuires with Frank Sinatra

tine and Dorothy were visiting Phyllis, who lived in New York City, her sisters would get together to visit her from time to time. Whenever they were seen together, their presence was constantly interupted by still adoring fans who would request autographs, always inquiring where they would be appearing.

"Why not?" was the question.

Like other performers, from Jolson to Sinatra before them, the girls came rigorously out of retirement and blazed a new chapter in their lives.

The McGuire Sisters were going to make a comeback.
The three began rehearsing their famous repertoire of songs at Phyllis' Las Vegas home. The effort persisted until the harmony and hard work brought back the old spark. When they were booked to appear, all the old fans once again stood in line and new fans began joining them.
The McGuire Sisters harmonies were a hit once again.

SINCERELY

This 59 track 2 CD set compilation covers many of the McGuire Sisters biggest hits. There are also some long lost tracks on this CD along with their major hits: "Sincerely," "Muskrat Ramble," and "Picnic."

- May You Always
- That's A Plenty
- Since You Went Away To School
- Do You Love Me Like You Kiss Me (Scapricciatiello)
- Volare (Nel Blu, Dipinto Di Blu)
- Ding Dong
- Summer Dreams
- Sweetie Pie
- Peace
- Achoo- Cha Cha (Gesundheit)
- I'll Think Of You
- One Fine Day
- Sugartime
- Around The World
- Weary Blues
- Banana Split
- Interlude
- Forgive Me
- In The Alps In The Alps In The Alps
- Kiss Them For Me
- Shame
- Livin' Dangerously
- Lovers Lullaby
- The Last Dance
- Nine O'Clock
- Anniversary Song
- I Love You
- Shuffle Off To Buffalo
- Do You Remember When?
- Sometimes I'm Happy
- June Night
- All By Myself

- Tiptoe Through The Tulips With Me
- Them There Eyes
- Mississippi Mud
- Cuddle Up A Little Closer, Lovey Mine
- Does Your Heart Beat For Me?
- Somebody Loves Me
- S'wonderful
- Blue Skies
- I'm In The Mood For Love
- Don't Take Your Love From Me
- My Darling, My Darling
- Moonglow
- Tenderly
- I Hadn't Anyone 'Till You
- If You Were Only Mine
- Wonderful One
- I'm Confessin'
- Moon Song
- Love Is Here To Stay
- Think Of Me Kindly

These standard and sometimes romantic melodies just inspire harmony, and the orchestrations are brilliant as well. "Tiptoe Through The Tulips" uses imitation among the horn and string sections to reinforce the vocal line, while "Them There Eyes" is punctuated by percussion and horn accents and a

half-time coda. The three voices, very similar in tone color and generally having a low tessitura in the female range, blend easily, and their vocal style is natural and without artifice. It's wonderful stuff.

THEIR GREATEST HITS

- Sincerely
- Something's Gotta Give
- Goodnight Sweetheart, Goodnight
- Picnic
- Muskrat Ramble
- Ev'ry Day Of My Life
- Sugartime
- It May Sound Silly
- Christmas Alphabet
- May You Always
- Just For Old Time's Sake

McGUIRE SISTERS/ANDREWS SISTERS: SING THE BIG HITS - BACK TO BACK

- Sincerely
- Sugartime
- Something's Gotta Give
- May You Always
- Beat Me Daddy Eight To The Bar
- Boogie Woogie Bugle Boy
- Well All Right
- Bei Mir Bist Du Schön
- I'll Be With You In Apple Blossom Time
- Muskrat Ramble

MAY YOU ALWAYS

May you always walk in sunshine
Slumber warm when night winds blow
May you always live with laughter
For a smile becomes you so

May good fortune find your doorway
May the bluebird sing your song
May no trouble travel your way
May no worry stay too long

May your heartaches be forgotten
May no tears be spilled
May old acquaintance be remembered
And your cup of kindness filled

And may you always be a dreamer
May your wildest dream come true
May you find someone to love
As much as I love you

(May your heartaches be forgotten)
(May no tears be spilled)
May old acquaintance be remembered
And your cup of kindness filled

And may you always be a dreamer
May your wildest dream come true
May you find someone to love
As much as I love you

THE GUMM SISTERS

It is not generally well-known that the girl who sang "Over the Rainbow" in the film *The Wizard of Oz* first made appearances with her two sisters, Mary Jane and Virginia, on vaudeville stages from the East coast to the West before she became a star on her own. They called themselves The Gumm Sisters: Mary Jane, Virginia, and baby Frances, later Judy. Judy Garland.

Mary Jane, Virginia and baby Frances
(later she would become Judy Garland)

The girls and their family set sail for California before Baby Frances was four and on the way earned about a needed $300.00 playing vaudeville houses from Grand Rapids to L.A. They loved the California climate and made the move permanent. Their father purchased an old rundown theater in a small town named Lancaster, renovated it with new seats and a cooling system and featured his family as the main act.

After her Mom and Dad's act Frances would dash to the pit piano in a costume with lots of spangles and bracelets, and entertain. She was billed as Baby Gumm. With her sisters, Frances would sing on the radio show, *The Kiddies Hour* and sang with cowboy star William S. Hart: the song? " There's a Long, Long Trail a-Winding." On a movie short called The Big Revue, vivacious and assured, Frances out- shouted her sisters and displayed a special screen presence. It was the beginning of Frances' and her sisters' screen debut and the start of an amazing career.

Frances Gumm: "Someday I will sing on the screen and become a movie star."

The girls continued singing, billed as The Hollywood Starlets Trio.

After an appearance at the Paramount Theater in Los Angeles, Variety, the show-business magazine declared:

A Young Frances Gumm - later Judy Garland

The Gumm Sisters, harmony trio, socked with two numbers. Selling end of the trio is the ten-year-old kid sister with a pip of a low-down voice. Kid stopped the show, but wouldn't give more."

With Shirley Temple stealing all the kiddy scenes in one movie after another, Frances and her sisters were in demand and was registered with Mrs. Lawlor's School for Professional Children where Shirley Temple had attended. It was here Mickey Rooney and Frances Gumm first met. He was already a star of the many Mickey Mcguire shorts. They immediately struck up a lasting friendship.

Mrs. Gumm began to book the girls in Portland, Oregon, Seattle, and then Chicago. "My mother was not a stage mom, but a serious person in anything she undertook."

Vaudeville star George Jessel introduced the girls as the Glumm Sisters, thinking they were a comedy act. He suggested the girls change the name to the Garland Sisters, named after his friend, Robert Garland, a drama critic for the New York World Telegram. Jessel, recognizing Judy's booming voice which did not need a microphone had their act moved up to second closing.

"She could make you tingle when she sang, make you laugh and cry with her, whether her name was Frances Gumm, Minnie Ha-Ha, or Algrene Handelpotz."

The three girls were picked up by the prestigious William Morris Talent and Booking Agency who represented many big stars. Frances performed torch songs partially hidden by her sisters, and at the end of her act revealed herself as a twelve year old winning over audience after audience with her unexpected, powerful, mature-sounding voice.

The newly christened Garland Sisters returned home to California and won an engagement at Grauman's Chinese Theater in Hollywood. George Jessel said that Judy sang with a hurt heart, even at the age of twelve.

Meanwhile, their father lost his Valley Theater because of the depressed economy and rejoined his family in L.A. He purchased another theater close by. He also changed his name to Garland. And, Mary Jane became Suzy, Virginia became Jimmy and Frances became Judy, the name taken from a line in a Hoagy Carmichael song;"If you think she's a saint and you find out she ain't, that's Judy." Judy's first screen test was ignored. Harry Askt, songwriter and Al Jolson piano accompanist who wrote "Dinah," played it while Judy sang and said: " I was playing three feet away. The volume nearly knocked me flat. Her pitch was perfect, her breathing and timing naturally flawless, and she had those saucer-shaped, brown eyes

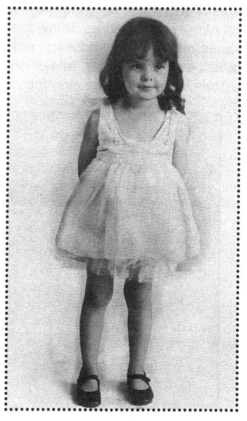

Frances Gumm at Three Years

swimming with anxiety and love."

Later, at the MGM studios schoolroom Judy hooked up with her friends Mickey Rooney and Donald O'Connor. When Judy sang "You Made Me Love You" to a Clark Gable photograph in the movie Broadway Melody of 1938, she felt like her knees would cave in. She also sang a jazzy number "Everybody Sing," and people began to notice her.

The Hollywood Reporter declared..."A certain new picture star." Her debut with Mickey Rooney had begun. The films were *Thoroughbreds*, *Don't Cry* and *Everybody Sing,* "Mickey helped me. He would tell me how to walk into a scene off camera and he would suggest to me how to get the best out of a line."

Judy and her mom embarked on a six-week, seven city studio promotional tour appearing before live audiences. She soon began appearing in the Mickey Rooney *Andy Hardy* films where she sang with Mickey, featured as Betsy, the girl next door. This led to future movies with Rooney and a few unforgettable duets. As well as a re-markable career in films, television, and stage appearances.
But, this is just the beginning for those two-Rooney and Garland.

THE CHORDETTES

"Mr Sandman" was the big hit for the Chordettes and has

become one of pop music's most popular recordings of the 1950s. The original group was comprised of four very lovely girls Jinny Osborn, Nancy Overton, Lynn Evans and Carol Buschmann. Succeeding members over the years 1946 through 1961 were Janet Ertel, Dorothy Schwartz, and Margie Nedham.

Another of their megahits was "Lollipop." The girls were generally known to be very much like their past heroes The Andrews Sisters, although they made their mark on the music scene during the doo-wop era.

The Chordettes began it all in Sheboygan, Wisconsin in the late forties and started emulating the Weavers group sound. Remember Pete Seeger, Ronnie Gilbert and Lee Hays and "Goodnight Irene?" Usually the girls sang *a capella* (which means without music accompaniment.) They wound up singing close harmony, almost like a barbershop quartet. Jinny's dad was involved with barbershop with the Barbershop Harmony Society, being its president.

The girls won their appearance on *Arthur Godfrey's Talent Scouts* program in 1949. They remained on Godfrey's very popular daily radio show. The orchestra leader on Godfrey's show was Archie Bleyer, who formed Cadence Records and signed some of Godfrey's current and former stable of stars.

Two notes of interest I'll bet you didn't know: Bleyer married Janet Ertel and later, their daughter Jackie married Phil Everly of the Everly Brothers. And it was Archie whose voice responded to the girls on the recording of "Mr. Sandman." ("Mr. Sandman.....Ye-s-s-s!) Well it was Archie who said that.

The Chordettes went along recording two theme tunes from the movies: *Zorro* and *Never on Sunday*. They also sang to King Curtis' saxophone. They appeared on *American Bandstand* in 1957 when the show went national on ABC television. The girls broke up and reunited in the early nineties and toured with the Tennessee Plowboy, my good friend, Eddy Arnold. They appeared in Branson, Missouri a number of times.

In 2001 The Group was inducted into the Vocal Group Hall of Fame. They certainly deserved the honor, most likely being the longest running vocal group of them all, and one of the groups who sang from both sides of the turntable: doo-wop, standard popular tunes, barbershop, and country, as well.

The Chordettes hit singles were "Mr. Sandman," "The Wedding," "Eddie My Love," "Born to be with You," "Teen Age Goodnight," "Lollipop," "Zorro." "Never or Sunday," and "Faraway Star." A wonderful tuneful legacy.

MISTER SANDMAN
W.M. PAT BALLARD

Bung, bung, bung, bung, bung
Bung, bung, bung, bung, bung
Bung, bung, bung, bung, bung
Bung, bung, bung, bung, bung
Bung, bung, bung, bung, bung

Mr. Sandman, bring me a dream
(Bung, bung, bung, bung)
Make him the cutest that I've ever seen
(Bung, bung, bung, bung)
Give him two lips like roses and clover
(Bung, bung, bung, bung)
Then tell him that his lonesome nights are over

Sandman, I'm so alone
Don't have nobody to call my own
Please turn on your magic beam
Mr. Sandman, bring me a dream

Bung, bung, bung, bung

Mr. Sandman, bring me a dream
Make him the cutest that I've ever seen
Give him the word that I'm not a rover
Then tell him that his lonesome nights are over

Sandman, I'm so alone
Don't have nobody to call my own
Please turn on your magic beam
Mr. Sandman, bring me a dream

Bung, bung, bung, bung

Mr. Sandman bring us a dream
(Yes)
Give him a pair of eyes with a come-hither gleam
Give him a lonely heart like Pagliacci
And lots of wavy hair like Liberace

Mr. Sandman, someone to hold
(Someone to hold)
Would be so peachy before we're too old
So please turn on your magic beam
Mr. Sandman, bring us, please, please, please
Mr. Sandman, bring us a dream

Bung, bung, bung, bung

The DeCastro Sisters

In 1945 the DeCastro family moved to the United States from their native Cuba and became proteges of 1940s movie star singer/dancer Carmen Miranda and formed as a singing trio in Miami, Florida. Peggy, Cherie and Babette De Castro's style emulated, like so many other groups, the Andrews Sisters, but with a slight difference, an added Latin flavor. Their biggest hit is "Teach Me Tonight,"

released in 1954 and reached the number two hit on the music charts in the United States. The recording sold over 5 million copies. The

girls appeared at the Copacabana in New York with the Will Mastin Trio (with Sammy Davis, Jr.) and then appeared with Groucho Marx and Carmen Miranda in the film *Copacabana*.

At one point in their growing career, the girls traveled with Tito Puente's band all across the country including a gig at the Hollywood Palladium. They were sort of an Andrews Sisters style act. The Andrews girls were their absolute singing heroes, and they sang like the Andrews girls, but with a latin beat.

Legend has it that it was the De Castro's who suggested to a young Bobby Darin at the Sahara in Las Vegas, that he should record "Mack the Knife." Good Advice, I would say!

The DeCastro's appeared on all the big-time TV variety shows including Ed Sullivan and Perry Como's, and on film shorts featuring some Big Bands including Harry James.

Cherie DeCastro was the only sister that appeared on every recording, TV appearance, films and stage show. She was the last of the girls to pass from us in March of 2010.

THE CLOONEY SISTERS

Rosemary and Betty

The Clooney Sisters, Betty and Rosemary, were very close at the point in their lives when their mother left them in care of their father while she took off for California with their brother Nicky. The girls did not see their mother or brother for four years.

During that time their father took them to see the big bands on Saturdays when the bands came to the Keith Albee Theater in Cincinnati, Ohio. The girls loved the big bands. It was at the high point of

World War II and the bands were the most prominent entertainment. Radio programs featuring the bands were very popular. And they were featured in a number of Hollywood films.

New York radio station WNEW, with Martin Block, was playing Tommy Dorsey and Glenn Miller recordings with the Pied Pipers and the Modernaires singing groups backing the band's boy and girl singers including Frank Sinatra, Bob Eberly, his brother Ray Eberle, Dick Haymes, Perry Como, and Helen O'Connell.

"My sister would cut school and ride the streetcar to the theater to attend the big band shows," Rosemary said. At home the girls would sit on the floor and listen to Harry James' records: "I've Heard that Song Before," and "I Had the Craziest Dream," sung by Helen Forrest, from the technicolor film *Springtime in the Rockies*.

At the Harry Chapin Outdoor theater in Huntington Long Island, I interviewed Rosemary Clooney, who said: "I listened carefully and realized I was becoming enamored by these performers and decided I might want to be a singer. But there were exacting rules to singing, and the fact that you needed a natural sense of timing. Listening to Helen Forrest's phrasing, I only knew I had to wait, and in my mind beat out the end of one phrase until it was over before I started the next one."

When the girls tried to audition for radio, Betty had more nerve than Rosemary and auditioned with more confidence. "If we get a job, I'll get an advance. If we don't get it, then we'll walk home. That's all there is to that," she'd say. Meanwhile, before one particular audition, they had but ten cents in their pocket.

"We heard they held open auditions at WLW radio station every Thursday. Our repertoire consisted of three songs." Betty had a very good ear for harmony and a lower voice than Rosemary. Betty would sing the second part in their duets. Rosemary would sing higher, so she sang lead.

Nothing would deter them. They sang their three songs, including Johnny Mercer's "Dream," the anthem of the Pied Pipers, and many years later, the theme song of the Society of Singers. It earned them a job singing for twenty dollars each. The station manager wanted the girls to submit the contract to their parents. For a change, Rosemary had moxie: "Our mother and father are in California and we live with my aunt."

"That's all right, he said. "You get your aunt to sign and you can go to work."

Thanks to Betty's nerve, the station manager advanced them one dollar. They cut school the next day, called their aunt and asked her if they could stay with her. They explained about the radio singing job. Their Aunt Jean was happy for the girls and allowed them to move in with her.

The station provided the girls with a singing coach. "We learned about six songs to do the *Moon River* show. It was on late at night and we sung mostly ballads like " How Deep is the Ocean," and "My Silent Love," and "Talk of the Town." With our salaries we bought summer dresses and saddle oxfords."

One show led to another for Betty and Rosemary. They began singing with a local band that played high school dances. "We were very happy being band singers." After two years with WLW they were being billed as The Clooney Sisters and became virtual celebrities in their hometown. When Barney Rapp's band came to town, he hired the girls, just like he once hired an unknown Doris Day. They performed big club dates at places like Castle Farms and several downtown Cincinnati hotels, one which performed on remote network broadcasts on weekends.

Now living with their Uncle George, who also managed their affairs, the girls were hired by the notable big band of Tony Pastor. Barney Rapp had arranged for the girls to audition for Pastor who just loved them. "Our first engagement was at the famous Steel Pier in Atlantic City. It was the first time we saw an ocean."

For the Clooney Sisters it was make -it -or -break -it -time. The place was jam-packed and the people applauded endlessly. " It was good, and there was so much excitement attached to it that it gave us a kind of a push."

The road beckoned and they took it. It was an education.

They learned a lot about performing and music during the Pastor years. The butterflies were starting, as they were in the big-time now. Rosemary was eighteen and Betty just fifteen. During the big band era many singers began their careers while teenagers: Billie Holiday, Ella Fitzgerald, Connie Haines, Doris Day, Helen O'Connell and Fran Warren, among others.

Rosemary and Betty at Home

"We always studied our lead sheets and rehearsed and re-hearsed faithfully," Rosemary told me, "We performed at one-night stands, at college proms, barn dances, subscription dances, hotel ballrooms, dance pavilions, and in theaters.

"After each show, we would climb aboard our chartered bus and sleep until we arrived at the next place. And, at last, we took our first plane trip. We were headed for the Hollywood Palladium." When Rosemary got off the plane, she instantly fell in love with California's soft air and warm climate and would come to love and live in California for the remainder of her life.

The girls were smart kids. They had a good ear for the music and easily met the arrangements and had some corny arrangements of their own. Ralph Flanagan, who was writing arrangements for them, gave them some good new arrangements, and they performed them very well.

After three years or so of band--bus traveling," Rosemary said, "Betty decided to quit and I remained with Tony Pastor as a single." Uncle George took Betty home with him and the mature, now experienced Rosemary Clooney began her tremendously successful solo career. However, that's another story now that the Clooney Sisters story was at an end.

The career of America's Sweetheart, Rosemary Clooney, had begun. 1983 - Rosemary Clooney: "I think I'm more in charge of my life now than I ever have been. When I was younger I had the tendency to listen exclusively to the person who was in charge, without trusting my own judgement enough. And I think that was a mistake at times in my life. But that was part of the female conditioning of the fifties. That was what we were supposed to do."

Rosemary Clooney at Harrah's - Lake Tahoe

THE LENNON SISTERS

The first question I posed to the lovely Lennon Sisters, after four solid kisses planted one by one on their cheeks, followed by a variety of giggles and smiles, was "Did Jimmy Durante really call you "My goils?" We were backstage at Westbury Music Fair on Long Island where the girls were appearing with the Tommy Dorsey Band under the direction of Buddy Morrow and the Texas Plowboy, Eddie Arnold.

Jimmy Durante and his goils!

"Oh Yes!" replied Kathy. " He loved us and we loved him. We appeared with him on our joint television show in 1969." It was now 1987.

Yes, it was such fun interviewing the Lennon's but, unfortunately, on our way home, my photographer discovered there was no film in the camera when he snapped about 25 photos of me and the girls.

The Lennon's were now grownup, so to speak, -Janet, Kathy, Diane, and Peggy, had already become group icons since their 1955 debut on the Lawrence Welk television show. "We still travel maybe four or five times a year- when it's beneficial money-wise for all of us to go together." They all began to talk at once: "We have to support our stageman and drummer, too. We usually back up people like Eddy Arnold, Andy Williams in places like Vegas and sometimes we are just our own act. We try to bring along some of the kids and husbands...but at different times."

They were headed for Atlantic City the following day. The Len-

Janet, Kathy, Diane and Peggy

non's never looked lovelier or acted more enthusiastic, like kids on a carousel, each trying to grab the ring. The familiar faces with those infectious smiles made an absolute Joy to be in their presence. "The youngest one is Janet, right? That's me," answered Janet from behind. We had interrupted "make-up" time.

"Is it true...at least that's what I have heard....that you quit (Lawrence) Welk because he would not give you a raise after a long time on a very low salary?" I asked.

"Basically, yes," answered Kathy. "We began with him---being four girls in one family ...and he paid us scale. But we were there a long time at group scale and felt we deserved solo scale." They argued, "But, when we got married and were raising children and so on...what we took home...simply wasn't enough for the time we were spending away, which was a full five days a week."

. The girls had been with Welk for almost twelve years. Welk had reasoned that they were gaining fame and attention appearing on his world-famous television show and that was to be considered a sort of payment, as well. The girls were receiving $ 100.00 each.

They began in 1955 on Welk's Christmas Show and surprised the experts by drawing 30 million viewers almost every week.

Welk felt they could make fabulous sums at appearances at state fairs on their own time with the publicity received from appearing on this show.

"Leaving the Welk show came at a time when we wanted to grow musically and didn't want to be treated as little girls," piped up Janet, "and so this allowed us to leave town these four times a year and make fifty times more money than to stay and do the Welk show.

"Was Welk upset?"

"We don't know. We were with him for twelve years and loved him very much, and we him. He raised us. We were just little kids. There are no hard feelings. We had to make a change and he didn't understand."

Lawrence Welk: "It was foolish to say that I was not hurt when they left. I was deeply hurt, but hurt by the parting itself, not by the fact they had decided to go. I missed them. They had been part of

Ralph Edwards and Lawrence Welk - *This is Your Life* with the Lennon Sisters

our lives for twelve years, and I hated to see those years end."

The Lennons sentimental ballads and sweet song executed in close harmony was a welcome contrast for viewers and listeners compared to the rock and roll being promoted to the public at that time.

"There are so many people we meet that played with our coloring books and now they're all the same age as we are and they are now parents like us. We grew up right alongside our fan," Peggy was saying.

"For the record, girls, I need you each to state who you are, how many children you have," said I.

"All right...I'll start....I'm Peggy and I'm married to Dick Catheart and we have six children. " Dick was a trumpet player in the Welk Orchestra and was currently freelancing." Married nineteen years this week.

"I'm Diane and married to Dick Gass and have three children, two girls eighteen and nineteen and a boy seventeen who plays in a rock band. Dick is a telephone repair man."

"I'm Janet and married to John Bahler--second marriage (first to ABC page Lee Bernhardi and had three children) and have five children and am raising them all."

"Oh, my God," I muttered aloud,"Little Janet, an American institution is married with teenage children." The girls infectious laughter brightened the room.

"I'm last...I'll finish off. I"m Kathy and married to Jim Derhris who is a chiropractor and we have no children and we've just been married one year. This is my second marriage. (The first to Mahlon Clark, another Welk musician who also played in Ray McKinley's band.)

These were the days of the *Ed Sullivan Show* on Sunday and *Lawrence Welk* on Saturday night. Everybody knew where to find the Lennon girls. "Now, when you go home and the show is over and all the lights are off---what do you do?"

"We do what every other housewife does. We scrub floors and take care of our children and husbands," agreed Kathy. "We all live in L.A. and see each other almost every day. One of us teaches school." None of the girls had a pool or grandiose house, even though they could have afforded it.

"We spend our evenings watching television and enjoying our families," declared Janet.

"We love our homes and family and we also love our careers," said Diane, "and all of our sons play in rock bands and perform at school."

"Did you all get along as sisters?"I treaded carefully on that one.

"Yes," said Diane, "We really do! We have seven other brothers and sisters, so we have a large family." "When you prepare for a concert tour, how do you get it all together?"

"When we put in new material, we learn the music, we learn the dancing. We rehearse and rehearse, but only the new stuff, otherwise we know our regular parts and need minimum rehearsing. Once it's up here," Janet said pointing to the brain behind her forehead, "we never have to rehearse it again."

The Lennon's appearance that night was a happy, upbeat, up tempo show with lots of close harmony. "We get to do our old songs, new songs, production numbers with four costume changes, and thoroughly enjoyable vignettes. "The audiences are incredible," the girls declared almost in unison, forever talking over one another, "there are always standing ovations every performance, every night. It's always a good, warm crowd," Janet said.

As I left the Lennon's in the year 1986, the girls were once again singing with the Lawrence Welk Big Band in Branson, Missouri. Today, they are celebrating 55 years as America's Sweethearts. They deserve it.

CONNIE HAINES

CONNIE HAINES AND *LES GIRLS*

Jane Russell, Beryl Davis, Rhonda Fleming and Connie Haines

DO LORD
TRADITIONAL

I've got a home in glory land that outshines the sun.
I've got a home in glory land that outshines the sun.
I've got a home in glory land that outshines the sun.
Way beyond the blue.

I took Jesus as my Savior, You take Him too.
I took Jesus as my Savior, You take Him too.
I took Jesus as my Savior, You take Him too, while He's still calling you.
Way beyond the blue.

I took Jesus as my Savior, You take Him too.
I took Jesus as my Savior, You take Him too.
I took Jesus as my Savior, You take Him too.
Way beyond the blue.

Chorus: Do Lord, O, Do Lord, O do remember me,
Do Lord, O, Do Lord, O do remember me,
Do Lord, O, Do Lord, O do remember me,
Way beyond the blue.

Connie Haines, Beryl Davis, Jane Russell, and Rhonda Fleming sang together as Les Girls, a quartet of well-known performers who got together to express their spiritual ideals in song and through the inspiration of the Holy Bible sang appropriate songs, the favorite and theme was "Do Lord."

Connie Haines and I were close friends the last 10 years of her life. She and I put together her biography, Snootie Little Cutie. The girls, all famous icons in their own genre, became first a gospel trio and then a quartet. Their first recording together was for the Decca-Coral label. "Do Lord" sold two million copies and reached number twenty-seven on the Billboard charts in 1954.

Connie, Jane and Beryl followed up with an album LP for Capitol Records, *The Magic of Believing*.

When they first got together to practice in the basement of Beryl's St. Stephen Episcopal Church, Della Russell (who was an early member and wife of crooner Andy Russell), and Jane Russell agreed to sing at a fund-raising event. Jane had just completed the movie *Gentlemen Prefer Blondes* with Marilyn Monroe.

Connie suggested they sing "Do Lord," an old church spiritual. Della was Catholic and said she didn't sing that song in her church. Beryl said," I'm from London. I never heard of it either."

That was the beginning of the gospel singing celebrities named the Four Girls.

Connie, of course, sang shoulder-to-shoulder with Frank Sinatra in the big bands of both Harry James and Tommy Dorsey. Beryl Davis, an English vocalist, was the last girl singer for Glenn Miller before he died on a flight over the English Channel on the way to Paris, to be followed by the band to entertain the troops. As we now know, Glenn was lost when a group of English planes accidentally hit his twin engine plane when they had to abort a bombing strike over Germany and were forced to abort their bombs in the Channel due to adverse weather. Beryl went on to sing with Sinatra on the *Lucky Strike Hit Parade* radio show.

Rhonda Fleming, the beautiful redheaded movie star who appeared in *A Connecticut Yankee in King Arthur's Court*, her first technicolor film, wherein she sang with Bing Crosby, and appeared in *The Spiral Staircase*, *Gunfight at the O.K. Coral*, and *Spellbound*, among many others quality films.

Jane Russell, a film superstar played in The Outlaw, *Gentlemen Prefer Blondes* (with Marilyn Monroe), and *Paleface*, with her friend Bob Hope. Jane wrote the foreword for my book on Bob Hope and contributed anecdotes about Bob. I enjoyed a friendship with Jane for many years thereafter. Earlier, Jane also sang with the Kay Kyser Band and once recorded with Frank Sinatra and the Modernaires on a single "Kisses and Tears."

Jane: "Connie and I knew all those spirituals. She was raised in the Baptist Church and I was raised in a non-denominational evangelical, so we taught the other two." The musical validity was that Connie carried the melody and the others provided the harmony. Jane sang bass and Beryl the equivalent of tenor harmony.

They performed on Abbott & Costello's *Colgate Comedy Hour* on Easter Sunday and appearances followed on a group of shows including Red Skelton, Ed Sullivan's, Milton Berle's and Arthur Murray's show. The press named them "Bosoms and Bibles."

While with the gospel singing group with Connie, Rhonda, and Beryl, guesting on television variety shows that sported a full band, Jane would call out to the musicians: "It's prayer time, fellows. Let's have a prayer."

The musicians came forward as the girls reached out their hands, guiding them into a circle. The musicians loved it and missed it when the girls went on tour.

"We four girls closed our eyes and bowed our heads...and the musicians followed suit," Jane said. Jane's words were like the command of a first sargeant.

"I peeked and caught a few roaming eyes and winks," Beryl remembered. "They didn't care whether the musicians were Jewish, Buddhist, or Christian. When Bing Crosby found us rehearsing in the Decca studios: That's it," he called out. "You gals have a hit...maybe a million seller. How about that!" Bing declared with enthusiasm. Years later, talking with Jane, Beryl, Rhonda, and Connie, they remember those incidents with loving kindness in voices that remain the same as they did in the 60s. Can you imagine four women living together, working together, starring together-and still loving one another?

"We had our differences, our fights, and some tears, but one overriding similarity transcended our differences---we lived by the scriptures," said Connie.

"Every night we would go back to our suite lined up in a row. Both girls were married, I was divorced from Bob (DeHaven), but we had eight kids among us," reminded Connie.

The girls frustrated the prying press. In a place like Las Vegas, the girls would remain in their room after a show. They had a refrigerator. We would have a bite to eat, talked, prayed,and then went to sleep," said Beryl. The press would have them painting the town, anyway, just to fill the papers."

After three years, Rhonda quit the group in 1957, reducing it to a trio. She was burdened with movie commitments. Beryl, Jane and Connie continued on and introduced some popular songs with a positive message into their repertoire, but kept on giving the bulk of their earnings to churches and charities.

The girls became the decade's leading pop gospel singers. They were the first to record spirituals on pop labels and launch the gospel trend of the time. They made twenty-four hit records with both Capitol and Decca Records. The girls returned to their regular career and family life.

Glenn Miller Bandleader Larry O'Brien, Connie Haines and Richard Grudens- 2002

I loved Connie and her wonderful outlook on life. She passed away too soon, but she is in the Lord's hands now. We just lost Jane Russell, and Beryl Davis' daughter tells me her mom has passed away. Rhonda Fleming is flourishing out there in California. She's contemplating a book about her life but just hasn't finished it at this writing. We talk regularly.

Those wonderful girls are and were wonderful girls and were a worthy and valid group of fine singers.

BRIAN SISTERS - 1935

THE BRIAN SISTERS
WITH DORIS AND BETTY BRIAN

This is the story of three little girls and their mother. Circumstances of family dynamics, beyond their control, thrust these girls into the drama of the Great Depression of 1929 to 39, which was the backdrop to this tale as was World War II. The incredible strength of the mother and her resolution are major parts, but the irrefutable fact of their own talent, their inherited genes, and pervasive ears for and the love of music, of these three children cannot be denied. Their parents stressed education in their development, so they all stretched a great deal beyond working on the family farm.

Top: Norma 13, Bernice18
Bottom: Gwen 4, Doris 6, Betty 8 -1932

Nineteen-year-old mom, Meda, determined early that farming was not in her future, so she was intrigued by a tall and handsome red-haired fellow, Frank Leslie Brian, whom she met in Rexburg, a semiprofessional baseball player by day, and ragtime piano performer in the dance band by night. These were activities as far removed from farming as she could imagine. Meda married Frank in 1912.

Mom - Meda Brian

Five daughters were born to the couple: Bernice in Rexburg in 1913, Norma in Twin Falls in 1918, Betty in Rexburg in 1923, Doris in Pocatello in 1926, and Gwen in Pocatello in 1928. Bernice and Norma were reared mostly in a home with both parents, but the younger three, close in age barely knew their father.

The indications that these girls - all five of them - were richly endowed with musical talent was obvious from their birth. From infancy they all could sing in tune and in perfect time. Willingly, but with little encouragement from their father and without any lessons, each girl performed alone and/or together at church meetings, parties, banquets, variety shows, at school and on local radio.

Bernice and Norma, absorbed with growing up and finishing their education, did not pursue further musical efforts, but the professional Brian Sisters trio was begun when Gwen, barely four years old, sang the melody, while Doris, six years old, and Betty, eight years old, formed the harmony parts. Soon they were in demand singing the popular songs of the time, "Bye, Bye, Blackbird" and "When the Red, Red Robin Comes Bob, Bob, Bobbin' Along," among many others. They learned these tunes by listening carefully to the radio.

Gwen 8, Doris 10, Betty 12 - 1937

After 1929, the Great Depression dragged the economy to a dead end. When Frank, always employable, left good-paying jobs to enjoy his pastime sports, Meda was forced to take in boarders to keep food on the table. Frank followed his own star, finally separated himself from the family in Salt Lake City in 1934, and Meda was left to finish the job of parenting alone.

The Brian Sisters' first paying job was on Amateur Night in a smoky, below-street-level speakeasy called the Brass Rail in Salt Lake City. The patrons, delighted at seeing this very young trio of performers belting out the popular songs of the day, tossed quarters, dimes and nickels onto the floor, and the girls gathered up their pay. That night they counted about eight dollars - an impressive sum for those desperate days. The rent was due, and food was scarce. Meda, a fine cook, seamstress and homemaker but with no career opportunities, soon figured that she had the dubious choice of

Brian Sisters - 1939

leaving the girls alone to find work for herself or putting her talented youngsters to work and staying with them.

The Shirley Temple phenomenon was in force and there were other children-oriented films being made, the *Our Gang Comedies* among them. Sunny California beckoned, with its radio, recording, theater, and movie industries. So, with only twenty dollars in her pocket but determination in her heart, Meda packed up the 1929 Model A Ford with whatever household goods she could fit in, gave the rest of their belongings to her sisters, and headed southwest with her brood. She was heard to say, "We can starve as easily there as here, and it will be a whole lot warmer."

Without the benefit of professional management, the Brian Sisters auditioned for radio shows, films, theater and night club engagements. Meda herself would present the girls - in their attractive homemade costumes - who would always enthusiastically and unselfconsciously perform, mostly without accompaniment. Almost immediately, they won small jobs and started to earn their way.

On their own they learned how to enter and leave a stage, how to bow graciously for applause, how to dance, how to stand quietly before an open microphone, how to read a dramatic script, and, most importantly, how to act as professionals, not as children. They learned early and well that producers, theater managers, and musical directors detested child performers and would not tolerate any extra noise, taciturn or temperamental outbursts, or other childish conduct. They learned that there are no excuses. And they learned not to cry. Their immaturity did not protect them from the realities and responsibilities of a tough life.

Gwen, Doris, Betty - 1943

Because their very existence depended upon the mastering of these lessons; they knew that, sick

L-R: Doris, Gwen and Betty, 1937 singing "Who Stole the Jam?" in a scene from *Sally, Irene and Mary*

or well, tired or rested, early morning or late night, like it or not, they must put smiles on their faces, stand up and sing out, and never, never lapse into youthful behaviors. They learned the hard way that if they misused their shoes, there were no new shoes. There were few toys, amusements or other trifles. They learned that if they wasted food, the next meal would be meager. They learned to forgo any but the barest necessities because the rent must be paid first. After they had been cheated by or imposed upon by ruthless adults, they learned to depend upon and trust one another exclusively, and they learned that The Show Must Go On.

With proceeds, they paid the rent and bought food and clothes. They even managed to pay tuition to a private school when the state of California took a dim view of their many absences from public school in order to rehearse, audition or perform and threatened to take them away from their mother and put them into orphanage care. Their income was sporadic and often had to last through dry times, but Meda's amazing ability to manage their assets kept them going until their next job. They were happy together, and grateful to be in warm California.

In the summer of 1935, Meda took the girls to the Hal Roach studios in Culver City. Their auditions started with assistant musical directors, then full directors and finally wound up in the offices of Hal Roach himself, who offered them an appearance in a musical episode of the *Our Gang Comedies* series. They were offered the princely sum of one hundred dollars a day for two days' work, and they were ecstatic! That film, *Our Gang Follies* of 1936, started a movie career.

At the time, radio, night clubs and theater were the primary sources of their activity and income. Among the preservation of their works are eight movies and two records, which have been collected, but they represent little of the actual career of the Brian Sisters.

The girls were featured in a couple of musicals: *New Faces of 1937* and *Swing While You're Able*. Late in 1937, they appeared in a film entitled, *Sally, Irene and Mary* starring Alice Faye, Jimmy Durante, Fred Allen and Tony Martin. This film, including a charming dancing scene with the female stars, was probably their best musical appearance.

Connee Boswell, of the famous Boswell Sisters, took an interest in the girls and assigned her brother-in-law to be their agent/ personal manager. Now Meda was released from the responsibility of finding jobs for them, and they were considered truly professionals. Their new manager procured appearances for them at famous Ciro's nightclub, The Mocambo, and The Trocadero. Miss Boswell arranged for a short musical film to be produced called *Sunday Night at the Trocadero*, which starred the Brian Sisters.

Their manager also scheduled benefit appearances for the Metro-Goldwyn-Mayer Studio Club and the Motion Picture Relief Fund. These benefits included appearances by Milton Berle, Fannie Brice, Mickey Rooney, Sophie Tucker, Eddie Cantor, Bing Crosby and many others.

On the basis of their success in *Sally, Irene and Mary*, the Twentieth Century Fox producers had them appear in a new Shirley Temple film, but Shirley Temple's mother balked at allowing little Gwen to be seen in the same movie with Shirley. "Too cute" was her reason. When told that Gwen would not be used but Betty

Twin Tones: L-R Alan Copeland, Gwen Wardrobe, Doris Brian, Bob Parker and Doris would sing with Shirley in their trio, Betty and Doris balked. However, when faced with the promise that Gwen would be paid for not appearing, Betty and Doris sang with Shirley Temple in *Little Miss Broadway*.

In 1938, also at Twentieth Century Fox, they performed in *Kentucky Moonshine* starring Tony Martin and the Ritz Brothers. In early 1939, the girls' appeared in *Second Fiddle* starring the Norwegian ice skating Olympic gold medalist, Sonja a Henie, Tyrone Power and Rudy Vallee.

Their next film was Tin Pan Alley, a lively musical from Twentieth Century Fox starring Alice Faye, Betty Grable and John Payne. And next they appeared in a Columbia film called *Music in My Heart*, starring Rita Hayworth and Tony Martin. The young and very dark-haired Miss Hayworth was just starting her career.

In 1939, the Brian Sisters' final movie appearance was in *Love Affair at RKO*, starring Irene Dunne and Charles Boyer. Although all three Brian Sisters recorded "Wishing Will Make It So" for the sound track, only Gwen appeared on screen. It was clearly pay back for her

nonappearance in Little Miss Broadway. As a result of the success of this movie, the Brian Sisters adopted the song "Wishing" and used it as a theme song for their weekly coast-to-coast radio broadcasts on NBC, accompanied by pianist Skitch Henderson. The girls appeared in fifteen movies, the last being, *Beautiful, But Broke*, in 1944 starring Joan Davis and Jane Frazee in which they sang their own arrangement of "I'm Just Another Blues."

While the little trio was growing up and gaining popularity, they were considered for the immensely successful radio show called *Camel Caravan*, but then were dropped because the sponsor, R. J. Reynolds

Top to Bottom: Bob Parker, Bette Bligh, Doris Brian and Alan Copeland

Tobacco Company, decided that children were not suitable for their product. They were again disappointed when they were chosen to appear as regulars on *The Kraft Music Hall* starring Bing Crosby, but at the last minute were told that the Mills Brothers had been selected because a black audience was important to the sponsors. In spite of these letdowns, they did appear on many famous radio shows including *Lux Radio Theater*, the Eddie Cantor weekly show *Texaco Town*, where the girls sang "Mister Paganini," and for two years on the very popular coast to coast *Eddie Lowry Show*. They continued with nightclub and theater appearances and sang on background sound tracks of several movies.

In 1941, war was on the horizon. . There were several radio shows devoted to young military servicemen including *Your Blind Date and Hollywood Victory Committee* and the Brian Sisters, who were by now teen-agers, were perfect for this type of entertainment. In late 1943, they were delighted to work with the talented songwriter/producer Johnny Mercer at Capitol Records and were asked to record the Jimmy VanHeusen/Johnny Burke song, "Swinging on a Star." Throughout the war years they sang often at the Hollywood Canteen and traveled with USO Camp Shows. They were regulars with the Bing Crosby/Bob Hope North Hollywood Marching and Chowder Club Clambake Follies which performed at many military bases around the Southern California area. They flew with this group in military aircraft throughout the western United States. They appeared with the zany Spike Jones Orchestra promoting the sale of War Stamps and Bonds.

In December 1945, Betty left the group to be married, so Gwen and Doris joined with two young men to form a quartet. They sang with the Jan Garber Orchestra on the road throughout the U.S., made several recordings with that band, and appeared at the Biltmore Hotel in Los Angeles for over two years.

When Gwen married in 1946, Doris carried the ball alone and joined with another girl and three young men to form a five-part harmony group. Considered "studio musicians," they recorded vocal background music for films and recordings. They also appeared in early television shows including Ed Sullivan's. In 1952, Doris left California to live in Ogden, Utah, but she continued to sing with a radio-advertising group in Salt Lake City called Notable Ads. Meda, finally able to turn her attention to herself, became an accomplished representative for a beautiful linens firm and retired in 1975. She lived with Betty until her death in 1995 at age one hundred and two. The lives of the Brian Sisters after their careers were successful, rearing bright and beautiful children of their own.

Author's Note:

Although underrated and frequently uncredited in the 15 films they performed, the Brian girls were excellent singers with an obvious, natural gift. No one could teach them what they were able to impart to audiences. Their motion picture performances in films are endearing, wholesome and enriched with charm. Had they produced an abundance of recordings like so many other groups, they would have reached the pinnacle of popularity enjoyed by their peers and had the strong historical presence the future has denied them. Find their works and enjoy the fine performances that have been isolated from the films.

From Doris: On behalf of myself, and my sister Betty, (unfortunately, Gwen passed away in 1990) I want to thank you for presenting our memories in your book. At eighty-five and eighty-seven years old, respectively, it is a pleasure for us to find ourselves included with these illustrious *Perfect Harmony* groups. Although our career lasted only from 1933 until 1944, we reached some loyal fans and we now hope to find more folks who would appreciate our efforts. With appreciation, Doris Brian Rounds.

MOVIE APPEARANCES

1. Our Gang Follies of 1936
2. New Faces of 1937
3. Sing While You're Able 1937
4. Thanks For Listening 1937
5. Sally, Irene and Mary 1937
6. Sunday Night at the Trocadero 1937
7. Little Miss Broadway 1938
8. Kentucky Moonshine 1938
9. Second Fiddle 1939
10. Love Affair 1939
11. Music In My Heart 1940
12. Tin Pan Alley 1940
13. Boogie Woogie Boogie Man 1942
14. High School 1940
15. Beautiful But Broke 1944

The Brian Sisters sing in *Sunday Night at the Trocadero* - 1937

FOLLOW THE BOYS

THE FOUR FRESHMEN

Ross Barbour, Don Barbour, Bob Flanagan, Hal Katzsch

The Four Freshmen group members consisted of Don Barbour, Ross Barbour, Hal Kratzsch, Ken Albers, Brian Eichenberger, Bob Ferreira, Curtis Calderon, Vince Johnson, Bob Flanagan, and Ken Errair-a total of ten, although eventually 24 voices were adopted into this fine singing group over the years.

Don and Ross Barbour began the barbershop-style singing group as the 1940s came to a close. They were originally named Hal's Harmonizers.

They were clearly influenced by Bing and the Mills Brothers, the Pied Pipers and Mel Torme's Mel-Tones. The Beach Boys, however, credit the Four Freshmen as their major influence, as well as Bing and The Mills Brothers, so there were close ties and influences among all these groups as they alternately became featured in the spotlight.

The Freshmen started out singing standards that were not exactly groundbreaking, but was established material like Mel Torme's "Christmas Song," and "Moonglow," (the theme from the film *Picnic*) while attending Butler University's Arthur Jordan Conservatory in Indianapolis, Indiana.

The group was self-contained instrumentally, each member playing more than one instrument besides their vocal skills. They struggled for some time before they were discovered by bandleader Stan Kenton, who was able to influence the producers at Capitol Records to allow them the needed chance to record their fine work. Arranger Pete Rugolo, who was closely associated with the Kenton band, being their innovative arranger, helped guide the Four Freshmen to their inevitable success at Capitol. Their first hit single was one of my favorite group hits " It's a Blue World," followed by "Mood Indigo," a pure Ellington piece of material they performed with a partial *a cappella* sound of voices instead of the well established entire Ellington big band ensemble effect. "Graduation Day" was another hit released in 1956 one year after the success of another hit, "Day by Day."

The Four Freshmen were, and still remain, a very smart and innovative outfit always working their instruments around their singing performances ever so smoothly and always proficiently. They created their own album concepts, similar to what Sinatra was doing at the time. The boys were consistently booked on the popular television shows. The original group performed for many years and through many personnel changes. Bob Flanagan, an original member who retired in 1992, recently passed away.

Over the years the group as been nominated six times for the Grammy. Today, Brian Eichenberger is lead vocal and guitarist; Curtis Calderon is second vocalist and trumpet/flugelhorn player, Vince Johnson is 3rd vocal and bass player and Bob Ferriera is 4th vocal and on drums. Their bookings extend into 2012 and beyond. Can you believe it? The Four Freshmen won Best Vocal Group of the Year in Down Beat Magazine's Readers' Polls in 1953, 54, 55, 56, 58,2000, and 2001.

Brian Eichenberger, Curtis Calderon, Vince Johnson, Bob Ferreira

PAST MEMBERS

Ross Barbour, Don Barbour, Marvin Pruitt, Bill Comstock, the late Bob Flanigan,Ken Errair, Hal Kratzsch, Ken Albers, Ray Brown, Gary Lee Rosenberg, Kevin Stout, Greg Stegeman, Autie Goodman, Alan MacIntosh, Newton Graber, Dennis Grillo, Rod Henley, Dave Jennings, Mike Beisner and Kirk Marcy.

There exists a Four Freshmen Society who held their 23rd convention in Toledo, Ohio during the second week of September 2011, during the production of this book. Back in 2009 the convention was held in Atlanta, Georgia. The show was well attended and featured the original group of Ross Barbour, Bob Flanigan, and the widow of Don Barbour. Former Four Freshmen, Ray Brown, Rod Henley, Kirk Marcy, and Greg Stegeman also attended and performed.

LIST OF ALBUMS:
Voices in Modern (1955)
4 Freshmen and 5 Trombones (1955)
Freshmen Favorites (1956)
4 Freshmen and 5 Trumpets (1957)
4 Freshmen and 5 Saxes (1957)
Voices In Latin (1958)
The Freshmen Year (1958)
Voices In Love (1958)
In Person (1958)
4 Freshmen and 5 Guitars (1959)
Love Lost (1959)
Freshmen Favorites Vol.2 (1959)
Voices And Brass (1960)
Road Show (1960)
First Affair (1960)
Voices in Fun (1961)
The Freshmen Year (1961)
Best of The Four Freshmen (1961)

Stars in Our Eyes (1962)
The Swingers (1962)
Day By Day (1962)
Got That Feelin' (1963, In Person, Vol. 2 (1963)
More 4 Freshmen and 5 Trombones (1964)
Funny How Time Slips Away (1964)
That's My Desire (1967)
A Today Kind of Thing (1968)
Today is Tomorrow (1968)
Four Freshmen in Tokyo '68 (1969)
Different Strokes (1969)
My Special Angel (1970)
Return to Romance (1971)
Mount Freshmore (1977)
Alive & Well in Nashville (1977)
Live At Butler University With Stan Kenton And His Orchestra (1986)
Fresh! (1986)
Freshmas! (1992)
Angel Eyes (1995)
Easy Street (1997)
Golden Anniversary Celebration (1998)
Still Fresh CD (1999)
Four Freshmen Live CD (2000)
First Affair/Voices in Fun Double CD (2002)
Live in the New Millennium CD (2002)
Live in Holland CD (2004)
In Session CD (2005)
Star-spangled Banner Single CD (2005)
Live from Las Vegas' Suncoast Hotel DVD (2006), Snowfall CD (2007)
Live from Las Vegas' Suncoast Hotel CD (2009)
Live from the Atlanta FFS Convention (members only) DVD (2009)
Four Freshmen and 'Live' Trombones CD (2009).

Dale Sheets still represents the Four Freshmen, as he has for many years. I first met him when he was representing Mel Tormé and arranged an interview with Mel and me back in the mid-eighties.

THEME OF THE FOUR FRESHMEN

IT'S A BLUE WORLD
BOB WRIGHT AND CHET FORREST

It's a blue world without you
It's a blue world alone
My days and nights that once were filled with heaven
With you away how empty they have grown
It's a blue world from now on, its a through world for me
The sea, the sky, my heart and I
We're all an indigo blue,
Without you it's a blue, blue world

THE AMES BROTHERS

The four Ames Brothers began it all in Maiden, Mass in a nonprofessional but musical family. The boys - Gene, Vic, Joe and Eddie were brought up on classical music by their parents who were Russian-Jewish immigrants from the Ukraine who read Shakespeare and semi-classics to their nine children. Being the first four children, their mother's plan for them was singing popular music as a quartet.

The very young boys performed touring Army and Navy bases and were offered a job in Boston at the Fox and Hounds Nightclub under the name the Armory Brothers and built a popularity base for themselves. They were hired by The Art Mooney's Orchestra and

were "discovered" by Milt Gabler of Decca Records who had them cut a few sides just before the recording ban was invoked. When the ban was lifted they were the first artists to record for Coral Records. They shortened their name to Ames from Armory when they recorded the sensational single "Rag Mop" with "Sentimental Me" on the "B" side, a tremendously popular single recording and their first hit. Their voices had a nice lilting, although crying, nasal sound. Ed sang lead, Gene was second tenor, Joe sang bass and Vic first tenor. They actually began singing in their inimitable style when they were in grammar school during the 1930s.

The boys originally had alternate aspirations. Gene had wanted to be a baseball player, and even made semi-pro in New England, while Vic wanted to become an actor, but wound up a comedian even within the group. Ed was actually a ping-pong (table tennis) professional player, and Joe's interests centered around singing opera.

Nevertheless, they became regulars on the Arthur Godfrey, Milton Berle, Jackie Gleason, Perry Como, and Ed Sullivan television shows. Not bad!

The boys recorded the popular "Undecided" with Les Brown's band of Renown. Billboard Magazine voted the boys Best Vocal Group of 1958.

The recordings, "Can Anyone Explain?," "You, You, You," (their # 1 hit), "The Naughty Lady of Shady Lane," and "Undecided" were all hits. It seemed as though every recording was a notable success.

Lead singer Ed Ames eventually went solo, which seems to be the case with many of the singing groups from Rosie Clooney, to Al Alberts, to Patty Andrews. However, Ed Ames, still with us, sparkled in the theater and on television. He appeared in the Fantasticks and Carnival on Broadway. Interestingly, Ames' unusually dark complexion won him many roles as an American Indian. You may recall his role playing Chief Bromden on Broadway in One Flew Over the Cuckoo's Nest? He performed on television in Daniel Boone as the Native American Mingo with Fess Parker. Ed continued singing and produced a number of albums through 1970, twenty-one in all.

The Ames brothers songs always hit the spot and the heart,

being refreshing- sounding and contained acceptable subject matter popular with appreciable audiences. Their recording of "Ragmop" will, for me, be the signature recording of the Ames Brothers.

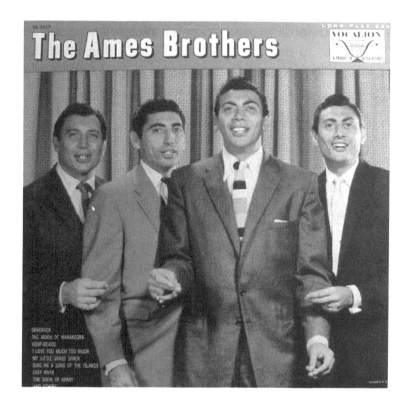

THE FOUR ACES
AL ALBERTS AND THE FOUR ACES: HARMONY AND INSPIRATION AND SOME COINCIDENCES

BY JOHN PRIMERANO

It was early summer of 1967. I was auditioning at J & A Catering in South Philadelphia to appear on a new television show due to air in the fall. It was to be *The Al Alberts Talent Hour*. I was a piano player and later added vocals to my act, although I had been singing and playing for a time in talent contests.

John Primerano

As a youngster in the 1950's our family 45 RPM player was playing artists like the Four Aces singing "Stranger in Paradise," "Three Coins in the Fountain," "Organ Grinder's Swing," and "Heart-of -My-Heart." For my audition, I was going to play my majestic arrangement of "Love is a Many Splendered Thing" that had served me well in other competitions.

For some unknown reason I had a vague idea Al Alberts and the Aces had recorded the tune. But we did not have a copy of the song by them or anyone and it remained a gnawing mystery.

All day long the idea continued to haunt me. Did they or didn't they record it? We should have had a copy of it at home. Well, I liked my arrangement and went with it.

When I performed, I played my heart out, hammering triplets with my right hand on the second chorus while my left hand played an active, flowing accompaniment. I was a veritable Ferrante and Teicher rolled into one. When I finished, I received an ovation from other auditioners and their families. But, I was aware that Al and his staff were chuckling. So I knew then I was right: "Love is a Many Splendored Thing" was not only a Four Aces hit, but they sang it on the movie's sound track and the song won the Oscar, Yes, the Academy Award.

Oh! Boy, was I embarrassed. Surely the judges had to think I was trying to score points with Al Alberts by choosing that particular song. Why hadn't I listened to my inner voice advice?

Al stood up with a good-natured smile and in a voice I swore could be heard in California: " You sure know what to play to pass an audition, kid." The rest of the room broke into laughter and I was sure

I was history regarding the *Al Albert's Talent Hour*. I was lucky after all: I made my appearance on the fourth show. It would be the first of many coincidences in the lives of Al Alberts and John Primerano.

But, I'm getting ahead of the story.....

Al Alberts was born Albert Albertini in South Philadelphia on August 10, 1922 to an immigrant father from Italy, named Vincent, but everyone called him Jim, and an American mother of Italian parents, Vincenzo, called Bessie. I was born on August 10, 1950 and my father's name was Vincent, whose Godmother called him Jimmy, as well. In Italian history there is some connection with the two names although I have never figured out why? (Coincidental, yes?)
Al had an older brother named Angelo, and a younger sister named Rita. Al was an excellent student at Drexel Elementary school and went on to Vare Junior High where Al had his first taste of performing in a dance band where he both played and sang: "We had three saxes, two trumpets, one trombone, bass, drums, and I played the piano and was the featured vocalist." said Al. (Coincidental again!) Incidentally, Buddy De Franco (who later directed the Glenn Miller Orchestra) was the band's clarinetist when they auditioned for the famous *Major Bowes Amateur Hour* and made it. "We didn't win, but what a great feeling to be in New York. Wow!" said Al.

The band accepted an appearance on the popular *Horn & Hardart Children's Hour*. They called themselves the Bandbusters. Here is where Al Albertini became Al Alberts. It was due to the show's host constant mispronunciation of Albertini.

The clouds of war now covered the country and Al Alberts joined the Navy, not serving in Special Services, but with distinction as a radio operator on a destroyer that escorted oil tankers, and was often attacked by German U-Boats.

After the war, Al enrolled in Temple University (Coincidence 4) and spent much time with Dave Mahoney, a friend he met in the service, and Lou Silvestri and Rosario (Sod) Vacarro, and formed a combo with Al on the piano and vocals, Dave on tenor sax, Lou on Drums and Sod on trumpet. They auditioned at Esther's Recreation in Prospect Park, Pa. Esther's husband was the proprietor and was playing solitaire while the boys auditioned. He liked what he heard

and the agreed salary was seven dollars per man.

      With all the work arranging and practicing, they had forget to coin a name for themselves. At that moment the proprietor turned over an 'Ace' from his playing card deck and asked "Why don't you call yourselves "The Aces?" Al instantly agreed but added the fact that there were four of them, so he named the four young singers from Philadelphia, The Four Aces.

During rehearsals, Al experimented with vocal harmonies and although the others had never sang before all had pretty good voices which brought Al's arrangements to life. At an engagement at the Ukrainian Club in Chester, Pa. a songwriter (George Hoven) with a handwritten lead sheet in pencil approached them with a song called "It's No Sin." And now things began to happen. "Sin" became their most requested song and although Al was saving money to get married to Stella Zippi, they both put their savings together and invested in producing a 45 RPM recording of the song with their own label. A Chester, Pa. radio disc jockey, Jimmy Lynn, played the record over and over. It's success spread wide enough to interest the producers of a Philadelphia radio station show *The 950 Club* with Joe Grady and Ed Hurst. The Four Aces were on their way.

Hit followed hit: "Garden in the Rain," "Tell Me Why," (to which Al wrote the lyrics), and "Written on the Wind," winning gigs on the popular television shows of Patti Page, Perry Como, Ed Sullivan, and Milton Berle's *Texaco Star Theater* and other top-rated variety programs.

During the ensuing years you could find the Four Aces virtually everywhere you could find a stage for them to fill with their magical performances. From Baltimore's Hippodrome to the New York Paramount, the Four Aces reigned. They performed with the great Gene Krupa Band, Count Basie's Big Band, Kate Smith and Johnny Ray, Frankie Laine, Perry Como, and their great friend Tony Bennett, Woody Herman's Band, and picked up a Gold Record for " Tell Me Why," on the way back to the Paramount again with Jerry Gray's Orchestra, then sharing the stage with Gordon MacRae and Kathryn Grayson on film with *The Desert Song*. They were a foursome sharing the spotlight on the highest mountain of show business with the creme-de la-creme of talent of their time.

After ten years of leading and managing The Four Aces, Al quit the group and went solo. First stop: Sciolla's Supper Club in Philadelphia where they booked only top acts (Coincidence 5 - that's where I started playing piano in the house band). For the following ten years Al Alberts toured the world many times, including entertaining our troops in Japan, Korea, and throughout the Far East. After a grueling trip to Korea, and playing extra dates, Al and Stella decided to return home.

Next: The *Al Albert's Talent Hour* first aired in September, 1967, on WKBS television in Philadelphia. After my initial appearance on the show, I became part of a select group of talented teens and young adults who would be called for special programs. Our Christmas show ran on Christmas Eve, a Sunday, Al's normal day for broadcasting his show. It was so successful that it was repeated on Christmas Day.

By now, everyone connected with the show were like a family and we wanted to present the best possible show. We taped from morning til 3 AM to do a one-hour show. It was an incredible experience.

Being associated with Al Alberts was a special opportunity as he performed an annual benefit at a convent in Media, Pa. I acted as accompanist for every act during these shows. We had rehearsed at Al and Stella's home in Media, Harmony Hill, and I couldn't believe my eyes when Al brought out his charts of the hits of the Four Aces. There I was, at seventeen, playing these great songs, reading the actual piano parts and hearing the voice, in person, the voice and recordings I had grown up listening to.

During one show, I was embarrassed when the arrangement called for a D seventh chord arpeggio. I had played an F seventh, which to a musician, is tantamount to being musically illiterate. Al calmly walked over to the piano and played the correct chord. After the show I apologized (with my parents watching) and Al simply put his arm over my shoulder to calm me.

"Let me tell you something, John. That was just a moment that can happen to anyone. I once gave these same piano charts to Count Basie and he couldn't even read them! Not a note. So don't be so hard on yourself. You did a better job than the Count himself." Al was a warm gentleman to me, an embarrassed seventeen year old kid.

Although the show was doing well, it was nevertheless canceled by WKBS without any explanation, but it was probably the best thing that could have happened to Al Alberts.

While Al was negotiating to move the show to another station in October, 1968, I joined the American Federation of Musicians to begin my professional career. By the summer of 1969, I was playing piano for singer Billy Mathews in Atlantic City before the casinos took over. Billy and his family stayed in Wildwood, New Jersey and I at an aunt's bungalow in Wildwood, and so we commuted the forty-six mile one-way trip every night or day. Our performance schedule was inhuman, but we did have one night off, a luxury, indeed, that I would not see again for five years.

Al was appearing at The Lucky Club in Wildwood. Being short of nineteen years, I went to see him perform with my parents. Al spotted us before the show and joined us at our table. My folks and he and his wife, Stella had always enjoyed one another's company. Al invited me backstage as he prepared for his appearance and we spoke about my professional future for a half an hour until it was show time. I rejoined my parents.

Al's performance was always his best. In the middle of his act he paused to introduce me and my folks to the audience, stating that I had once been a part of his show and that I was beginning my own career and wished me success. The audience applauded and I took a shy bow, all of this was heady stuff for a promising nineteen year old.

In 1970, Al Alberts was back on television WPVI, now ABC-6 in Philadelphia, with a new show, *Al Albert's Showcase*. He had retained most of the original group, then eventually catered to a younger group over time, some of whom became future stars on Broadway. The show traveled to Hershey Park, Pa. and Wildwood, New Jersey. Its success led to a thirty-two year run.

I saw Al Alberts just one more time after our Lucky Club encounter. By then I had become a popular tri-state act, performing a songwriter/singer/pianist act in lounges throughout those areas in and around around Philadelphia, Atlantic City, and related areas. In 1975, Al and the Aces reunited, although through the years other members joined the group as original members resigned. Al and the original members lost the title to the name Four Aces by a quirky Court decision. He was forced to settle on the name Al Alberts and the Originals. What had started as a reunion turned into many professional appearances together.

On November 27, 2009, Al Alberts passed away at the age of eighty-seven (coincidence 7) . My dad, who had been ill for some time passed on the exactly the same day. My dad was also eighty six and left us at 8:00 AM that very morning, which leads to coincidence 8. Both Al and I were born on the 10th day in the month of August. Stella Alberts, Al's true love, passed away in January, 2011. I had heard the news when I was pulling into a hospital parking lot to visit my mother, who was a critically ill patient.

In February 2010, I learned about a tribute to Al Alberts by a former show regular. My dad was ill and I was not in a mood for attending the tribute. However, I was invited and was eventually drawn to it and became a guest speaker and performed "Three Coins in the Fountain" because the scheduled performer had to cancel. Indeed, there was no doubt that I felt I was supposed to be there.

The day came and I spoke glowingly of my friend Al Alberts, recounting stories and played an instrumental version of "Three Coins in the Fountain," keeping it pure by omitting a vocal. During the second chorus of the song, I mentioned the distinctive Four Aces sound....the Four Aces Shuffle, a slowing down of the traditional shuffle rhythm that many bands like Louis Prima used on fast tunes. After playing that second chorus, I received a standing ovation. My attendance at the tribute, I believe, was meant to be, and as Stella had always said, "There are no coincidences."

I shall always cherish my association with Al and Stella Alberts and the Four Aces.

THE FOUR LADS

"In 1946, while still students at St. Michael's Cathedral Choir School in Toronto, Canada, Connie Codarini and I, Bernie Toorish, decided to form a vocal quartet. Along with Rudy Maugeri and Jackie Perkins.

We called ourselves The Otnorots (Toronto spelled backwards.) Enamored by a black jubilee spiritual group, The Golden Gate Quartet, we changed our name to the Jordanaires (years before the group that backed up Elvis Presley existed). By 1947, Perkins and Maugeri (who later formed the Crewcuts) had been replaced by Jimmie Arnold and Frank Busseri.

"In 1949, our idols, The Golden Gate Quartet came to Toronto to play a theater date. We wrangled our way backstage and sang our version of several of their songs. Orlandus Wilson, their bass singer was so impressed that he called Michael Stewart, their manager, who soon brought us down to New York City. "There we were booked into an East side supper club, Le Ruban Bleu, and were renamed The Four Dukes. But there was already a group in Detroit by that name, so Julius Monk, the impresario of the club, coined us as The Four Lads.

"In 1951 I was asked to work up the arrangements for a new singer that Columbia A & R man Mitch Miller had discovered. It was Johnnie Ray and the songs were "Cry," and on the "B" side "The Little White Cloud That Cried." Two blockbusters to start our career. "Our backing Johnnie on that recording propelled The Four Lads into a contract with Columbia Records.

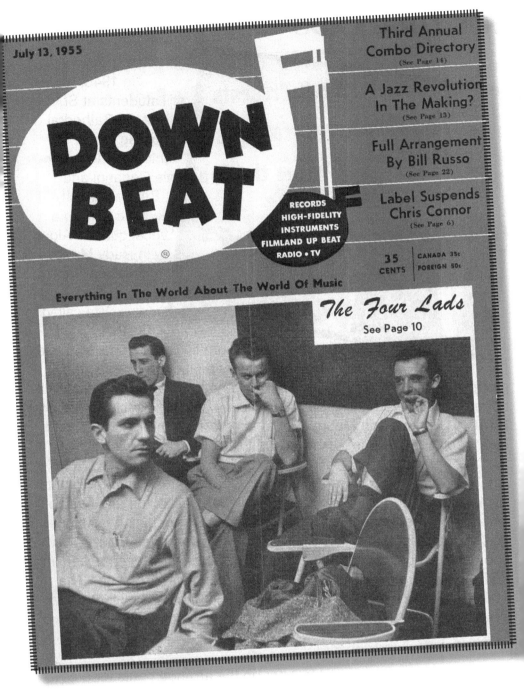

July 13, 1955

DOWN BEAT

RECORDS
HIGH-FIDELITY
INSTRUMENTS
FILMLAND UP BEAT
RADIO • TV

Everything In The World About The World Of Music

Third Annual
Combo Directory
(See Page 14)

A Jazz Revolution
In The Making?
(See Page 13)

Full Arrangement
By Bill Russo
(See Page 22)

Label Suspends
Chris Connor
(See Page 6)

35 CENTS | CANADA 35c
FOREIGN 50c

The Four Lads
See Page 10

"We got lucky with a string of notable hits: "Down by the Riverside" in 1952, "Istanbul" in 1953, "Skokiaan" in 1954, "Moments to Remember" in 1955, "No, Not Much" and "Who Needs You" in 1956, and the very notable "Standing on the Corner" from the Broadway show *The Most Happy Fella,* written by Frank Loessor.

"During this period we produced five gold records and appeared on virtually every network variety television show. We performed endlessly at State Fairs, on college campuses, in theaters and night clubs located just about everywhere, including gigs from Tokyo to Las Vegas to Honolulu, and even to Glasgow in Scotland. We also sold over 50 million records.

"However, like life itself, many of the good things in our career came to an end. Connie left the group in 1962, and I in 1970.

"Richard, with Jimmie Arnold and Connie Codarino gone, it leaves Frankie Busseri and I as the sole survivors. One thing we took pride in was the fact that we strived to be good role models to all our young fans. That was as important as every song we sang and every record we made."

Bernie Toorish, January 2012

Richard Grudens notes: Today, the Four Lads continue bringing exciting and those truly golden performances to audiences on cruise ships, dinner theaters, night clubs and hotel casinos. The current members of the group features original member Frank Busseri (bass),

Don Farrar (lead tenor), Aaron Bruce (second tenor), and Alan Sokoloff (baritone), For over fifty years, the Four Lads' singing has lit up stages and recalled many a memory for their legion of fans. It's amazing, how, after all the years the Four Lads are still providing many wonderful "Moments to Remember."

"This photo was taken at The Buttery - a showroom/restaurant at the Ambassador West Hotel in Chicago. We were there for three months from December 1950 to March 1951. It was great. Peggy Lee was a guest at the hotel for several weeks. We became friends with Peggy and even took her two daughters to the Chicago Stadium to go ice skating. We had lots of fun skating and falling. We appeared later on Peggy's network radio program in New York City where we sang "Shrimp Boats are a Comin' " Peggy Lee was a beautiful class act singer and an even better person." - Bernie Toorich

STANDING ON THE CORNER
W.M. - FRANK LOESSER

Standing on the corner watching all the girls go by
Standing on the corner watching all the girls go by
Brother you don't know a nicer occupation
Matter of fact, neither do I
Than standing on the corner watching all the girls go by
I'm the cat that got the cream
Haven't got a girl but I can dream
Haven't got a girl but I can wish
So I'll take me down to Mainstreet
And that's where I select my imaginary dish
Standing on the corner watching all the girls go by
Standing on the corner giving all the girls the eye
Brother if you've got a rich imagination
Give it a whirl, give it a try
Try standing on the corner watching all the girls
Watching all the girls, watching all the girls go by
Saturday and I'm so broke
I couldn't buy a girl a nickel coke,
Still I'm living like a millionaire
When I take me down to Mainstreet
And I review the harem
Parading for me there
Standing on the corner
Watching all the girls go by
Standing on the corner
Underneath the springtime sky
Brother, you can't go to jail
For what you're thinking
Or for the oh-o-o-o-h look in your eye
You're only standing on the corner
Watching all the girls
Watching all the girls
Go by

THEIR BIGGEST HITS

Istanbul - 1953
Moments to Remember - 1955
No, Not Much - 1956
Standin' on the Corner - 1956
Who Needs You? - 1957

The Hi-Lo's

Once upon a time, Clark Burroughs and Bob Morse sang with the Billy May band as the Encores. When the band stopped touring they added the voices of Gene Puerling and Bob Strasen and formed the fabulous voices known as the Hi-Lo's.

This quartet of fine singers had no category. During the 50s and the 60s they sang pop, jazz, barbershop, calypso, and musical theater as well. Their unusual arrangements set them apart from all other male groups. Members Gene Puerling, Bob Strasen (replaced by Don Shelton in 1959), Clark Burroughs, and Bob Morse excelled on such compositions as "June in January," "Fools Rush In," and "Whatever Lola Wants," with their incredible vocal range. They recorded a great album with Rosemary Clooney: *Ring Around Rosie*. Clark sang lead, Bob and Bob were tenors, and Gene on bass, this stellar group became one of the most innovative vocal groups of all time.

"Gene Puerling (arranger and group leader): "We were influenced by the Four Freshmen, the Modernaires and the Meltones. This was happening at a time when the Beach Boys, the Mamas and the Papas, the Gatlin's, and Manhattan Transfer were finding their own way, too."

The Hi-Lo's opened for the great voice of Judy Garland while she performed on tour, and they sang at Madison Square Garden, the Hollywood Bowl and in London at Royal Albert Hall. The boys signed with Columbia Records in 1956. Their first album sold 100,000 copies, not bad for unknowns. It was named *Suddenly It's the Hi-Lo's*.

This brought them lots of work that included filling their harmonic efforts with their trademark adventurous vocal acrobatics. Along the way they also worked with Frank Sinatra, Steve Allen,

Don Shelton
August 28, 1934 -

Herb Jeffries, Peggy Lee, and Nat "King" Cole. Their appearances on the *Rosemary Clooney Show* catapulted them to even a higher level of exposure nationally as small screen regulars.

With the arrival of the Beatles in America, along with other English groups, the Hi-Lo's lost lots of hard won ground. They were badly damaged by that musical barrage. They never really had

Milton R. Chapman
September 9, 1932 -

a hit record which caused Mitch Miller, Columbia Records A & R man, to council

Robert B. (Bob) Morse
July 27, 1923 - April 27, 2001

them to dress down those complicated arrangements and join the more popular Hit Parade material.

The ensuing albums in the early sixties did not succeed. Although they were more upbeat, they ultimately failed. Frank Sinatra called upon them to join his new Reprise label. Nothing worked out there, either. The

Clark Burroughs
March 3, 1930 -

British had out done the Hi-Lo's and so they scattered and quit, each one doing different things. Bob Morse settled down and opened an antique store. Gene Peurling formed Singers Unlimited and finally in 1977 Gene

Eugene Thomas (Gene) Puerling
March 31, 1929 - March 25, 2008

reunited the quartet at his San Francisco home to prepare for a reunion album after fourteen years, beginning with "Georgia" which got them very excited. The album was released a year later and was called The Hi-Lo's - Back Again and contained a great selection of Hi-Lo favorites. The album was launched at the Monterey (California) Jazz Festival and a year later

in 1980 they followed with *The HiLo's!- Now.*

Over the next fourteen years the Hi-Lo's played in colleges and music schools. The last performance was at the Betty Ford Center in Palm Springs, California. Health issues finally put the Hi-Lo's voices to rest. Of course, you can listen to the skills and innovative sounds of the Hi-Lo's on compact disc. The Hi-Lo's influential singing qualities were to singing groups what Frank Sinatra was to vocalists.

Robert Martin (Bob) Strasen
April 1, 1928 - February 28, 1994

Frank Allen Howren

January 21, 1928 - December, 21, 2003

THE LETTERMEN

The original Lettermen were three terrific vocalists: founder Tony Butala, Donavan Tea and Bobby Poynton, became one of the most popular harmony groups of the late 50s and on to fifty years of success that still carries through today, even with personnel changes over the years.

Today I played one of their signature tunes "See You in September," and that was enough for me to bring their story into this book.

Back in the late 50s, most groups were named after school types. "When we named ourselves we should have chosen a more startling or exciting name, but, in the end it didn't matter," said Tony, "Today, to achieve notoriety and to be novel, you have to dye your hair purple or pink, multi-pierce your face, ears and tongue."

Well, it was pure talent and great musical choices that Tony and his partners possessed that allowed the Lettermen to achieve immortality in music harmony. The Lettermen wore signature letter sweaters. When the group joined up with Capitol Records it was too late to change their name, as they were already an established group with a worldwide following. So the name remained.

Their first big-time gig was in 1958 at the famed Desert Inn Hotel in Las Vegas, where they performed in a revue with legendary bandleader Paul Whiteman, who gave Bing Crosby his start in the Rhythm Boys trio back in the 20s; Rudy Vallee, an earlier innovative crooner who became a film actor of note, and vaudeville legend Harry Richman. Besides singing, the three Lettermen had natural acting and performing abilities.

"Our mentors, were those we followed and who influenced us. There were The Modernaires, The Pied Pipers, The Mills Brothers, The Four Freshmen, The Ink Spots, and others," said Tony. Tony Butala had had considerable experience as a member of the Mitchell Boys Choir, who appeared in over one hundred films and dozens of radio and television programs. Tony, therefore garnered an appearance in *White Christmas*, the Irving Berlin musical with Bing Crosby, Rosemary Clooney, Danny Kaye, and Vera-Ellen; *War of the Worlds*, and *On Moonlight Bay*, with Gordon MacRae and Doris Day, among others.

By 1960, Tony, with Jim Pike and Bob Engemann, the revised Lettermen, were signed by Capitol Records, an association that lasted twenty-five years. Their debut single was "The Way You Look Tonight" and "That's My Desire," followed by "When I Fall in Love." They were immensely successful, establishing the Lettermen as the romantic singing group in a do-wop world, the 1960s.

The 1968 recording success of "Goin' Out of My Head/Can't Take My Eyes Off You" and "Hurt So Bad" designated the Lettermen as Best New Group and Best Vocal Group, especially after adding to their romantic repertoire the evergreen "Smile," "Put Your Head on My Shoulder," "Shangri-La" and "Traces/Memories."

The group toured with George Burns, Jack Benny, and Bob Hope and performed on an endless list of variety shows including Ed Sullivan's *Toast of the Town*.

The Lettermen performed on over two hundred shows and enjoyed success touring the world stages from China to Saudi Arabia.

Being the clean-cut, no drugs, all-American image won them much success and admiration in the world of music harmony.

The Lettermen Singles

1961 - "The Way You Look Tonight"
1961 - "When I Fall in Love"
1962 - "Son of Old Rivers"
1962 - "Come Back Silly Girl"
1962 - "How Is Julie?"
1962 - "Turn Around, Look at Me"
1962 - "Silly Boy (She Doesn't Love You)"
1962 - "Again"
1963 - "Heartache Oh Heartache"
1963 - "Allentown Jail"
1963 - "Where or When"
1964 - "Put Away Your Tear Drops"
1964 - "You Don't Know Just How Lucky You Are"
1965 - "Girl with a Little Tin Heart"
1965 - "Theme from A Summer Place"
1965 - "Secretly"
1965 - "Sweet September"
1966 - "You'll Be Needin' Me"
1966 - "I Only Have Eyes for You"
1966 - "Chanson D'Amour"
1967 - "Our Winter Love"
1967 - "Volare"
1967 - "Somewhere My Love"
1967 - "Goin' Out of My Head / Can't Take My Eyes Off You"
1968 - "Sherry Don't Go"
1968 - "All the Grey Haired Men"
1968 - "Holly"
1968 - "Medley: Love Is Blue/Greensleeves"
1968 - "Sally le Roy"
1968 - "Put Your Head on My Shoulder"
1969 - "I Have Dreamed"
1969 - "Blue on Blue"
1969 - "Hurt So Bad"

1969 - "Shangri-La"
1969 - "Traces/Memories Medley"
1970 - "Hang On Sloopy"
1970 - "She Cried"
1970 - "Hey Girl"
1971 - "Morning Girl"
1971 - "Everything Is Good About You"
1971 - "The Greatest Discovery"
1971 - Feelings"
1971 - "Love"
1971 - "Oh My Love"
1972 - "Spin Away"
1973 - "Sandman"
1973 - "Summer Song"
1974 - "The You Part of Me"
1974 - "Touch Me in the Morning/The Way We Were"
1975 - "Eastward"
1975 - "You Are My Sunshine Girl"
1976 - "If You Feel the Way I Do"
1976 - "The Way You Look Tonight"
1977 - "What I Did for Love"
1979 - "World Fantasy"
1980 - "In the Morning I'm Coming Home"
1985 - "It Feels like Christmas"
1986 - "Proud Lady of America"
1987 - "One More Summer Night"
1988 - "All I Ask of You"

The Lettermen have been an important part of the American culture for over 50 years, singing quality harmony music the whole world can enjoy.

Tony Butala fulfilled his dream of establishing the Vocal Group Hall of Fame and Museum in his home town of Sharon, Pennsylvania in 1998. This nonprofit organization honors the best vocal groups of the world in every conceivable genre.

THE WILLIAMS BROTHERS

Did you know that Andy Williams of " Moon River" fame was once part of a quartet with three of his brothers. In fact, the boys, Bob, Don, Dick and Andy were the backup voices on the famed Decca-Bing Crosby recording of "Swinging on a Star."

The boys began singing in the mid-1930s in Wall Lake, Iowa and were managed and directed by their father, Jay. They sang on radio stations in Des Moines and in 1943 were under contract to MGM where they appeared in several movies. They soon found themselves as part of a traveling act with Kay Thompson in the late 1940s.

With their jazzy harmonies and appealing performances they appeared prolifically on television and radio until the act broke up in 1951. Each brother went his own way but would always appear together annually on brother (Andy's) *Andy Williams Show*.

Andy Williams is famous for two singles that I love: "Moon River" which is his signature song and "The Village of St. Bernadette." His version of "The Bilboa Song" is another favorite as well as "The Hawaiian Wedding Song." Obviously Andy Williams enjoyed a great career equaled to Presley, and even Sinatra, selling many albums and spending twenty years performing in Las Vegas nightclubs, and now, with his own Moon River Theater, which he owns in Branson, Missouri, he still performs.

ANDY WILLIAMS SINGS

MOON RIVER
W. JOHNNY MERCER, M. HENRY MANCINI

Moon River, wider than a mile,
I'm crossing you in style some day.
Oh, dream maker, you heart breaker,
Wherever you're going I'm going your way.
Two drifters off to see the world.
There's such a lot of world to see.
We're after the same rainbow's end--
Waiting 'round the bend,
My huckleberry friend,
Moon River and me.

HENRY MANCINI PLAYS

Bob, Dick, Andy and Don

WHERE THEY PERFORMED

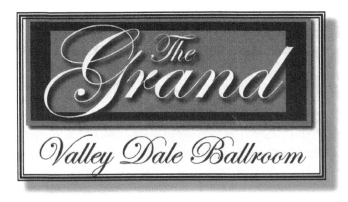

VALLEY DALE
THE GREAT BALLROOM

During the Big Band Era there were many great ballrooms where the big bands played and where the singing groups were either featured with a band or booked alone as an unattached special attraction.

The Valley Dale Ballroom, which is still operating on Sunbury Road in Columbus, Ohio, under the ownership and operation of Marty Finta IV and his son Marty V., since 1989. The ballroom has actually been operating for over 100 years. Today, besides being a ballroom for dancing, the Valley Dale is the area's long-favorite source for special events, weddings, corporate events, fundraisers and public events, as well. And, it will become the future home of the National Big Band and Jazz Hall of Fame Museum.

STILL STANDING-STILL OPERATING

The Perfect Harmony Groups Performing at Valley Dale were:

Bing Crosby And The Rhythm Boys
The King Sisters

The Mills Brothers
The Platters
The Kingsmen
The Modernaires
The Andrews Sisters
The Pied Pipers
The Ink Spots

As well as many of the famous big bands from Artie Shaw, Benny Goodman, Glenn Miller, Tommy and Jimmy, the Dorsey Brothers, and almost all the creme-de-creme of the Big Bands and their Big Band vocalists including, Dick Haymes, Frank Sinatra, Perry Como, and Bing Crosby. As the Gershwin's once asked the world, "Who could ask for anything more?"

OUR FEATURED BALLROOM

THE GRAND VALLEY DALE BALLROOM COLUMBUS, OHIO
Once a stage coach stop and inn in the 1880's.

THE NATIONAL BIG BAND AND JAZZ HALL OF FAME MUSEUM
AT VALLEY DALE

The National Big Band and Jazz Hall of Fame Museum Inc., was formed in October 2011 to help preserve the history of America's Popular music. The goal of the National Big Band and Jazz Hall of Fame and Museum is to continue the music legacy for present and future generations through the display of various exhibits and musical artifacts reflecting the musical genre and its evolution.

The purpose is to establish a national Big Band and Jazz Hall of Fame Museum to commemorate the famous bands, vocalists, musicians, arrangers, songwriters and their All-American popular music with an emphasis on the Big Band Era.

Jazz is America's true art music, and in the history of this music, one period of time stands out as the magnificent "Golden Age," the era in which songwriters Irving Berlin, Cole Porter, George and Ira Gershwin, Richard Rodgers, Hoagy Carmichael, Harold Arlen, Johnny Mercer and many others were creating the music played by the great "Big Bands" of Glenn Miller, Benny Goodman, Harry James, Tommy and Jimmy Dorsey, Duke Ellington, Count Basie and so many more.

The historic Valley Dale Ballroom will become the home of the National Big Band and Jazz Hall of Fame and Museum and is a huge piece of history itself, with national value. It is most appropriate building to house the Hall of Fame and Museum within the walls of the very same building in which they performed. This is one of the places where popular music got its start, a time when the Big Bands first put the stomp in the teenagers step and the swing in their stride. The Valley Dale Ballroom was a must-stop for the famous Big Bands who were touring the country in the 1930's and 1940's.

Valley Dale is significant as being one of the nationally renowned ballrooms of the Big Band Era of that time. All of the famous Big Bands and entertainers including Bing Crosby, Frank Sinatra, Dean Martin, Cab Calloway, Ella Fitzgerald, Andrews Sisters, the King Sisters, and more have appeared at Valley Dale. Established in 1918, Valley Dale remains as one of the last few great American ballrooms from this era. While its admission to the National Register of Historic Places preserved its history, its ongoing extensive renovation secures its future.

During the early 1940's Columbia Broadcasting Company (CBS), and Mutual Broadcasting (MBS), broadcasted simultaneous coast-to-coast radio shows from the Valley Dale. Radio, not records, was the star-maker of the day, with shows emanating from the Valley Dale being broadcast live across the country. The original radio booths that once housed the broadcasting equipment from where the announcers, who declared "*From the beautiful Valley Dale on Sunbury Road in Columbus, Ohio, we bring you the music of Benny Goodman,*" still flank the stage and are hidden behind burgundy curtains, but will be revealed during museum events. Valley Dale was the only ballroom in the nation from which broadcasts from two different radio networks were delivered simultaneously throughout the country through its affiliate stations.

With the loss of the World War II generation, it becomes necessary to generate new ideas and creative ways directed to a new generation who has had limited exposure to this creative and lasting music. From a historical standpoint, the music represents a time period in American history which has set the standard for all popular music that currently exists. Without the effort of these musicians, bandleaders, vocalists, arrangers and songwriters, today's popular music would not exist in its current form. It is our responsibility to preserve the legacy of the artists and performers who created it.

MISSION STATEMENT:

THE NATIONAL BIG BAND AND JAZZ HALL OF FAME MUSEUM INC. IS THE NONPROFIT ORGANIZATION THAT EXISTS TO EDUCATE VISITORS, FANS AND SCHOLARS FROM AROUND THE WORLD ABOUT THE HISTORY AND CONTINUING SIGNIFICANCE OF BIG BAND AND JAZZ MUSIC. IT CARRIES THIS MISSION THROUGH ITS OPERATION OF A FIRST CLASS MUSEUM THAT COLLECTS, PRESERVES, EXHIBITS AND INTERPRETS THIS ART FORM FOR ALL TO SEE AND HEAR.

L-R: Paul Tanner, Jimmy Priddy, Frank D'Anolfo, Glenn Miller

GLENN MILLER AND THE BOYS

A Short History of Dance Ballrooms

One of the first hotels to host a dance band was the St. Francis Hotel in the heart of San Francisco way back in 1913, when it hired Art Hickman's small band to play its prestigious Rose Room. In 1915, a patron, famed theatrical producer Florenz Ziegfeld heard them play and brought the eight piece band to New York to play in the Ziegfeld Follies revues, perhaps initiating the dance band craze at the dawn of the Big Band Era. The Hickman band later showcased a string and sax section and is believed to be the first dance band to employ the use of saxophones. Glenn Miller's and Tommy Dorsey's big bands played the very popular Meadowbrook in

The Meadow Brook

GLEN ISLAND CASINO - Home of the Big Bands

Cedar Grove, New Jersey, which was owned by Frank Dailey, who in 1941, and for only one year, leased our featured, historical ballroom, The Valley Dale.

Here are the names of some of the great ballrooms operating during the big band era:

- The Meadow Brook In Cedar Grove, New Jersey
- The Sunnybrook, Pottstown, Pennsylvania
- The Tune Town Ballroom, St. Louis, Missouri
- The Starlite Ballroom, Hershey, Pennsylvania
- The St. Francis Hotel, San Francisco, California
- The Valencia Ballroom, York, Pennsylvania
- The Graystone, Detroit, Michigan
- The Savoy And The Grand Terrace Cafe, Chicago, Illinois
- The Palomar, Hollywood, California
- The Benjamin Franklin Hotel, Philadelphia, Pennsylvania
- The Cafe Rouge, In The Pennsylvania Hotel, New York City
- The CocoaNut Grove, Los Angeles. California
- The Trianon & Aragon Ballrooms, Chicago, Illinois
- The Ritz Carlton, Boston, Massachusetts
- Roseland Ballroom, In The Heart Of New York City
- The Rainbow Room, Rockefeller Center, New York City
- The Hopkins And Palace Hotel, San Francisco, California
- Glen Island Casino, New Rochelle, New York

SPECIALTY MIXED GROUPS

Lambert, Hendricks & Ross

A short lived, yet magnificent singing group, Lambert Hendricks & Ross began in 1957, their first album being *Sing a Song of Basie*, which was successful enough to put them on the map and even won a Grammy Hall of Fame Award in 1998, mostly because of the association with Count Basie and the content of the album.

Dave Lambert, John Hendricks and Annie Ross

Their albums added up to seven, one each in 1957 Sing a Song of Basie, 1958 *Sing Along with Basie*, 1958 *The Swingers*,

1958 *The Swingers*, 1960 *Lambert, Hendricks & Ross*, 1960 *Lambert, Hendricks & Ross Sing Ellington* (My favorite), 1962 *The Ambassadors*, and also in 1962 *High Flying with Lambert, Hendricks & Ross*.

It was Dave Lambert, Jon Hendricks and Annie Ross in the beginning, then Annie left and Yolande Bavan replaced her and forced a name change to Bavan instead of Ross. Later the last name was Moss, for Anne Marie Moss, who replaced Bavan.

The group was crushed when Dave Lambert died as a result of an automobile accident in 1956.

Their great songs were "Moanin'," "Twisted," "Cloudburst," "The Doodling Song," "Every Day I Have the Blues."

THE MANHATTAN TRANSFER

There was a cab driver who had dreams of a singing career. His name is Tim Hauser and his aspirations came true in the fall of 1972 when his taxi fare, a young singer named Laurel Masse had many of the same dreams. They talked music.

Tim had sung in doo-wop groups and even in an early group named The Manhattan Transfer, a quintet that was not quite what he envisioned, and so it did not last. Tim's dream was of creating a four part harmony group with the sounds of jazz, salsa and even swing from the past.

At a party he met a girl from Brooklyn named Janis Siegel, who was in a group, but she worked with Tim and shortly became the third member of Tim's aspiring harmony quartet. They began rehearsing and invited Alan Paul, a pit band drummer on Broadway and boyfriend to Laurel Masse at the time, to join the group now known to the world as The Manhattan Transfer.

The four fledgling singers/musicians combed through many venues in New York City and became a favorite attraction. *Newsweek Magazine* to Reno in Greenwich Village and the result was a contract with Atlantic Records and the first album yielded their first hit "Operator." "Operator" was a favorite with radio jocks. Add many appearances on all the popular variety shows and then Hollywood was brought into the mix, making *The Manhattan Transfer Show's* first broadcast on CBS, Sunday's at 8, in the old Ed Sullivan Show slot.

The following albums produced hit singles, one of which, "Chanson D'Amour," became the U.K.'s number one hit, although it failed to be charted in America. The live album *The Manhattan Transfer Live* reached far and wide in the U.K.

When Laurel Masse was injured in an auto accident, she was replaced by Cheryl Bentyne.

Extensions was released in 1979 and the track "Twilight Zone/ Twilight Tone" which was a disco hit, was written by my old friend Joe Graydon, (who also managed singers, including Helen Forrest,) and Alan Paul. The single from the album *Birdland* won a Grammy for the group, "Until I Met You" won in 1981, and won still another for "Route 66," in 1982, from the film *Sharkey's Machine*.

And again, another Grammy in 1987 for "Brasil," and their 10th Grammy was won for the song "Sassy." Their first Christmas Album came along in 1992. After switching to Atlantic Records, one of their best was a dedication to Louis Armstrong, The Spirit of St. Louis in 2000.

The Manhattan Transfer is a remarkable group that literally does it all, swing, jazz, folk, *a capella*, and even doo-wop. Recent projects include works with symphony orchestras right up to 2009 with an album with Chick Corea and the Chick Corea Songbook that featured many fine jazz musicians.

Front: Janis Siegel, Tim Hauser
Back: Alan Paul and Cheryl Bentyne

Today's Manhattan Transfer is composed of Tim Hauser, Cheryl Bentyne, Alan Paul, and Janis Siegel. Former members over the years were Erin Dickens, Marty Nelson, Gene Pistilli, Pat Rosalia, Laurel Masse, and Larry Heard.

ALBUMS

Jukin' - 1971
The Manhattan Transfer - 1975
Coming Out - 1976
Pastiche - 1978
The Manhattan Transfer Live - 1978
Extensions - 1979
Mecca for Moderns - 1981
The Best of the Manhattan Transfer - 1981
Bodies and Souls - 1983
Bop Doo-Wopp - 1985
Vocalese - Live - 1987

Brasil - 1987
The Offbeat of Avenues - 1991
The Christmas Album - 1992
Anthology: Down In Birdland - 1992
The Very Best of the Manhattan Transfer - 1994
The Manhattan Transfer Meets Tubby the Tuba - 1994
Tonin' - 1995
Man-Tora! Live in Tokyo - 1996
Swing - 1997
Boy From New York City And Other Hits - 1997
The Spirit of St. Louis - 2000
Couldn't Be Hotter - 2003
Vibrate - 2004
An Acapella Christmas - 2005
The Symphony Sessions - 2006
The Definitive Pop Collection - 2006
The Chick Corea Songbook - 2009

SIX HITS AND A MISS

You may recall the popular singing group Six Hits and a Miss: Bill Seckler, Tony Paris, Marvin Bailey, Howard Hudson, Jerry Pre-shaw, Vincent Degen, and Mac McLean. The Miss, Pauline Byrns, performed for Capitol Records and on Bob Hope's show backed Dick Haymes on some of his Decca discs.

The group began as Three Hits and a Miss. Martha Tilton was the Miss. In the movie Topper with Cary Grant and Roland Young they sang "Old Man Moon," written by Hoagy Carmichael. Martha Tilton later became a vocalist with Benny Goodman.

The group started as 3 Hits in 1936 and expanded to 6 Hits in 1937. During the war the group acquired Lee Gotch and Tony Paris when Jerry and Howard left. By 1943, Vince and Tony left, the re-maining group comprised of just 4 made a few recordings for Decca backing Bing Crosby and Jimmy Durante.

After the war, Degen, Hudson and Paris formed a new group called the Starlighters, a new quintet. The fifth new singer was Andy Williams, who remained for a short time. The Starlighters recorded for

Mercury, Capitol and Columbia Records mostly backing other groups and especially worked with Jo Stafford and bandleader/arranger Paul Weston, Stafford's husband. Jo Stafford was an original member of the Pied Pipers.

A lot of the information above may not be exact, although it probably is mostly true with respect to members and the staff changes and comings and goings of individual members over the years.

THE MEL-TONES WITH MEL TORMÉ'

Mel Tormé's first recording with the Mel-Tones and Decca Records was his own composition "Stranger in Town," a song he wrote that was a torch song similar to the Willard Robison tune "Cottage for Sale." He also recorded with Bing Crosby, who was a big fan of Mel. The Mel-Tones with Mel sang on the *Hires Root Beer Show*.

Clockwise from Bottom - Bernie Parke, Betty Beveridge, Mel, Ginny O'Connor and Les Baxter

"I had been a long time fan of the Pied Pipers and the Modernaires" Tormé said, and so he organized a group of singers he called the Schoolkids. Bernie Parke suggested the Mel-Tones would be a better name for the group which included: Betty Beveridge, Ginny O'Connor and Bernie Parke, Les Baxter, Sheldon Disruhd (who left for military service and was replaced by Les), and, of course, Mel himself.

Mel Tormé and his Mel-Tones were chosen for a part in the movie Let's Go Steady, -- a "B" movie about amateur songwriters. When the movie was released, it was a hit and Columbia made Mel an offer to become regulars with his group on a show called Swingtime that starred Martha Raye.

At the same time, Mel, also a drummer, was offered a chair in both the Gene Krupa and Stan Kenton's bands, but what was he to do with the Mel-Tones? He was still in High School for goodness sake.

During an interview with Mel in the late nineties, Mel said this to me: "Later on, just when the Mel-Tones and I reached some sort of a career dead end, a wonderful thing happened: The Mel -Tones became regulars on the Fitch Bandwagon radio show that featured host Dick Powell and cowboy sidekick and character (graveled voice Andy Devine,) and was signed to Musicraft, a new label that had also signed Duke Ellington, Artie Shaw, Kitty Kallen, Dizzy Gillespie, and the great Sarah Vaughan.

"At Artie Shaw's house, we worked out a couple of tunes for Musicraft's first album, 'What is This Thing Called Love,' for the Mel-Tones, and a solo number for me to sing 'Get Out of Town.'" Mel wrote the arrangements.

The Mel-Tones broke up when Mel was drafted. By the way, it was Mel Tormé who co-wrote the very popular and enduring Christmas Song "Chestnuts roasting on an open fire, Jack Frost nipping at your nose," with Bob Wells, which is popularly believed to have been written in "forty minutes."

Mel with the Mel-Tones and Bing Crosby

The Manhattans

Molly Brady, Bob Maxwell and Lee Hale were a successful singing trio in the early '50s. They were the outgrowth of another vocal group, The Sunnysiders, a quartet which included Molly and Lee.

Miss Brady was an exceptionally lovely young lady and a topnotch lead singer. Bob Maxwell took on most of the male solos, while Lee Hale wrote the special musical material for the trio. Unlike other groups of the era, The Manhattans had a distinct Broadway style. They were often called a smaller version of Kay Thompson and the Williams Brothers.

They were especially proud of the fact that they averaged 48 working weeks every year. They appeared at New York's Palace Theater five times, when that legendary showplace offered vaudeville and a movie, with a change of live show appearances each week.

The Manhattans were on the bill at many other theaters, hotel showrooms and nightclubs around the country, as well as in Canada, Mexico and the Caribbean, including the Latin Quarter in New York, the Biltmore Bowl in Los Angeles, Amato's in Portland, the Magic Inn in Seattle, the Old New Orleans in Washington, D.C., the Elmwood Casino in Windsor, Canada, Cotton Carnival in Memphis, Barclay Hotel in Toronto and others.

They guest starred on many TV variety shows of the day, performed in stacks of industrial shows, recorded countless singing commercials, and had a hit recording, "Kiki."

Just before the group broke up, they headlined a highly successful USO tour of service bases in Germany and England.

Lee Hale connected with the *Dean Martin Television Show* and helped manage the musical aspects for the entire nine years they were in the air, and as stand-in for Dean, script and skit writer, and musical and rehearsal director.

Lee's book about his experiences with the Dean Martin Show are highlighted in his book *The Lee Hale Story-An Entertainer's Life Among the Stars.*

Bob Maxwell, Molly Brady and Lee Hale

ROYAL DUETS

Fred Astaire and Ginger Rogers

Fred Astaire and Ginger Rogers

There was Fred Astaire and Ginger Rogers who introduced more songs known now as respectable members of the the Great American Songbook, and they sang them as duets on a long line of recordings and films.

And how about the musical combination of Mickey Rooney and Judy Garland's endearing performances in Strike Up the Band among a series of others. Remember Crosby & Hope sitting on the back of a camel singing "We're Off on the Road to Morocco," or Jimmy Van Heusen and Johnny Burke's "Put It There Pal, Put it There," from the Road to Utopia.

As a special feature, we present this chapter on Duets reminding us of the couples who were featured on records and in the movies without musical assistance from a third or fourth member. Although Ginger Rogers and Fred Astaire were known for their outstanding dancing skills and their immense popularity exhibiting that ability on the silver screen (in a handful of excellent and entertaining musical films), you cannot ignore the fact that they also introduced a number of original songs. Those songs have scored what's now known as the great songs that help formed the American Song Book,

America's classical music performed by singers Frank Sinatra, Bing Crosby, Tony Bennett, Ella Fitzgerald, Jerry Vale, Helen Forrest, Lena Horne, Peggy Lee, and a handful of brand new singers that include Michael Bublé, Tony Babino, Julia Keefe, Tony DeSare, Diana Krall, Jane Monheit, and Dana Marcine, and a host of others headed for musical stardom.

Here, to remind you, is a list of the songs and the films in which Astaire and Rogers performed them, most as part of the introduction to their inimitable dancing sequences:

1933 *Flying Down to Rio* - "Music Makes Me" - w. Gus Kahn/Edward Eliscu, m. V. Youmans
1934 *The Gay Divorcee* - "The Continental" - Cole Porter
1935 *Top Hat* - "Cheek to Cheek," "Isn't This a Lovely Day?" - Irving Berlin
1935 *Roberta* - "Yesterdays," "Smoke Gets in Your Eyes," Lovely to Look At," "I Won't Dance" - Jerome Kern and Otto Harbach
1936 *Follow the Fleet* - "Let's Face the Music and Dance," "Let Yourself Go," "I'm Putting All My Eggs in One Basket" - Irving Berlin
1936 *Swingtime* - "A Fine Romance" and "Pick Yourself Up" - Jerome Kern and Dorothy Fields
1937 *Shall We Dance* - "They All Laughed," "They Can't Take That Away from Me," "Let's Call the Whole Thing Off" - Ira and George Gershwin
1938 *Carefree* - "Change Partners" - Irving Berlin

These, of course, are not the only songs featured in the above films, but just the songs that helped create the distinquished Great American Song Book -- sung as a duet and quasi-duet with Astaire and Rogers. What a great list of tunes sung by two of films most iconic actors-dancers-singers.

BING CROSBY - BOB HOPE

Aside from the standard three-member and four-member majority of group singers of the past 50-60 years, there were a number of two-member creative singers that may not have formed an established, premanent group, but have clearly demonstrated their collective ability as singers over the course of their careers, known as duets. A few years ago, Columbia pictures sent a crew to Long Island to film me narrating the features which appear on the Bing Crosby and Bob Hope Road Pictures Tribute Collection. Ann Jillian and Phyllis Diller also participated in the adventure. Of course, Diller had worked with Bob Hope forever and ever, and my friend, singer/actress Ann Jillian, traveled with Bob Hope, sharing the stage when he was entertaining the troops overseas.

Bing and Bob sing "Harmony"

My qualification is my book The Spirit of Bob Hope, and my association with Bing's wonderful wife, Kathryn Crosby, and my book Bing Crosby-Crooner of the Century.

During those Road films Bob and Bing polished off quite a number of songs. Some of them were duets, which endeared them to their vast audiences even more, adding to the success of the seven films.

Life-like caricature sculptures of Bing and Bob by Al Myers

Here are those seven songs they sang together in those films. I'm sure you'll never forget them:

SONGS IN FILM
"Put It There Pal" - Road to Morocco
"Road to Morocco" - Road to Morocco
"Chicago Style" - Road to Bali
" Hoot, Man" - Road to Bali
"The Merry Go Round" - Road to Bali
" Nothing in Common" - Road to Hong Kong
"Team Work" - Road to Hong Kong

Bob Hope and Richard Grudens

Dorothy Lamour, Bing Crosby and Bob Hope in Road to Morocco

ROAD TO MOROCCO
W. JOHNNY BURKE M. JIMMY VAN HEUSEN

We're off on the road to Morocco

This camel is tough on the spine (hit me with a band-aid, Dad)

Where they're going, why we're going, how can we be sure

I'll lay you eight to five that we'll meet Dorothy Lamour (Yeah, get in line)

Off on the road to Morocco

Hang on till the end of the line (I like your jockey. Quiet)

I hear this country's where they do the dance of the seven veils

We'd tell you more (uh-ah) but we would have the censor on our tails (Good boy)

Were off on the road to Morocco

Well look out, well clear the way, 'cause hare we come

Stand by for a concussion

The men eat fire, sleep on nails and saw their wives in half

It seems to me there should be easier ways to get a laugh (Shall I slip on my big shoes?)

Off on the road to Morocco

Hooray! Well blow a horn, everybody duck

Yeah. It's a green light, come on boys

We may run into villains but we're not afraid to roam

Because we read the story and we end up safe at home (yeah)

Certainly do get around

Like Webster's Dictionary we're Morocco bound

We certainly do get around

Like a complete set of Shakespeare that you get

In the corner drugstore for a dollar ninety-eight

We're Morocco bound

Or, like a volume of Omar Khayyam that you buy in the Department store at Christmas time for your cousin Julia

We're Morocco bound (We could be arrested)

MICKEY ROONEY AND JUDY GARLAND

Mickey and Judy were an awesome twosome, to coin a phrase. They were adorable in their ten pictures together and sang some precious duets, but not exactly in what we would call perfect harmony, nevertheless they sang together and deserve this minor tribute in a book about group singers although the group consisted as a *group of only two*, and sometimes a mere smattering of verse-not the full tune together.

1948 -----"I WISH I WERE I LOVE AGAIN" - from the film *Words & Music*

1946-----"HOW ABOUT YOU" - from the film *Babes on Broadway*

1945-----"THIS LOVE AFFAIR" - from the film *Strike Up the Band*

1945----- "DO THE LACONGA" - from the film *Strike Up the Band*

1945----- "DRUMMER BOY" - from the film *Strike Up the Band*

1943----- "COULD YOU USE ME?" - from the film *Girl Crazy*

Strike Up The Band
George and Ira Gershwin

Let the drums roll out.
Let the trumpet call.
While the people shout, Strike up the band.
Hear the cymbals ring. Calling one and all.
To the martial swing, Strike up the band.
There is work to be done,to be done.
Theres a war to be won, to be won.
Come you son of son of a gun. Take your stand.
Fall in line, yea bo. Come along, lets go.
Hey, leader. Strike up the band.

ROY KRAL AND JACKIE CAIN

Kral and Cain were a memorable duo, quite different from most of their contemporaries. When bandleader Charlie Ventura moved to RCA Victor Records, he considered himself a "Bop" performer and one of the appeals of his band was the "Bop" singing of Jackie Cain and Roy Kral.

Roy studied piano from the age of five--yes, five! His classical studies turned to jazz after listening to Earl Hines' band playing at the Grand Terrace in Chicago. Roy formed his own band when he was merely seventeen. After a stint in the Army during World War II he returned home to Chicago, but settled in Detroit working in a band on the radio. He returned to Chicago and joined a quartet with George Davis. There he met Jackie Cain, who taught him how to sing, who later became his wife and musical partner. A great musical duo was born.

Early *Today Show* host Dave Garroway was in Chicago and used the band with Jackie and Roy, who once shared the stand with Charlie Ventura, who was once a featured player in the Gene Krupa band. In fact, they were the reason for Ventura's popularity. Roy's "Bop" arrangements became very popular with the fans. "I'm Forever Blowing Bubbles" was a favorite, as was "Whatta Say We Go," "Birdland," "Lullaby in Rhythm," and "For Boppers Only".

After Ventura, they worked as simply Jackie & Roy. They appeared in concerts and cabarets and on TV to become one of the most important vocal groups in jazz, always winning many prizes and polls.

A note about Jackie Cain. Jackie was always a cheerful teenager and always a very good singer. Her special sound and superb, swinging style would always attract critics to imprint her as very special. In 1955, the song "Spring Can Really Hang You Up the Most" really established her and her lifetime husband, Roy. This wonderful duo kept it going for 53 years.

Jackie Cain was born in Milwaukee, Wisconsin. At that time, (1928), life was very difficult for many people, including her family. Mainly because of financial problems, her parents divorced when she was eight. Jackie lived with her grandmother and mother. "My mother played piano in our rooming house, located in a mansion. She played all the tunes of the times that she learned from the radio. I knew I could sing. I always sang with her and always joined the school chorus."

Jackie could not, and still doesn't read music, but she had a good ear and could follow through with her natural pitch and intonation qualities. She caught a job with the Wurlitzer Melody Kids in a local band and always continued to sing in her own way. She sang with a society dance band, then got a job with Jay Burkhart's band, known as the Jay Burkhart Jazz Cradle. The band also featured the great Joe Williams and Roy Kral's sister, Irene. Jackie continued singing in clubs and and hooked up with Roy when she visited a jazz club in Chicago where Roy was the piano player in the George Davis Quartet.

Her friend, musician Bob Anderson, who brought her to the club, suggested she sing with Roy as accompanist, but he refused, saying," I don't like to play for girl singers, because they never know what they want to sing, and when they tell you their key, it's usually in the key of Z."

Well, Roy changed his mind after hearing Jackie sing "Happiness is a Thing Called Joe," which she sang in the same key that Frances Wayne, girl singer with the Woody Herman Band, recorded it. The place went wild over her performance of the song.

Jackie is now reaching eighty-four. Roy is gone. For Jackie, happiness was a thing called Roy.

A CHANCE FOR
· STARDOM ·

INTERLUDE
THE HIT MAKERS

ARTHUR GODFREY

Many of the subjects in this book were contestants on the Arthur Godfrey Talent Scouts program. This show featured entertainers and the winner was selected by the live audience applause registered on

a meter. Several winners are now among my friends including Julius La Rosa and Carmel Quinn. La Rosa was fired while he was on the air by Godfrey because La Rosa hired an agent and a manager which was against the policy of Godfrey. Godfrey didn't want to deal with agents considering the high number of performers on his show. However, the act against La Rosa became the beginning of the end of Godfrey's career. The Mc Guire Sisters were also winners on the show. My longtime friend Johnny Mince was one of the musicians on the show.

Arthur Godfrey was a popular radio and television broadcaster who was an excellent salesman for the products his sponsors offered

on the program. Lipton Tea was one of his sponsors. He was also a great spokesman for Chesterfield Cigarettes, which eventually caused him to suffer with lung cancer because he smoked heavily.

Carmel Quinn told me many stories about him while she was a performer on the show. She was always in awe of him. He loved Carmel's singing and the stories about her family she told when she lived in Ireland.

His show was very enjoyable and spawned many successful performers like the singing group The Chordettes, bandleader Archie Bleyer, Pat Boone, Tony Bennett, comedians Don Adams & Lenny Bruce, opera's Marilyn Horne, country singer Roy Clark, Janette Davis, and country singer Patsy Cline. Godfrey's relaxed and informal, personal manner won over audiences at a time when announcers and hosts were mostly stiff-sounding. He also played the ukulele, a four string, guitar-like instrument and sang along on the air. His recording of "She's Too Fat for Me" ("Two Fat Polka") and his theme " Seems Like Old Times" were very successful recordings.

Godfrey appeared in several movies including *The Glass Bottom Boat* in 1966.

ED SULLIVAN

Ed Sullivan was a syndicated newspaper columnist for the New York Daily News before he became the host of the television show Toast of the Town, later renamed The Ed Sullivan Show. He was the first to showcase England's Beatles in the United States. Almost every living entertainer performed at least once on his show. Rodgers and Hammerstein first introduced their new show South Pacific, before it opened on Broadway.

It was a sign you had made it when you garnered a spot on the Sullivan show. Dean Martin and Jerry Lewis opened the first show when it changed its name to The Ed Sullivan Show. Many breakthrough acts got their start with Sullivan including the Beatles, Elvis Presley, The Supremes, the Beach Boys, the Jacksons and Rolling Stones and other rock and roll acts among the established acts of the time that included songwriter Tonight Show host, Steve Allen, bandleader Tommy Dorsey, and vaudeville and television comedian Milton Berle, and hundreds more.

Probably, most of the subjects of this book had appeared on the Ed Sullivan Show at one time or another. Nothing wrong with that. Those appearances helped many of our celebrity idols secure record contracts and quality positions on television and on Broadway.

Ed Sullivan

TED MACK AND MAJOR BOWES GAVE HOPEFUL STARS A CHANCE - ONE OF THE CONTESTANTS WAS FRANK SINATRA.

HELP MORE AMATEURS GET THEIR CHANCE

Every Purchase of Chase & Sanborn Dated Coffee helps Another Amateur to Fame and Fortune

FAME OVERNIGHT—The three talented Youman brothers—Jack, Skippy, George — imitate famous bands. They were overwhelmed with votes after their appearance on the Amateur Hour. Have been able to contribute three much-needed salaries to the family exchequer.

TAPPING FEET CLIMB LADDER OF FAME—You heard Gloria Rich, 18-year-old singer and toe-tap dancer, on the Amateur Hour. Gloria's dancing teacher thinks she has the strongest toes of any of his pupils. They carried her right into an Amateur Unit.

MAKING FACES, MAKING MONEY –Michael Ballero practiced making faces in the basement with a mirror. It never got him anywhere until he was heard on the Amateur Hour. Then the votes rolled in, and he rolled out to success on a tour.

Copyright, 1936 by Standard Brands Inc.

MORE THAN 1300 TELEPHONE OPERATORS given jobs. This happy young lady got a much-needed job on the Amateur Hour. For every amateur you hear, 2 to 3 people get work handling the great volume of votes you send in!

MAJOR BOWES' Amateurs get a real break—and *you* get a deliciously fresh, fine-quality coffee—when you buy Chase & Sanborn *Dated* Coffee.

Every pound of *Dated* Coffee is rushed fresh to your grocer—marked with the date of delivery to him. Our *Dating* Plan keeps it always *fresh* and full flavored. And every pound saves you money in its economical new bag.

Keep on doing yourself—and others—a good turn! Buy a pound of Chase & Sanborn *Dated* Coffee tomorrow. Listen in over the N.B.C. Red Network every Sunday evening.

CHASE SANBORN Dated Here COFFEE

FINE GROUPS OF DISTINCTION

MARY KAYE TRIO
FONTANE SISTERS
HILLTOPPERS
DINNING SISTERS
DELTA RHYTHM BOYS
GAYLORDS
THREE SUNS
CHARIOTEERS
ANITA KERR SINGERS
THE MOON MAIDS
STAFFORD SISTERS
THE SENTIMENTALISTS
DEJOHN SISTERS
BARRY SISTERS
KIRBY STONE FOUR
PAULETTE SISTERS
MERRY MACS
FOUR PREPS
CREW CUTS
LANE SISTERS
PETERS SISTERS
THE DANDRIDGE SISTERS
OSMOND BROTHERS
THE STARLIGHTERS

Mary Kaye Trio

Mary Kaye, a singer and guitarist was descended from Hawaiian Royalty . She was literally born into a show business family. She formed a trio playing her Fender guitar she named the Mary Kaye Strat, an expensive guitar with ash blonde body and maple wood neck adorned with gold hardware. It was both Mary Kaye and Louis Prima, who were the two performers credited for creating the Las Vegas lounge environment as an all-night party where the stars and their fans shared a stage around the clock.

The singing group was a very popular Las Vegas act in the 50s and 60s. Mary and her brother Norman started out very young in Hawaii on the carnival circuit. Mary actually started at three years old wearing a grass skirt in St. Louis, while Norman played he ukulele. The trio was composed of Mary, Norman, and their dad,and called themselves the Kaiihue Trio., but soon changed their name to the Royal Hawaiians.

When Norman joined the army in 1943, Frank Ross took his place. "When Norman returned two years later he rounded out the trio, adding his beautiful baritone voice plus the myriad instruments he played so well: piano, trombone, bass, guitar, and added to the singing part, ad libbing as well." according to Mary.

The Mary Kaye Trio played Las Vegas for over 20 years and was a household name in Las Vegas.

The Fontane Sisters

The Fontane Sisters, who backed Perry Como all the way, were Bea, Geri and Margi Rosse, originally from New Milford, New Jersey. They first performed with their guitarist brother, Frank, who they lost in World War II. They joined together with Perry Como on his radio show from 1945-1948 and con- tinued on Perry's tele- vision show through the 1950s and

on many subsequent recordings, usually with Ray (the other) Charles and the Ray Charles singers.

The Hilltoppers

They were just a couple of kids attending Western Kentucky State College when they were singing barbershop pop on campus. This was 1952, when Don McGuire (bass), Jimmy Sacca (lead), Seymour Spiegelman (tenor), got together. When they met pianist Billy Vaughn, who played for the band of Ace Dinning and who was also the brother of the Dinning Sisters, the no-name group became a serious contender. Billy had written a song called "Trying" and invited the group to back up his tenor voice on a recording of the song.

After some radio exposure, Vaughn took the song to Dot Records who promptly signed the boys and created the name Hilltoppers. "Trying" hit the spot and led to a shot on Ed Sullivan's *Toast of the Town* television Sunday night show.

With their college Sweaters and white buck shoes, they per-formed with college "beanies" and were a great success, so much that they continued wearing the same signature outfits at live gigs. Their next single "I Keep Telling Myself" was also a hit and the flip side "Must I Cry Again," was even better.

1968

The Hilltoppers
featuring Jimmy Sacca

Karl Garvin   Jimmy Sacca

Chuck Ayre   Jack Grebel

Some of their tunes were "P.S. I Love You," "Love Walked In," "If I Didn't Care," (an Ink Spot treasure), "Til Then," an earlier Mills Brothers hit, and later, a calypso winner called "Marianne."

The group broke up in the seventies with members pursuing other ventures like real estate, hotel food and beverage management. Billy Vaughn remained with Dot Records and arranged and conducted for many recording stars like Pat Boone and, guess who-The Dinning Sisters, Ace's very own sisters.

DINNING SISTERS

A popular close harmony group were the Dinning Sisters, real sisters at that, whose names were Lucille, alto, and the twins, Virginia, who sang lead, and Jean who sang soprano. The girls were instilled with perfect pitch, sang in the church choir and also had a local radio show. As they grew musically they toured the midwest's clubs and theaters with Herbie Holmes' Orchestra.

They were signed by NBC in Chicago and sang their way on shows like the *National Barn Dance* and the *Garry Moore Show*. In Hollywood, they appeared with Ozzie Nelson's band in the film *Strictly in the Groove*.

The girls also backed some short Walt Disney films. One of the tunes was "Blame it on the Samba." They soon signed with Capitol Records and recorded "My Adobe Hacienda", "I Wonder Who's Kissing Her Now." and "Beg Your Pardon," and their million-seller "Buttons and Bows," a tune originated by Bob Hope and Jane Russell in the film, *Paleface*.

Singing with Hoagy Carmichael

Lucille also recorded solo with Paul Weston's Orchestra "The Little White Cloud That Cried," "Trust in Me," (an Eddie Fisher hit) and "Just Friends."

After their retirement, their brother Mark found success with a tune called "Teen Angel." Another brother, Ace, had a successful orchestra for many years.

THE DELTA RHYTHM BOYS

When you listen to the Delta Rhythm Boys you feel the joy they project to their listeners. For example, "Take the A Train," that catchy masterpiece tune from the Duke Ellington songbook, written by Billy Strayhorn, this is perhaps the best version of the song I've ever heard. This cheerful foursome has backed the First Lady of Song, Ella Fitzgerald and

shared the stage with the great Nat "King" Cole on many a program.

First organized in Langston, Oklahoma in 1934, Elmaurice Miller, Traverse Crawford, Essis Joe Adkins, and Otha Lee Gaines worked as the New Orleans Quartet. The group lost Miller and Adkins who were replaced by Carl Jones and Hugh Bryant, and they added a pianist named Rene DeKnight.

The boys appeared on the radio with Amos and Andy and in film with Bing Crosby, and backed the big band of Charlie Barnet, and even backed the first big band singer, Mildred Bailey, and also Ruth Brown. Their best recording was a vocal version of the hit "I Dreamt I Dwelt in Harlem," written by Jerry Gray with lyrics by Buddy Feyne. The group seemed to do better in Europe than in the U.S. For over 50 years they performed beautifully, but unfortunately, and over a short span, most of the group passed on in the 60s and 70s. They were, however, inducted into the Vocal Group Hall of Fame. I loved the way they handled a lyric with their mellow and melodious, fully harmonic phrasing.

THE GAYLORDS

This is a different kind of group singing as they were famous for singing American song hits in Italian. They were a duo composed of Ronnie Gaylord and Burt Bonaldie, who sang mostly in lounges delivering mostly nutty parodies of songs like "Charlie Brown," "Only You," "Tom Dooley," "Yakety Yak," "Blueberry Hill." and "Itsy Bitsy Teenie, Weenie Yellow Polka Dot Bikini." You had to enjoy the shenanigans they performed for that special audience. They started out as a threesome and wound up as a twosome, with their most successful recordings " Tell Me You're Mine" which sold one million copies. The original song title was "Per un bacio d'amor," "From the Vine Came the Grape," (this was also a hit for the Hilltoppers), "Ramona," "Isle of Capri," and "The Strings of My Heart ." Ronnie continued performing with his son, Ron Jr., after the passing of Burt, who had changed his name to Burt Holiday.

THE THREE SUNS

"Twilight Time," and "Peg O' My Heart" were the two top tunes recorded by The Three Suns. The Suns were the Nevin brothers: Al who played guitar and Morty who played accordion. After a year or so kicking around New York City, the boys joined up with their cousin Artie Dunn who played organ and all emigrated into Philadelphia's Adelphia Hotel in 1939, and then headed back to New York into the Circus Lounge at the Hotel Picadilly where they remained musical stars for seven years.

Players worked their way in and out of the Suns depending on the concept of the time. As a quintet they added Marty Gold on organ and Larry Green on piano. They were, at different times, a sextet and septet. When Al Nevins changed to arranger and composer, the Three Suns went on without him. He formed a music publishing company with Don Kirshner and placed over 200 songs into the system including "Up on the Roof," and "Will You Still Love Me Tomorrow," and Neil Sedaka's "Breaking Up is Hard to Do."

Recordings of the Three Suns:
- Twilight Time, Rondo-lette (Reissue of 1940s material)
- The Three Suns in Three-Quarter Time, RCA Victor
- Hands Across the Table, RCA Victor
- The Three Suns Present Your Christmas Favorites, RCA
- The Happy-Go-Lucky Sound, RCA Camden
- At the Candlelight Cafe, RCA Camden
- Continental Affair, RCA Camden
- The Sounds of Christmas, RCA Victor (reissued on RCA Camden)
- My Reverie, RCA Victor
- High Fi and Wide, RCA Victor
- Soft and Sweet, RCA Victor
- Midnight for Two, RCA Victor
- Things I Love, RCA Victor
- Let's Dance with The Three Suns, RCA Victor
- Love in the Afternoon, RCA Victor
- Having a Ball with The Three Suns, RCA Victor

- The Three Suns Swingin' on a Star, RCA Victor
- A Ding Dong Dandy Christmas!, RCA Victor
- Twilight Memories, RCA Victor
- On a Magic Carpet, RCA Victor
- Dancing on a Cloud, RCA Victor
- Fever and Smoke, RCA Victor
- Fun in the Sun, RCA Victor
- Movin' 'n' Groovin', RCA Victor Stereo Action
- Warm and Tender, RCA Victor
- Everything Under the Sun, RCA Victor
- One Enchanted Evening, RCA Victor
- A Swingin' Thing, RCA Victor
- Twilight Moods, RCA Victor
- Busy Fingers, RCA Victor
- Three Suns Christmas Party, RCA Victor
- Slumbertime, RCA Victor
- The Three Suns Present Pop Concert Favorites, RCA Victor
- Country Music Shindig, RCA Victor
- This is the Three Suns, RCA Victor
- 16 Greatest Hits, Musicor

The Charioteers

When you hear the soft strains of the Mills Brothers-like group, the Charioteers on numbers "If I Could Be with You," "Ooh, Look-a -There Ain't She Pretty," you know you're listening to quality, soulful renditions of these songs.

The Charioteers began their gospel-like pop singing with tenor, Billy Williams in 1930. The group was organized by Professor Howard Daniel in Wilberforce University in Wilberforce, Ohio. Originally the Harmony Four, borrowed from a gospel song "Swing Low, Sweet Chariot," and renamed themselves the Charioteers. Members were Billy Williams, Edward Jackson (second tenor), Ira Williams (baritone), Howard Daniel (vocal), Herbert Dickerson (vocal), Peter Leubers (vocal), John Harewood (vocal), and Jimmy Sherman (piano).

Billy went on to form his own group in 1950 as he was always the lead vocal. With Decca Records the Charioteers performed with Pearl Bailey and four recordings backing Frank Sinatra, including "Lilly Belle" and " Jesus is a Rock," then they switched to Columbia. The boys performed on Broadway in the long-running show *Hellzapoppin'*, and was the back up chorus for Bing Crosby on his *Kraft Music Hall radio show.*

Members of the group drifted from one label to another and recorded over 75 singles over twenty-two years and made their final recording "The Candles" with MGM records in 1957. The Charioteers were indeed in perfect harmony.

Their most popular recordings were:
"So Long" in 1940
"On the Boardwalk in Atlantic City" in 1946
"Open the Door Richard" in 1947
"Ooh! Look-a-There Ain't She Pretty" in 1948
"A Kiss and a Rose" in 1949.

Billy Williams moved on to form his own quartet with Eugene Dixon, Claude Riddick and John Ball. They appeared on many television programs including *Your Show of Shows* that starred Sid Caesar and Imogene Coca. Unfortunately Billy had lost his voice from diabetes, moved to Chicago and became a social worker until his death in 1972.

ANITA KERR SINGERS

Quality and quaintness, smooth and light, perfection in tone and phrasing. These are some of the adjectives to describe the phenomenon of the Anita Kerr Singers. Kerr and her group graduated from the country song scene where they played with all the great ones then moved over to L.A. to further their beautiful sound backing everyone from Perry Como, Rosemary Clooney, Bobby Vinton, Ann Margaret, Roy Orbison, and Willie Nelson.

Here is the girl who, with her clear soprano vocals, is a singer, arranger, composer, conductor, pianist and producer, who organized and recorded with her vocal harmony groups over many years. Her group added to their strength after the 1950 success of "Our Lady of Fatima." The group consisted of Carl Gavin, Jim Hall, Doug Kirkham, Mary Ann Puckett, Evelyn Wilson, Mildred Kirkham, and Don Fotrell. In those days they backed country artists, (and my personal friend for 25 years), Eddie Arnold, Burl Ives and Ernest Tubb. After winning an *Arthur Godfrey Talent Scouts* competition as a quartet with Gil Wright, Louis Nunley, Dottie Dilliard, and Kerr as soprano and arranger, their demand widened and they grew from there. They disbanded when Kerr went to Los Angeles to seek her proverbial fortune. And that's just what she did.

Kerr and her many different singing groups covered a career with Warner Bros Records, Dot Records (The Anita Kerr Singers Reflect on the Hits of Burt Bacharach & Hal David), and in

Anita Kerr (bottom front) with her group of fine singers.

Switzerland she organized a new group and recorded in London the albums *A Christmas Story* and *A Tribute to Simon and Garfunkel* of "Mrs. Robinson" fame.

Musically, Anita Kerr has done it all and with everyone. She has even written books on music for the giant Hal Leonard Music Publishers. Kerr has won the ASCAP award and several Grammy's, one for We Dig Mancini, Southland Favorites, with George Beverly Shea, and other Grammy awards, as well.

There are endless singles and albums, many with deeply religious overtones and those with her group, Anita Kerr Singers, the Living Voices, the Mexicali Singers, and the San Sebastian Singers, including "Amazing Grace," "Welcome to My World," and Bacharach's "I Say a Little Prayer for You." Wonderful listening, honestly.

VAUGHN MONROE'S MOON MAIDS
THE BIG BAND'S BACK-UP SINGERS

THE MOONMAIDS

Vaughn Monroe's female vocal group, which was first hired as a quartet, was increased to a quintet, with the addition of Mary Lee, a former member of the Lee Sisters. The four girls, who were discovered by Dixon Gayer, a NY publicity agent, had a variety of tags. First, they were to be known as The Moonbeams but it was discovered that Kay Kyser used a group of the same name so they switched to The Moon Racers, dropped that and became The Moon Maids, backing the wonderful recordings of bandleader Vaughn Monroe. Remember "Racing with the Moon," and "There, I've Said it Again," and the most memorable "Ghost Riders in the Sky."

MARY JO

Mary Jo was one of Vaughn Monroe's original Moon Maids from March, 1946 to late December, 1949. " What a great experience! Being on the weekly *Camel Caravan* radio show kept us constantly reading music and learning! We met many celebrities who were guests on the radio show. There were long stints at The Meadows night club, The Commodore Hotel, Atlantic City and Asbury

Park, as well as theaters across the country. And there were those one-nighters all across America! We were featured on more than fifty Victor recordings with Vaughn and the band."

For the Moon Maids those days with Vaughn Monroe were fun, and tiring,but exciting! The Moonmaids lugged around heavy luggage, as they lived out of a suitcase and a trunk! They had make-up kits to take along and also kept their gowns in hanging bags. Much of what they used was carried in the equipment truck that went to the jobs separately from the bus.

"We traveled by bus most of the time, and occasionally by train. I can remember only a time or two that we flew to a job. We would arrive in the town where we were to appear, in the wee small hours of the morning---after playing a job somewhere else, then riding all night to the next venue. We checked into a hotel, bedraggled and groggy, and tried to get a little more sleep."

Some of the time the girls had a dressing room, but usually they dressed in a restroom, or even in the back of the instrument truck. "We did our own hair and make up, and took care of laundry and cleaning. I think the entertainers of today have a much different life style. Our bus was just that with no TV, or restroom, or beds!"

One nighters were the most common types of jobs. The girls traveled all over the U.S., and performed on the *Camel Caravan* radio shows every Saturday night from a different University. Vaughn Monroe was not always with us on the bus. He owned his own private plane which he piloted himself.

TINKER CUNNINGHAM

"When Mary Jo left in January of '50, Ruth Winston was hired to be our new lead singer. But the next six months was a grueling and continuous time of one-niters, with a week stand in one or two of the places, so it was no wonder that June and I were ready to pack it up and head back home. However it was the hardest decision I ever had to make!!!

Band

Female Vocalists - Moonmaids

Years with Vaughn Monroe
1946 - 1953

Summary of Group

Maree Lee
(see Lee Sisters)

In Memory of
Katie Myatt

In Memory of
Arlene Truax

Mary Jo Thomas

Tinker Cunningham

June Hiett

Ruth Wetmer

Lois Wilber

Betty McCormick

Kathleen Carnes

Dee Laws

Arlene Truax, Maree Lee, Katie Myatt
Mary Jo Thomas, Tinker Cunningham
photo courtesy of Jay Montague

Maree Lee, Mary Jo Thomas,
Tinker Cunningham, June Hiett

Ruth Wetmer, Maree Lee (top), Lois Wilbur,
Betty McCormick (bottom)
photo courtesy of Maree Lee Eger

Kathleen Carnes and Dee Laws

Main
ORCHESTRA
Musicians
Photographs
FEMALE VOCALISTS
Marylin Duke
Rosemary Calvin
Cece Blake
Del Parker
Murphy Sisters
Norton Sisters
Lee Sisters
Moonmaids
Shaye Cogan
Betty Johnson
MALE VOCALISTS
Ziggy Talent
Moonmen

DEE LAWS

We were the last group of Moon Maids! Vaughn gave up the touring band with a last date at West Point. Eydie Gorme was the guest singer and it was a *Camel Caravan* radio show. Eydie was just starting out in those days and had worked with us before in "borrowed gowns!" Whenever I saw her later in NYC she always called me the 'Moon Maid.'

To Summarize the group, singers included Maree Lee, Katie

Myatt, Arlene Truax, Mary Jo Thomas, Tinker Cunningham, June Hiett, Ruth Wetmer, Lois Wilber, Betty McCormick, Kathleen Carnes, and Dee Laws.

Thε Stafford Sisters

Jo Stafford was, of course, a popular singer who sang shoulder-to-shoulder with Frank Sinatra as part of the Pied Pipers with the Tommy Dorsey Orchestra. Very few are aware that before all that fame and fortune, Jo and her sisters Christine and Pauline formed the Stafford Sisters who made their first recording with Louis Prima in 1936. They performed on Los Angeles radio KHJ after a stint on KNX with *The Singing Crockett Family* of Kentucky radio show. Jo was just eighteen. The girls obtained work in the movie studios that included backing Fred Astaire in the film *A Damsel in Distress* on the Gershwin song "Nice Work If You Can Get It."

At Twentieth Century Fox they were searching for a singing group for the film *Alexander's Ragtime* Band that starred Tyrone

Jazz Zither On Jo's 'Shrimp Boats'

Hollywood—The search for a "new sound" seems to lead in the direction of old instruments. Here's Paul Mason Howard with the keyboard zither he used to flavor Paul Weston's orchestral backing for Jo Stafford (right) on her *Shrimp Boats* recording. Paul, who did the backing for Leadbelly on some of his records, can claim with some justification to be the only "jazz" zither player in the business.

Power, Don Ameche and Alice Faye. Many groups worked on the film and in-between takes Jo joined a new group called the Pied Pipers which consisted of eight members. Without her sisters, Jo drove to New York to audition with the Pied Pipers. The group consisted of Hal Hooper, Chuck Lowry, John Huddleston (who became Jo's first husband), Bud Hervey, George Tait, Woody Newbury, and Dick Whittinghill, later becoming a top-notch Los Angeles D.J.

Paul Weston, who talked Dorsey into allowing the interview, eventually married Jo Stafford. Jo became a single act in 1944 and enjoyed a great singing career.

The Sentimentalists
The Original Clark Sisters

The Clark girls, Mary, Peggy, Ann, and Jean, made up the Sentimentalists, who were the back-up singing group for the Tommy Dorsey Orchestra. They began their tenure with Dorsey after the Pied Pipers left the orchestra in 1944 because they had professional differences with the incendiary bandleader. The Clark girls were but seventeen when they joined with Dorsey. They auditioned for him in his apartment and were hired on the spot.

The Clark girls' style was very Andrews Sisters and McGuire Sisters in their style of singing. However, they had a very unique sound of their own. Collectors have agreed the works they created are highly collectable because they are very jazz-oriented, unlike their predecessors.

The Clarks began singing at a very young age. Their mom brought them to New York to compete in the *Major Bowes Amateur Hour* competition, the very same show that gave Frank Sinatra his first start when he and his fellow singers won the prize and toured with Bowes.

The Clark girls lost the competition but remained in New York to sing with a USO show, singing for servicemen. Dorsey gave the Clark Sisters the name The Sentimentalists because of his fear of them eventually leaving and taking the name with them as did the

Pied Pipers.

The girls were pretty, with agreeable personalities, and enjoyed great success with Dorsey fans. Dorsey arrangers Nelson Riddle and Sy Oliver arranged special musical numbers for the girls that really suited and enhanced their singing abilities. The girls best song with Dorsey was the everlasting treat "On the Sunny Side of the Street," and "I Should Care," "Why Do I Love You?" (from the Broadway musical *Showboat* by Jerome Kern and Oscar Hammerstein), and Johnny Mercer and Harry Warren's "On the Atchison Topeka, and the Santa Fe."

The girls left Dorsey because they felt he underpaid them, but could not retain the name Sentimentalists so they continued on as the Clark Sisters. The three albums they made after Dorsey are now available as a single CD, entitled *The Clark Sisters Swing Again*. Peggy Clark Schwartz worked with the Society of Singers for many years helping other, less fortunate singers when they were in need. She eventually married Willie Schwartz, a musician who played saxophone in the World Famous Glenn Miller Orchestra.

THE DEJOHN SISTERS

With a family name of DeGiovanni, Julie and Dux, whose dad operated a dry Cleaners store, sang at the same club where the Four Aces first made their mark in music. A Scout for Epic Records discovered them and they were signed up to record.

Their big hit was "My Baby Don't Love Me No More." which was written by the sisters and their brother Leo in 1955. The recording was a major hit, but their career seemed to fizzle out except for a single with United Artists and another with Sunbeam Records.

I recently heard the DeJohn girls perform on a cute little "Hotta Chocolotta," which should have made the charts, but it didn't. Nevertheless, the two sounded very much like the Andrews Sisters.

THE BARRY SISTERS

Here, in the Bronx, New York existed two Yiddish singers, who performed on the popular radio show *Yiddish Melodies in Swing*, singing Yiddish translations of popular tunes like "Raindrops Keep Falling on My Head." Clara and Minnie Bagelman, later known as Claire and Merna Barry, performed on Ed Sullivan's and Jack Paar's television shows, and in the late fifties, even toured the unlikely venue of the Soviet Union. I'd say that's unusual, wouldn't you. But they did exactly that.

From left: Claire and Merna Barry.

Naturally, they were popular in the dominant Jewish community of the Bronx, New York, and also recorded with Barbra Streisand and other noted Jewish singers. They performed the "Passover Medley," a popular Yiddish collection of tunes, including the traditional favorite "Hava Nagila."

Interestingly, there existed yet another duo also named the Barry Sisters who hailed from Australia. That group never lasted very long and never charted any of their recordings. The two groups became friends and recorded a single in the late 60s entitled "No Hesitation" and it actually charted in Sydney, Australia.

I wonder if there are any copies existing of either of the Barry Sisters, or the single collaboration they performed together?

The Kirby Stone Four

Kirby Stone, Eddie Hall, Mike Gardner and Larry Foster comprised the Kirby Stone Four, whose bouncy, bubbling recordings became a hit right after World War II. The song "Baubles, Bangles and Beads," from the Broadway Show *Kismet* became a hit for them on Columbia and was actually nominated for a Grammy in 1958. It was their signature song.

The group had some notable musicians backing their recordings including Alvino Rey, Shelly Manne, Kai Winding, and Al Klink. They regularly appeared on a number of television shows, including Judy Garland's, because their style was a sort of swinging jazz which became popular for a short period. Their vocalese may have been influenced by the musicians that backed them. Their staccato, punctuated singing style was the precursor to early rock & roll. They even recorded a rock & roll album with The Tokens under the name The United States Double Quartet.

Listening to the Kirby Stone Four involves back up singers supporting almost every recording keeping the bounce going all the time. Nice, lively and different.

THE PAULETTE SISTERS

In 1952 the Paulette Sisters recorded a cute, fetching version of "Oh Johnny, Oh Johnny, Oh" with the Larry Clinton Orchestra on Columbia Records. (Bea Wain was one of Larry Clinton's best-known vocalists with the band recording "Deep Purple.")

Gloria, Betty, and Jane formed the catchy singing group known as The Paulette Sisters. You have to love their rendition of "Oh Johnny, Oh" by those girls, who sang much like the Chordettes, but a little less perfect,although some say many of their recordings were quality tight harmony and as good as any group who performed before them.

The Paulette Sisters worked their way through a handful of recording studios that included Columbia, Capitol, Decca, Aamco, and the Ribbons label. The girls appeared on *The Kraft Music Hall* radio show in one segment to back Connee Boswell, who was, by then, apart from her sisters and performing as a single, and was appearing on the famed radio show, a show that featured Bing Crosby, and earlier, the great Al Jolson. When Crosby was on the Kraft show he would invite his hero Jolson to be a guest and they would sing duets and mimic each other.

There is little known about the Paulettes except for the legacy of their music. It is a treat to listen to them sing "Your Love Captured Me" and "Lips That Lie," a single from Decca released in 1956. You'll love it.

Girls, if you are still around, let us know. Many fans would be so happy to find and celebrate your life and career.

The Merry Macs

The Merry Macs were a close harmony quartet consisting of three men and a girl, whose personnel did not remain constant for any length of time. But the group was very popular during the later part of World War II. They recorded for RCA Victor with Jack Hylton's Orchestra in 1933, and later with Victor Young's Orchestra. They also recorded with Bing Crosby around 1940 on "You Made Me Love You," and "Do You Ever Think of Me."

Their signature recordings and best sellers were "Praise the Lord and Pass the Ammunition" in 1942 and "Deep in the Heart of Texas" in 1941. The group also made an appearance at the London Palladium in 1948.

The group originally were the three McMichael brothers, Judd, Joe and Ted. They added a lead singer named Cheri McKay and changed their group name to The Merry Macs. The group was very active in radio, appearing on a number of radio shows over the years. Cheri dropped out and was replaced by Helen Carroll.

It is said that the Merry Macs revolutionized vocal harmony with the use of singing with closer harmonic chords. This apparently inspired succeeding groups like the Modernaires, who sang with Glenn Miller's Orchestra.

1939 saw Mary Lou Cook replace Helen Carroll just as the group began being featured in movies, including *Love Thy Neighbor* that starred Bing Crosby, and *Ride 'Em Cowboy* with Abbott and Costello, performing musical interludes.

The Merry Macs were inducted into the Vocal Group Hall of Fame in 2003.

The Four Preps

The old Four Preps are now the New Four Preps, starring the lead singers, Skip Taylor, Bruce Belland, Bob Duncan, and Michael Redman, from a collection of three old groups: The Association, The Four Preps, and The Diamonds, in which all four were lead singers. Collectively, they garnered 29 hit singles, 15 gold albums, 13 Grammy, Emmy and Golden Globe nominations, and the Presidential Medal of the Arts. Whew!!!

The Four Preps are now inductees in the Vocal Group Hall of Fame.

Looking back a bit, the original Four Preps lineup were Bruce Belland, lead, Ed Cobb, bass, Marv Ingram, high tenor, and Glen Larson, baritone, who were fellow students at Hollywood High and fortunately began recording with Capitol Records after being spotted by a Capitol executive at a talent show. They appeared on *The Edsel Television Show* with Lindsey Crosby, one of Bing's kids.

The group's big hit was "26 Miles-Santa Catalina" and climbed up high on the charts in 1957. Belland and Larson were the authors of that tune, as well as "Down by the Station" which also fared very well.

In 1960 they recorded a parody tune that imitated the song "Tom Dooley" a Kingston Trio hit. The group switched a number of re-placement vocalists, finally breaking up, although Belland and David Somerville performed as a duo now and then.

Bruce Belland's talented daughters Tracey and Melissa formed Voice of the Beehive, two beautiful and talented chips off the old block.

THE CREW CUTS

The Crew Cuts, a Canadian vocal quartet, had been members of St. Michael's Choir School in Toronto. The group was composed of Rudi Maugeri, baritone, John Perkins, lead, Ray Perkins, bass, and Pat Barrett, high tenor.

A Toronto disc jockey put them on a local teen show. The audi-ence renamed the group The Canadaires. The boys worked clubs in and around Niagara Falls. They headed for New York City and the *Arthur Godfrey's Talent Scouts* competition, where they came in second.

Shortly, they returned to Toronto and opened for singer Gisele MacKenzie at the Casino Theater. Not much luck there, but drove to Cleveland, Ohio and appeared on a show where disc jockey Bill

Randle re-named the boys The Crew Cuts. They auditioned for Mercury Records and were signed to a contract.

Their version of "Sh-Boom" hit number one on the charts, followed by "Earth Angel," a 'cover' recording rose to number two on the charts. The boys broke up after a short stint with RCA Records. For a short-lived group the Crew Cuts recorded a number of popular cover songs, listed here alphabetically.

Recently the three remaining members of the Crew Cuts have

appeared on PBS fund-raising television shows.

"All I Wanna Do" (1954)
"Angels In The Sky" (1955)
"The Barking Dog" (1954)
"Bei Mir Bist Du Schön" (1956)
"Be My Only Love" (1957)
"Carmen's Boogie" (1955)
"Chop Chop Boom" (1955)
"Crazy 'Bout You Baby" (1954)
"Dance, Mr. Snowman, Dance" (1954)
"Don't Be Angry" (1955)
"Earth Angel" (1955)
"Gum Drop" (1955)
"Halls Of Ivy" (1956)
"Hey! Stella" (1958)
"I Like It Like That" (1957)
"I Sit In The Window" (1957)
"Ko Ko Mo (I Love You So)" (1955)
"Legend Of Gunga Din" (1959)
"Love In A Home" (1956)
"Mostly Martha" (1955)
"Oop-Shoop" (1954)
"Over The Mountain" (1959)
"Seven Days" (1956)
"Sh-Boom" (1954)
"Slam Bam" (1955)
"A Story Untold" (1955)
"Suzie Q" (1957)
"Tell Me Why" (1956)
Twinkle Toes (1953)
"Unchained Melody" (1955)
"Whatever, Whenever, Whoever" (1957)
"The Whiffenpoof Song" (1955)
"Young Love" (1957)

The Lane Sisters

There were five Lane Sisters. Priscilla, Rosemary and Lola (actually Dorothy) were the three who achieved success as a singing act and Priscilla wound up as a popular movie star in a number of successful films. Leota and Martha never entered the arts. The family name was actually Mullican and all except Lola were born in Iowa.

In 1972 Cora Lane, the mother of the five Lane girls wrote an article about her and her girls for Liberty Magazine, a blithe, moving story of struggle and success. The girls dad was a dentist. Their mother encouraged and fostered their playing various musical instruments. They lived nearby Simpson College in Indianola. Lola played the piano for a silent movie theater at the age of twelve.

"I always wanted to be a big-city reporter," said mother Cora," I had such ambition, but I married and reared five children, like Eddie Cantor, all girls. Rosemary once said that if I adopted four children we'd have a baseball team."

In order to get the piano, Leota went all over town gathering coupons for a small mail-order house.

"In order to get other things for the girls, I rented spare rooms to girl college students, which bought bicycles and a trapeze for the girls. We used to have kitchen conferences, and we discussed everything from soccer to skirt hems - and even a lively debate about boys." Martha, with her poetry and her books, was not one of our singers. She would write poetry:

I WISH YOU WERE A CUP OF TEA,
SO I COULD POUR YOU DOWN THE SINK!

Leota was the family pioneer. She began singing at various events around the state, then eventually began singing on the stage, an idea recommended by the new singing teacher who just came to Simpson College. While Leota was visiting her friends flower shop, in came famed showman Gus Edwards, " Mr. Edwards, you should hear this girl sing, pointing to Leota."

FIVE HOLLYWOOD DAUGHTERS

The five Lanes and their mother try out a song at their home in Indianola, Iowa.

BY CORA B. LANE

READING TIME ● 9 MINUTES 55 SECONDS

AT seventeen, when I was working on my brother's newspaper in Indiana, I had one ambition: To become a big-city reporter.
So I married and became a small-town housewife. In the course of time, mother of five girls: Leota, Martha, Lola, Rosemary, and Priscilla.
"If you'd just adopt four children," Rosemary suggested once, very hopefully, "we'd have a baseball team!"
But we had plenty of problems without worrying about full-sized teams. Indianola, Iowa, where we lived, was the typical insular American town. Thirty-five hundred inhabitants in the heart of the corn belt. We had our county fairs, church bazaars, our rigid moral principles and even more rigid prejudices. (I'll never forget the furor it created when I first put the girls in basketball bloomers!)
We also had a singular advantage. The best conservatory of music in the state, Simpson College, was located in Indianola. The air was charged with Beethoven sonatas, Bach fugues. Even the iceman whistled arias. But I don't know how our family would have managed a piano if Leota hadn't won it. Money was disturbingly scarce. My husband was a dentist, and Iowans are noted for their excellent teeth. So there were times when we wondered where the next penny was coming from. To get that piano, Leota went all over town gathering coupons for some mail-order house.

In order to get other things for the children, I rented rooms to girl students. An easy enough matter, since we had a rambling old-fashioned house of sixteen rooms. Out of that extra change came bicycles for the youngsters, the trapeze in the back yard—and the music lessons.

I wanted two things for those girls of mine. First of all, I wanted them healthy, to love outdoor games and sports. Even during the four and a half years that Rosemary and Priscilla were with Fred Waring's band, I tried to find places where they could exercise in each city. And the older girls have kept it up no matter where they went.

My second hope was that each of the girls would excel in something, because I didn't have that chance. They had every opportunity to study music. "But money comes too hard to waste on lessons," I explained to them, "if you're not going to apply yourselves." If they wanted anything, they learned to work for it.

We used to have what the girls jokingly called "kitchen conferences." And we discussed everything from soccer to skirt hems. Once, I remember, we were having a lively debate about boys, when Rosemary, too young to be interested, punctuated it with a scream. She had fallen in the flour bin!

On Saturdays I did nothing but cook. Chickens, huge pans of baked beans, fudge cake. . . . Then, on Sundays, all the young crowd gathered around our table. Home has to be fun if you want to keep the youngsters in it. As the girls grew older they brought their boy friends to the house as a matter of course. I well recall Martha's first beau. Martha, with her poetry and books, was the literary light of the family, and she nearly dazzled the poor boy by such gems of verse as

I wish you were a cup of tea,
So I could pour you down the sink!

If they began going with the Wrong Boy, I'd encourage them to bring him home until they were tired of him. It worked every time.
Last summer, when Lola, Rosemary, and Priscilla were working in the picture Four Daughters, they used to come home chuckling. "Why, mother, all these funny homey things we're supposed to do—pillow fighting, borrowing each other's clothes, having jam sessions in each other's rooms—that's really us!" And it was.
I knew that if I could teach them to like the simple, small things in life, the big things would take care of themselves. Just the other day Priscilla, or Pat as the girls call her, came home from the studio after doing what I believe they call "dress shots"—wearing an elaborate gown and furs in some sophisticated night-club scene. After a while we missed her. I went outside to look, and there was Pat in old slacks, with a great smudge of white on her face, painting the picket fence. "This," she announced, "is the most sport I've had in years!"

Originally published in LIBERTY May 13, 1939

Fred Waring

"Well, here's no time like the present," said Mr. Edwards. And that's how it happened for the Lane Sisters. Edwards renamed the girls The Lane Sisters.

Leota and Lola appeared on Broadway. Lola in *War Song* and Leota in *Babes in Toyland*.

Rosemary and Priscilla joined Fred Waring's fine orchestra as singers and remained with him for over four years. He had heard them harmonizing at a music publishing house in New York. They appeared regularly on Waring's radio show with his musical group known as The Pennsylvanians. The entire ensemble appeared in the film *Varsity Show* with Dick Powell. The girls were awarded special roles. Rosemary was Dick Powell's romantic interest and Priscilla was a comedienne college girl.

Collectively, the Lane girls appeared in over 85 films including *Four Wives* in 1939, *The Boys from Syracuse*, *Gold Diggers in Paris*, *Hollywood Hotel*, *Arsenic and Old Lace*, *Yes, My Darling Daughter*, and *Brother Rat*. In the film, *Four Daughters* the Lane girls performed marvelously, and the film introduced and launched the upcoming star, John Garfield. What a charming film it is.

The Lane girls talents were stellar and far-reaching, especially during their film career which, I am sorry to say, replaced their fine singing career. As Frank Sinatra sings: "That's Life!"

THE PETERS SISTERS

Three genuine sisters were Mattye, Anne and Virginia, The three Peters Sisters, who began their career in the 1930s. Just listening to their recording of the song "Sweet, Sweet, Sweet," guarantees you'll enjoy their exceptionally clear and precise close harmony skills.

Copies of the recording may be hard to find. They recorded that tune in March of 1949 under the Columbia Label, recorded and produced in France.

"The girls harmonies," as one person exclaimed, "are as good as it gets."

Some of their recordings were performed in French. Their other releases were "Saint Louis Blues," "Mama Wants to Know Who Stole the Jam," "Les Soeurs Etienne: Lamb of God." They recorded "Some of These Days" with the great Louis Armstrong, and made an appearance on the *Ed Sullivan Show* sharing the stage with Kate Smith.

The Peters sang their way into the 1960s. Their Capitol Album is entitled *The Swingin' Peter Sisters*, backed by Geoff Love's Orchestra, is an album of standards sweetly performed.

Catch them if you can!

THE DANDRIDGE SISTERS

The Dandridge girls were very different from one another. There was Dorothy, who later achieved great fame as a singer and dancer in films, Vivian, and Etta Jones, who sang together on tour with the Jimmie Lunceford jazz band from 1934 through 1940 when they disbanded as a group.

Now Etta was not actually a sister, nor was she the famous Etta Jones who was born in 1928 and enjoyed a career as a jazz singer.

The girls won an amateur singing contest on KNX radio in L.A. defeating twenty-five other contestants.

As a result Joe Glaser, the famous promoter who represented Louis Armstrong and a number of other performers, invited the girls to sing at New York's Cotton Club and they got to perform regularly with W.C. Handy, Cab Calloway, and the dancers Fayard and Harold Nicholas. The girls were booked into the London Palladium and other English dates. Their famous recording of "Undecided" was recorded in London with the Charlie Shavers Orchestra in 1939.

The end of the Dandridge Sisters singing group came quickly after they got back to America, after a short stint with the Lunceford band. Dorothy left to go it alone and sought stage and film work. Dorothy married dancer Harold Nicholas, and Vivian appeared in a few films and as an "extra" uncredited in the great film Stormy Weather. The girls few recordings were "Minnie the Moocher is Dead," "You

Ain't Nowhere," "Ain't Going to Study War No More," and "That's Your Red Wagon."

Of course, Dorothy appeared in the film *Sun Valley Serenade* with the Glenn Miller Orchestra and sang and danced to the song "Chattanooga Choo Choo" with the Nicholas Brothers. The girls also appeared in a handful of films, one performing with Louis Armstrong and Maxine Sullivan.

THE OSMOND BROTHERS

Well, it's a good thing that Jay Williams, father of Andy Williams and his brothers, spotted the talent of the Osmond Brothers at Disneyland in California, shortly after their act was rejected by the Lawrence Welk show producers, and suggested that his son Andy invite the Osmonds to be a guest on his show. And Andy did just that. Earlier, the Osmonds began as a barbershop quartet that included Alan, Wayne, Merrill, and Jay, joined later by the younger Donny and Jimmy. Their only sister, Marie, went out and made it on her own. The Osmond boys became regulars on the *Andy Williams Show* for seven years.

The very clean cut appearance of the Osmonds endeared them to audiences when they decided to perform more popular music as a band. They secured a record contract with MGM Records with the help of producer Mike Curb, who felt they were talented and would succeed as a pop  group. And they did. And when they brought sibling Donny into the group, it became a quintet, and gained even more popularity. Donny, who usually sang second-lead and the chorus of the song, became popular with the teen-age female audience, and as a result, became the main attraction of the act.

Over the years the Osmonds produced 22 albums and 29 singles. They have toured Europe, and in 2007-8 they toured Europe to celebrate 50 years in show business. They appeared on PBS in 2008, and their mentor, Andy Williams, showed up as a surprise. It was a great show.

Donny and Marie have had their own act and appear on television and in Las Vegas today. They have succeeded in all forms of entertainment over many, many years.

THE STARLIGHTERS

A musical researcher from Australia by the name of Adrian Duff came up with information and some detail about another group we just squeaked in to the final draft of this book. The group is the Starlighters.

The Starlighters consisted of Pauline Byrns, Vince Degen, Howard Johnson, and Andy Williams. Yes, it's a very early Andy (an 18 year old,) before the days with his brothers and Kay Thompson's cabaret act. He left the Starlighters in early 1947 to join Thompson. The Starlighters recorded nine tracks with Matty Malneck's orchestra. It included "When Johnny Comes Marching Home," a popular post-war tune, and "The Banana Boat Song."

Andy Williams

The recordings were a unique series of radio entertainment for the service men and women in the American Armed Forces during World War II, known as the AFRS Jubilee Series.

The Starlighters recorded for those transcriptions produced by Standard, Capitol and World Records on 33 1/3 -16" discs. These discs were licensed to radio stations and were not available to the general public. The discs had a fifteen minute playing time per side,

Here is the interesting list of songs the Starlighters recorded in mid-1946.

"There's No One But You"
"Love On a Greyhound Bus"
"Iowa"
"I Don't Know Why"
"When Johnny Comes Marching Home"
"Banana Boat Song"
"On the Boardwalk" (In Atlantic City)
"A Little Kiss Each Morning"
"Yes, We have No Bananas"

Also thanks to Carl Hallstrom for his input. Carl lives in Uppsala, Sweden and has compiled a vast book on Tommy Dorsey' recording career. Their version of Cole Porter's "Night & Day" on Capitol Records is perhaps one of the best group recordings I've ever heard. Paul Weston's Orchestra backed this wonderful recording.

Richard Grudens and Radio DJ Jack Ellsworth discuss their favorite singers, songwriters and groups of the big band era at WLIM Radio - Long Island, New York

GOSPEL QUARTETS

The Golden Gate Quartet

There are three gospel-style groups who stand out among many. The Golden Gate Quartet, The Deep River Boys, and The Four Knights are the most successful of the jubilee quartet style.

The Golden Gate Quartet was originally the Golden Gate Jubilee Quartet founded by Robert Ford, A.C. Griffin, Willie Johnson, William Langford, Henry Owens, and Orlandus Wilson. Starting as barbershop and segueing into rhythms of blues and jazz. Jazz enthusiast and promoter John Hammond presented them to Carnegie Hall audiences where they achieved reasonable fame. They also appeared in some notable films; *Star Spangled Rhythm* in 1942,that featured Bob Hope and Bing Crosby; *Hit Parade of 1943, Hollywood Canteen*, and *A Song is Born* in 1948 with Danny Kaye and Virginia Mayo.

Their rendition of the World War II song "Comin' In on a Wing and a Prayer" may have been their most popular recording and one of the war's most inspirational songs. They were inducted into the Vocal Group Hall of Fame in 1998.

The Deep River Boys

Similar to the Golden Gate Quartet, The Deep River Boys performed musical material from the 1930s through the 80s. The first group enlisted Harry Douglass who sang baritone, Vernon Gardner who sang first tenor, George Lawson, second tenor, and Edward

Ware who carried the bass parts. They performed mostly Christian gospel songs where they began at Hampton University in Virginia. Their first hit was "Recess in Heaven" in 1948, and they went on to appear with the great Bill 'Bogangles' Robinson, William "Count" Basie's Band, and piano-playing vocalist Fats Waller of "It's a Sin to Tell a Lie" fame.

They performed successfully in Europe, Sweden and Norway and sang to translated words in both countries. They also performed on Ed Sullivan's *Toast of the Town* television show.

Personnel changes wound up with Jimmy Lundy surviving until 2007, and later, members Ronnie Bright and tenor Eddie Whaley have retired. Whaley was born in England and now lives in Florida.

THE FOUR KNIGHTS

The third of our tribute groups are the Four Knights formed in 1943. Original members were Gene Alford who sang lead, Oscar Broadway who sang bass, Clarence Dixon who sang baritone and John Wallace -tenor and guitarist.

The first two years they performed on *Carolina Hayride* on radio WBT, Charlotte, North Carolina. By 1945 they had moved to New York to sing on Arthur Godfrey's show. With Decca Records they recorded a few singles and appeared on comedian Red Skelton's show and subsequently toured with Bill "Bojangles" Robinson.

The boys signed with Capitol Records and released the beautiful song "I Love the Sunshine of Your Smile." On television they appeared on Ed Sullivan's show and renewed their relationship with Red Skelton on his television show, and also accompanied Nat "King" Cole on two single releases, "My Personal Possession" and "That's All There is to That."

The Knights broke up gradually after the death of Gene Alford in 1960 due to his epilepsy illness.

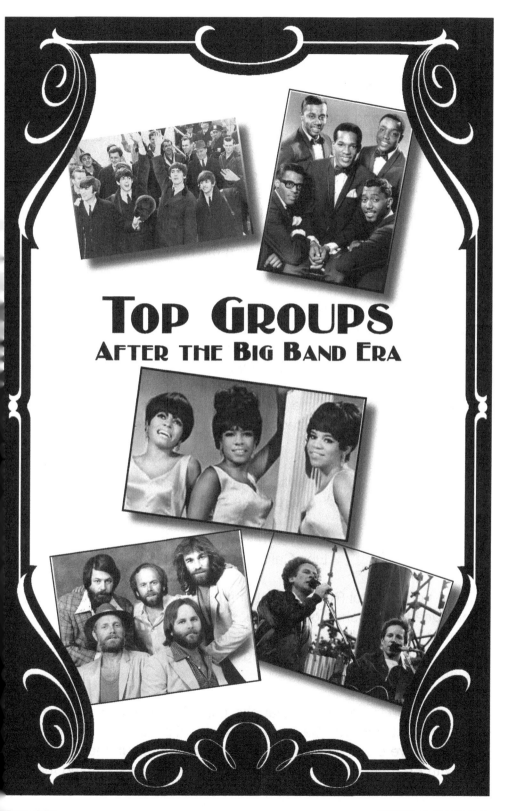

TOP GROUPS
AFTER THE BIG BAND ERA

The Beach Boys

America's Band

The amazing saga of the world-renowned singing Beach Boys is strictly a California story. It began in 1961 in Hawthorne with the very musical Brian Wilson playing bass, organ and piano, his brothers Dennis on drums and Carl on guitar, Al Jardine (a high school friend) on rhythm guitar, and Mike Love, (Brian's cousin), playing the saxophone. All of them sang and played gigs around their hometown as Kenny & the Cadets, Carl & the Passions, and even the Pendletons with various personnel. "Including my mother," Brian said with pride.

The group's first recorded success as the Beach Boys was "Surfin' Safari," which became a national hit and had "409" (a Chevrolet auto slang word) on the "B" side. In popular terms, this song was really something different. It was Dennis' idea to write songs about surfing. But it was Brian, who, a few months later, took Chuck Berry's already popular "Sweet Little Sixteen," retained the form and, in one masterful stroke, universalized the surfing phenomenon with their "Surfin' USA."

"If everybody had an ocean
Across the USA,

Then everybody'd be surfin'
Like Californ-nye-aye."

Then, Capitol Records, not entirely sold on the surfing craze, about-faced and rushed out another Beach Boys album, investing a quarter-million dollars in promotionals. Satisfied with success, the boys quickly released a sweet song entitled, "Surfer Girl." It became the top tune of 1963.

Now on top of the popular chart, the Beach Boys took to the road. The first stop was Sacramento, California's capitol, far away from the wave craze, but nevertheless a hotbed of summer surfin' fervor. With Brian taking over production, the work was sounding more sophisticated with the boys' uniquely full-bodied harmonies. Imitators

were legion, but never as acceptable. You can't imitate and earn success. You have to be original. Great success was looming. Radio disc jocks loved every tune and played them over and over til everyone was singing and swinging Beach Boys tunes.

Remaining with the successful teenage material, Brian began to tackle new themes. There was " Fun Fun Fun" in 1964 with the Chuck Berry inspiration. It was a peppy little song that moved up to the Top Five and remained steadfastly on top of the charts. "We're sticking to surf and hotrod stuff, but when a new fad comes along, we'll be the first to ride it," said Brian.

In the early '60s California was the epitome of teenage existence to everyone everywhere else. All the elements were present: affluence, leisure, permissive parental attitudes, weather – all combined to create a sort of Teenage Nirvana, where summer meant fun and the beach was the place to be.

Leader Brian Wilson was in his 20s and had no real interest in surfing, but he was an athlete with a wise eye. Most of his musical ideas, according to his wife, Marilyn, were based on the two of them growing up. "California's atmosphere and its people were his total inspiration," she said.

Of course, he had the lyrical aid, from time to time of Mike Love, Gary Usher and a local disk jockey, Roger Christian, whose cumulative efforts produced much of the words to both the surfing and automotive songs that were the catalyst for the Beach Boys' career. Most of the songs glorified California, its residents' way of living and emerging cultural experiences. California was the leader in national car trends and actual surfing mystiques, and was considered by many residents as being close to heaven. But influence from the 1950s teenage singers and vocal groups, like Chuck Berry, the Four Freshmen, faint echoes of Dion and the Belmonts, and Roy Orbison-styled vocal backgrounds must be acknowledged.

Most of the Beach Boys songs, however, were 1960s originals relating chiefly to teenage concerns: acceptance, rejection, complexion and hotrod cars.

"Surfer Girl" was, of course, the great romantic song of the surf era, with the boys' achingly pure harmonies and melodies shining through all the competition's releases.

In 1964, Brian Wilson was motivated to surpass the invasion of the British groups by recording, "I Get Around," backed with "Don't Worry Baby." It may very well be one of the strongest two-sided singles in pop history. "I Get Around" was a brilliant upbeat recording with a stunning vocal arrangement and ultimate teenage cruising ex-

Carl Wilson   Dennis Wilson   Mike Love   Al Jardine   Brian Wilson

THE Beach Boys

pression, a overwhelming assurance mixed with territorial pride. The record was California in spirit and inspiration.

After the album, *Shutdown Vol. II* (which included "I Get Around" and "Don't Worry Baby,") the Beach Boys reached a transition point between musical eras. With few exceptions, they never again shared the easy, comfortable, we-belong-together rapport with their audiences. Things were changing now, the culture influenced by long hair, drugs, political issues and economic belt-tightening. The boys became more personal and inspiring with their music, but the early zest and initial unself-conscious character that permeated their previous material was gone.

The one-night stands and every increasing workload was getting to Brian. And the record companies, who regarded the group as a childlike money machine, ran them ragged. It was, according to Al Jardine, "two hours of sleep a night with a few tranquilizers." The strain seemed life-threatening. En route to Houston in December

1964, Brian suffered a severe breakdown and had to quit the road trips.

"I used to be Mr. Everything," he said at the time. "I felt I had no choice. I just can't do it any longer." Brian's replacement was guitarist Glen Campbell, who could sing falsetto parts but who really wasn't a Beach Boy at heart. He was later replaced by Bruce Johnston, who more closely fit the group's image and remained with the group until 1972.

Even without Brian's performance efforts, the group was still immensely popular, and their *Beach Boys Concert* LP became their first chart-topping album. However, fans of the hot British groups considered them a bit outdated, and the group became more a "girls group," being primarily supported by dedicated females.

Well removed now from their cars and surfing pieces, the boys needed a musical change and Brian came up with "Barbara Ann" It was an old Regents hit from 1961 and came off that group's *Party* album. In "Barbara Ann," Dean Torrence shared the lead vocals

with Brian, then quickly followed with something still different in "The Sloop, John B," which gave them their second 1966 Top 5 hit.

"I write to explore my musical capabilities," said Brian Wilson. But the new Bob Dylan cult was a driving force and Burt Bacharach's unusual musical style was the hot commercial sound. Brian needed a new approach because Capitol Records was growing impatient for a new product.

Brian couldn't come up with anything quick enough, so the group's first live package, "Beach Boys Concert" album, was released. It produced the enormously successful "Little Old Lady from Pasadena" single and a host of musically competent takes borrowed from peers' albums. Capitol also released a Christmas album and the *Beach Boys Today*, mostly created at home by Brian and Phil Spector, his producer. It included the megahit, "California Girls." Brian was at last relieved of his touring burden.

While Carl, Dennis, Mike, Al and Bruce were on tour, Brian worked on a new album, *Pet Sounds*, in 1966. The sounds on that album were remarkable as keyboard textures unveiled in "California Girls" were everywhere. It was a dense, dreamy mix unlike anything they had ever done before. The opening song, "Wouldn't It Be Nice," exhibited a healthy dose of energy and a new drive, and each song was homogeneous with the next. It was a casual, sociable, play-it-at-parties success and quickly reached the top ten.

Then the masterful single, "Good Vibrations," was released, attaining new heights of complexity. It went from hymnal to solemnity to good old California exuberance in seconds. It was the Beach Boys biggest hit and their first million seller. "Good Vibrations" was a watershed, and the global flood of admiration for the group was in full swing. Critics raved, and in England the accolades were so great that the California Boys unseated the Brits' Beatles in popularity polls all over Britain and the United States.

In 1967, the group formed its own Brother label in association with Capitol, and Brian was appointed to the Board of Directors for the planned Monterey International Pop Festival, a move that would galvanize their rapport with the new, progressive-minded followers of late 60s rock.

Brian, however, was gradually destroying himself with psyche-delic drugs, and being called a genius, placed himself under even more pressure to produce and excel. He was absorbing everything around him at a killing pace, and he was becoming reclusive and introspective.

Mike Love, upset by the changes in Brian, including all the complex new music, didn't want to abandon the tried-and-true formu-la of the Beach Boys. Capitol Records, too, was unhappy with all the changes and the inability of the group to turn out new, timely record-ings. To bridge the lost time and revenue, they compiled two *Best of the Beach Boys* albums, which temporarily satisfied the record com-pany and the boys' fans.

If things weren't wrong before, everything now went from bad to worse. Brian's new material was being poorly received by Top 40 radio stations so the group pulled out of the Monterey Festival, miss-ing out on priceless opportunities. Brian believed local fires were mystically triggered by his music so he destroyed valuable, newly produced tapes. The new album *Heroes and Villains*, although re-leased, lost out to the lack of momentum from "Good Vibrations" some nine months before; and Brian scrapped a bunch of his new work fearful of it being judged in the wake of Sgt. Pepper's release by the Beatles.

Brian went to work on the album *Smi-ley Smile* with Val Dyke Parks, musician/lyricist. It was released in 1967, but followed just one month later with the *Wild Honey* album because *Smiley Smile* was perceived as anti-Beach Boys so the boys had rushed back to Brian's studio and pushed it out. Both albums were disconcerting to the group's new audiences, who felt the Beach Boys' artistic sights had been lowered.

The Friends album followed, but this one really divided fans.

Songs like "Little Bird" by Dennis and "Busy Doin' Nuthin'" by Brian proved musically trivial compared to past albums. It was a loser but it was Brian's favorite, nonetheless. With no major hits, it fared badly on the charts, so Brian and Mike rushed out a single entitled, "Do It Again," in time to catch the end of summer.

It was a triumph, like "Jumpin' Jack Flash" for the Rolling Stones and "Get Back" for the Beatles, and it marked a familiar return to the Beach Boys' surfing roots.

But hard rock stations were really ignoring the boys and they considered changing their name to Beach. The group and their music seemed hopelessly outdated, but they finished a final album for Capitol, *20/20*, in 1969.

The album was a smorgasbord of talents and it produced their most beautiful *a cappella* voicings, harking back to their 1963 version of "The Lord's Prayer." They were now finished with Capitol (after one last single, "Celebrate The News"/"Break Away"). In 1970, Warner/Reprise picked up Brother Records, with Brian, Carl, Dennis, Mike, Alan and Bruce.

The first single under the new label, the ill-fated "Add Some Music to Your Day," was pushed, but   it really didn't make the grade for Reprise, nor did the first album, *Sunflower*, although it was really an aesthetic triumph. It was filled with vibrant and stunning vocals. "Cool-Cool Water," much like "Good Vibrations," did well.

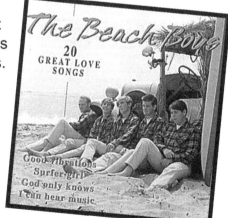

The 1970-71 season was hopeful, for as they resumed touring the United States, including the 1970 and '71 Big Sur Festival in California, Brian decided to make a stage appearance at the Whiskey-Go-Go in Los Angeles – and it was a disaster. On the second night, Brian succumbed to the lights and noise levels.

"I had trouble focusing on anything," he later admitted. "Faces out there were swimming at me… my eardrums ached… I felt like I was killing myself." That ended his stage comeback and he retreated to his Bel Air refuge to get back to composing.

But the Beach Boys triumphed anyway and the group was once again enthusiastically received by the crowds. Back in form, the

Surfin' U.S.A.

Words and Music by
CHUCK BERRY

group released *Surf's Up* in the fall of 1971 with a new style. Songs like Bruce Johnston's "Disney Girls" and Mike Love's "Riot in Cell Block #9" passed over easily and other cuts were far from their best work. But the Beach Boys mystique drew lots of airplay and, therefore, success again, and the album reached the Top 30.

In 1972, an album contained songs by the newest members of the Beach Boys, Blondie Chaplin, and Ricky Fataar, Carl Wilson's South African protégés. Carl wanted to infuse the Beach Boys music with the "Black Sound," but it just didn't work.

Still going and growing, however, they released *Holland* in January 1973. Through Jack Rieley's maneuverings, it was recorded in Holland and contained the songs "Sail On Sailor," "Big Sur" and "California Saga." The album was accepted readily since fans knew it contained better performances than usual.

In the ensuing years, the Beach Boys released a number of new albums and continued to tour (without Brian). They racked up impressive sales and continued popularity including a No.1 rating for *Endless Summer*, with their oldies continually reaping the rewards of the past. Unlike many other groups of their era, they remained together and spanned a generation. Their songs are appealing; their harmonies brilliant, comfortable and listenable; and their fans are undisputedly loyal.

Tragically, Dennis Wilson drowned in 1983 – and the heart of the group was gone. But the Beach Boys' songs – and popularity – didn't die and in December 1986 they celebrated their 25th anniversary with a hit television special from Hawaii.

The group recorded the hit single, "Kokomo," from Tom Cruise's successful movie and it quickly sold a million copies.

Then their *Still Cruisin* album by Capitol Records, which included "Kokomo," hit the music stores and has sold 700,000 copies to date at that time.

Over the years, the Beach Boys have joined forces with megastars like Elton John, Chicago, and other groups and personalities, almost always proving more popular with audiences that the headliners themselves. They've backed movie sound tracks and, much like Simon and Garfunkel, Peter, Paul and Mary, and other musical innovators. The replaying and reissuances of their work seem to increase in popularity over the originals.

The Beach Boys were still a top attraction in 1993, in fact, when they released a new album, *Summer in Paradise*, it attracted new fans as well as delighting long-standing followers. Also, Capitol Records released 30 Years of the *Beach Boys Best*, a five-hour, five-CD music extravaganza which chronologically covered all of the group's songs over three decades.

Past and current Members of the Beach Boys have been Brian Wilson, Carl Wilson, Dennis Wilson, Mike Love, Bruce Johnston, David Marks, Al Jardine, Ricky Fataar, Blondie Chaplin and Glen Campbell.

In 2011, the Beach Boys celebrated their 50th anniversary and at this writing they were to appear at the NBYC Theater in Westbury, Long Island, New York, a place well familiar to them over the years. Good Vibrations continue.

THE BEACH BOYS ALBUMS

- Surfin' Safari (1962)
- Surfin' USA (1963)
- Surfer Girl (1963)
- Little Deuce Coupe (1963)
- Shut Down Volume 2 (1964)
- All Summer Long (1964)
- The Beach Boys' Christmas Album (1964)
- Today! (1965)
- Summer Days (and Summer-Nights!!) (1965)
- Beach Boys' Party! (1965)

- Pet Sounds (1966)
- Smiley Smile (1967)
- Wild Honey (1967)
- Friends (1968)
- 20/20 (1969)

- Sunflower (1970)
- Surf's Up (1971)
- Carl and the Passions – "So Tough" (1972)
- Holland (1973)
- 15 Big Ones (1976)
- Love You (1977)
- M.I.U. Album (1978)
- L.A. (Light Album) (1979)
- Keepin' the Summer Alive (1980)
- The Beach Boys (1985)
- Still Cruisin' (1989)
- Summer in Paradise (1992)
- Stars & Stripes (1996)

THE ORIGINAL BEACH BOYS SANG AT THE 2012 GRAMMY AWARDS (INCLUDING BRIAN WILSON).

"To Infinity & Beyond"

Some Thoughts by Stephanie Jendrzejewski
Fan and Blogger - Tumblr - "ShoutThis"

Stephanie - Just 15

"Individuals all over the world have been affected by Beatlemania. There are multiple reasons why people love The Beatles. Their music talks to you; you, the "individual," and you feel like the songs they have composed are written for you/meant for you. They get you through the day. No one seems to understand exactly why. It makes me believe in something again, like there is still hope for something more to come.

"Their music is magical. It has the power to brighten up your life. That is why they are, indeed, the greatest band on earth. No matter if the song is sad or totally whacky, it gives me a mysterious pleasure.

John Lennon, Paul McCartney, George Harrison, and Ringo Starr are brilliant legends. Elvis may have changed music, but The Beatles changed the world. To this day no one can match them in talent and charisma. This is why The Beatles music will last to infinity and beyond.

Stephanie

George, PAUL, John, Ringo

A side note from Stephanie's Aunt:

"I grew up in the 70's listening to the Beatles, because my mom was always playing and dancing to *Obladi Oblada* - that was my introduction, (which would make Stephanie a third generation Beatles' fan.) Soon after, I discovered my own favorites like 'Day Tripper,' 'Paperback Writer,' and 'Michelle' - and the list goes on. Fast forward to 2012: since my niece started her Tublr blog, I've discovered great songs I never heard before, and forty years later, I still like my favorites. Whenever I hear them, my mind is instantly flooded with memories of my mom dancing to her favorite song in our living room. Music has such tremendous power to bring back clear recollections of past events and connect generations of listeners."
> **Madeline Grudens, Editor**

THE BEATLES

At first they were just an ordinary, struggling English rock and roll group singing in ale houses and on stages in the poor areas of Liverpool. Today, over 50 years later, the Beatles have emerged as the greatest rock and roll singing group of them all.

First there was John Lennon, Paul McCartney, Stuart Sutcliffe, and Pete Best. George Harrison and Ringo Starr soon replaced Sutcliffe and Best. Who could doubt the musical performance power and the eventual glory of this great group of vocalists, musicians and songwriters. Like the early power of Frank Sinatra's growing career, the Beatles moved consistently upward until they reached the absolute top.

Later, the Beatles iconic fame was advanced with the unfortunate, murder of John Lennon, songwriter and vocalist, who had created his own legend. He was gunned down by an American, Mark Chapman, in1980, outside Lennon's popular New York City apartment house, the famed Dakota, on Central Park West. The Dakota has and still houses many famous personalities from Judy Garland to Leonard Bernstein.

Everyone knows their songs: "Michelle," "Yellow Submarine," "Yesterday," "All My Loving," "Let it Be," "Eleanor Rigby," "Penny Lane," and many, many more, and some were composed by the members themselves.

Paul, John, Ringo, George

After the first fledgling years they were joined by manager Brian Epstein and producer George Martin, who molded them into a more professional group by enhancing their musicality, introducing more influential material into their repertoire, and allowing them to expand and grow from their early, singular and otherwise lightweight material.

The introduction of the group to the vast United Sates television audience via the Ed Sullivan Variety show *Toast of the Town* helped to make them the best-selling band in music history. The albums *Revolver* in 1966, *The Beatles* in 1968, and *Abbey Road* in 1969 were very influential in the rock and roll marketplace.Those albums, without doubt, easily catapulted them to the top.

Interesting to note that early member Stuart Sutcliffe who suggested a change to their original title name, The Beatals, then the Beetles, later to The Silver Beatles, and as Stuart suggested, coined the final name of The Beatles. Sutcliffe passed away shortly thereafter.

PERFECT HARMONY

Another ironic note: When Epstein presented the group to Decca Records, their response was "Guitar groups are on the way out, Mr. Epstein."

Meanwhile Martin signed the group to EMI's Parlophone label. Epstein professionalized them by encouraging them to stop eating, smoking, swearing, and wearing sloppy jeans on stage, that is, if they were going to achieve a more professional stature.

Their first million-selling recording was "She Loves You" that sold three-quarters of a million copies in a few weeks. With the amazing response on U.S. radio of the recording "I Want to Hold Your Hand, " which sold two and a half million copies, their entrance into the American marketplace through their appearance on the Sullivan show, was nothing short of phenomenal. The crowds at their arrival at Kennedy Airport were estimated at over three thousand. A few days later America showcased them to seventy-five million viewers which performed miracles and added significantly to their fan base.

Newspaper critics, however, tongue-lashed them about their haircuts and claimed they could not carry a tune. Nevertheless their popularity surged. Billboard had them in twelve positions on their Top 100 list, and the first four top hits were, of course, recordings by the Beatles.

By 1965 the album *Rubber Soul* reinforced the groups maturity

and the introduction of more critic's acceptance and approval. Their foray into introducing more classical instruments in their backgrounds on recordings included "Yesterday" and "Norwegian Wood" and became an "introduction to a time for the Beatles to expand," according to Paul McCartney. *Rubber Soul* was hailed by *Rolling Stone Magazine* and *All Music's Guide* as one of the top albums ever produced. Unfortunately, after a while you may come to expect the members of a singing group experience conflicts among themselves on somewhat trivial and sundry issues: Who gets top billing or credit for co-written songs, and you may include personal conflicts which would eventually break them up like so many groups before them. They would frequently open their big celebrity mouths on various issues and subjects which inevitably invited controversy: "Christianity will go. It will vanish and shrink," said Lennon in an interview," I needn't argue about that. I'm right and I will be proved right. We're more popular than Jesus now: I don't know which will go first, rock 'n' roll or Christianity." Lennon later refuted the comment saying it was taken out of context. He apologized. It was accepted.

The Beatles were involved in numerous incidents of drug use in many dimensions, creating alleged facts and stories that will go unpublished in this tome. Our interests have always involved the mu-

Sir Paul at work

sic and the history minus most controversy which we strive to leave to biographies written by others.

Later, after concluding over 1,400 personal concerts in the U.S. the Beatles seemed settled and free from the harsh effort required for such travel and performances. Their final live U.S.show was at Candlestick Park in San Francisco.

The album *Revolver* is considered by many as one of the best music albums of all time. It included Paul's "Eleanor Rigby" which employed the use of special musical instruments.

Earlier, in 1970 Paul had released "The Long and Winding Road" which effectively marked the end of McCartney's interest in the partnership. For Paul, the last straw was American Producer Phil Spector's heavy-handed wrecking of the arrangements of that recording.

To wrap it up: Paul Mc-Cartney filed suit to dissolve the Beatles partnership during December of 1970. Because of the complex legal disputes the dissolution became effective a long five years later in 1975.

John Lennon

The Beatles opened the door for many rock and roll groups that followed. Their works were fresh and new and experimental, and therefore successful, and thus widely imitated, although they also imitated many musical acts when they first entered the world of rock and roll. That fact is historic with all musical performers from the great entertainer Al Jolson to the great and first popular singer Bing Crosby, to the Sons of the Pioneers, and the four Mills Brothers. The Beatles openly declared their influences to be Elvis Presley, Chuck Berry, Carl Perkins, Buddy Holly, the Everly Brothers, and even the Beach Boys, Bob Dylan and The Byrds, all of whom set the stage for the Beatles. Many acts were an extension of the their past influences and present admirers when they emerged on the scene with a ton of originality and prolific material added to the mix.

Sgt. Peppers Lonely Hearts Club Band Album

Among my Beatles favorites are "Eleanor Rigby," "Here Comes the Sun," "Yesterday," "Norwegian Wood," "Blackbird," "Let It Be," "Penny Lane," "Octopus's Garden," "Strawberry Fields Forever," but I like and enjoy many more than are listed here.

Some interesting facts about George

REVOLVER

Martin: It was George who brought his classical training to the Beatles, like the string quartet accompaniment to " Yesterday." The result was amazing to the boys. Martin was sort of a music teacher to the group. He could play a variety of instruments including organ, bass and piano, as well as brass instruments. Martin was a stabilizing influence to the Beatles. "George Martin was our straight man and us the loonies. He was our anchor. He communicated our needs to the engineers when we recorded," according to George Harrison.

In 1965 the Beatles were appointed Members of the Order of the British Empire by Queen Elizabeth II. They also won seven Grammy Awards along the way.

Original United Kingdom LPs.

1963 Please Please Me
1963 With the Beatles
1964 A Hard Day's Night
1964 Beatles for Sale
1965 Help!
1965 Rubber Soul
1966 Revolver
1967 Sgt. Pepper's Lonely Hearts Club Band
1968 The White Album (The Beatles)
1969 Yellow Submarine
1969 Abbey Road
1970 Let It Be

THE KINGSTON TRIO

In the late fifties the incessant sound of the continuing airplay of a simple recording by the Kingston Trio called "Tom Dooley" was heard throughout the land following the awesome and influential power of the Weavers tunes, songwriter Leadbelly's "Goodnight Irene," and "Tzena, Tzena, Tzena" and "On Top of Old Smokey."

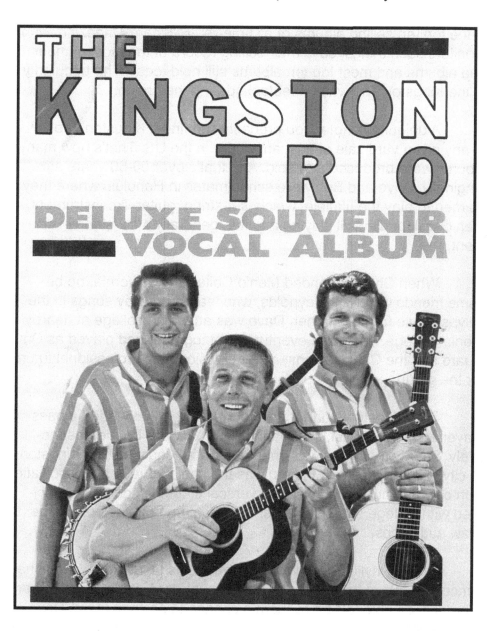

The Weavers had started the craze of American style folk singing and the Kingston Trio took up the torch and ran with it creating a trio with a handful of tunes, whose phenomenal success with them are now legendary.

Beginning in a San Francisco nightclub, Dave Guard, Bob Shane, and Nick Reynolds, as the Kingston Trio, cut their first album which included "Tom Dooley," a recording that sold three million copies as a single. Over the years four of their nineteen albums landed in the top ten selling albums of all time list. *Billboard Magazine*, who monitors such things, says their selling record of the most number one albums and most top ten albums still hold today. The popularity of the Kingston Trio was unbeatable during their reign.

A ubiquitous note: You probably can find a Kingston Trio LP at any given yard sale almost anywhere in the US. That's how many albums were produced and sold. And that's over 50-60 years ago. Originally, Dave and Bob were schoolmates in Honolulu where they learned to play the ukulele, which is 4-string, guitar-like instrument, then developed a skill playing a guitar, generally a six-string instrument.

When Shane attended Menlo College in California, he became friends with Nick Reynolds, who learned to play songs in the calypso style from his father. Dave was attending college at nearby Menlo College. The three eventually got together and played as Dave Guard and the Calypsonians, never envisioning a professional future for the group.

The Kingston Quartet was formed when they added a bass player and girl vocalist, Joe Gannon and Barbara Bogue, respectively. Shortly the name was changed to the Kingston Trio. Kingston (a city in Jamaica, West Indies) was the choice due to the association with calypso music, and wearing vertical striped shirts was associated with college students shirts, representing both factors in order to draw audiences.

Enter: Phyllis Diller, who confirmed this fact to me: When she canceled a gig at the Purple Onion club in Frisco, the trio's rep, Frank Werber, was able to secure them a chance to perform there. Dave Guard sent out hundreds of announcement post cards to friends and local musicians, and they posted leaflets all over the area. When show time came they were ready with their polished act and remained on the bill for six months.

They were booked into Kelly's in Chicago; the Village Vanguard, in New York's Greenwich Village, where I first saw them perform in 1958; Storyville in Boston; and in San Francisco at the Hungry i. Summoned there by an associate, Voyle Gilmore, one of Capitol Records execs, saw them perform and immediately had Capitol sign the group to an exclusive seven -year contract that sent them on their way.

I loved the Kingston Trio, who filled my life with acceptable music that was joyful to my ears. I was playing and teaching guitar in those days. The Kingston Trio's recordings influenced my students who wanted to play the songs "Tom Dooley," "Where Have All the Flowers Gone," "Scotch and Soda," "Greenback Dollar," "MTA." "Worried Man Blues," "This Land is Your Land," "Lemon Tree," "Scarlet Ribbons," and "It Was a Very Good Year," (written by my good friend Ervin Drake, and later on became strongly associated with Frank Sinatra, who would call Drake periodically offering personal financial assistance if needed.) Drake told me he always appreciated Sinatra's his calls.

Epilogue: At the height of their career, the Kingston Trio performed about 200 engagements a year. It was also a time when the trio became divided because, it was said, that Guard had two unhappy partners. Guard led the group but the others felt equal and there were other issues that finally split them up, physically and financially. John Stewart replaced Guard and the success nevertheless continued until 1967 when it finally ended.

Shane formed The New Kingston Trio in 1969 without too much success. The original trio became wealthy from the music and investments beyond the music, but still pursued their first love- singing and performing. In November of 1981 the group, as follows, performed a reunion concert with Dave Guard, Nick Reynolds and John Stewart, sharing the stage with the Shane-Gambill-Grove Trio and Mary Travers of Peter, Paul and Mary, Tommy Smothers, and Lindsey Buckingham of Fleetwood Mac, performed at the Magic Mountain amusement park near Los Angeles, California, as The Kingston Trio and Friends.

It gets complicated after that fine affair and so we close with favorable notes in that the Kingston Trio's influence on popular music was unanimously considerable and Dave Guard, Nick Reynolds, and Bob Shane were wonderful performers of folk music and American traditional music who entertained the world for a brief, shining moment.

TOM DOOLEY
BILL HANSON

Hang down your head, Tom Dooley
Hang down your head and cry
Hang down your head, Tom Dooley
Poor Boy, you're bound to die

I met her on the mountain
T'was there I took her life
Up there on the mountain
I stabbed her with my knife

Hang down your head, Tom Dooley
Hang down your head and cry
Hand down your head, Tom Dooley
Poor boy, you're bound to die.

Simon & Garfunkel

You cannot deny the fact that the duo, Simon & Garfunkel, was one of the most popular singing groups in popular music throughout the 1960s, although, by all accounts, they produced only a handful of recordings, but those recordings were sensational objects of music material.

Art Garfunkel and Paul Simon

Among them, consider "Sounds of Silence," "Parsley, Sage, Rosemary and Thyme," "I Am a Rock," and the iconic "Mrs. Robinson." All the songs they introduced were their own and were embellished with eclectic electric guitars and fine arrangements.

The boys first named themselves Tom & Jerry, but split up with Simon moving to England and successfully touring folk-singing circuits.

Meanwhile, one of their early record producers, Tom Wilson, re-released the boys version of "The Sounds of Silence," and it achieved success enough to permit the duo's singing production strength to continue. Thus, in 1967 they released "Homeward Bound," "I am a Rock," and "A Hazy Shade of Winter." Every song a winner!

The boys efforts, however, were somewhat erratic, although they began to improve due to Simon's prolific songwriting talents. Here is where their greatest success "Mrs. Robinson" surfaced and elevated into prominence, as it was the main theme of the popular film *The Graduate*. Simon & Garfunkel sang throughout the film that included their various themes of earlier recordings as further background to the film. This punctuated and elevated their career to a point of everlasting fame as a singing duo.

The Simon & Garfunkel phenomenon ran hot and cold time and again. They had known each other for almost all their lives and were performing together for over ten years, and they became tired of one-another. Simon wrote their material while Garfunkel had aspirations of becoming a film actor. Otherwise, and obviously they performed masterfully with Garfunkel's high tenor, and tasteful background accompaniments. Their work enhanced their magical singing abilities on recordings.They had the world at their feet.

Paul Simon and Art Garfunkel

Their final album *Bridge Over Troubled Waters* was a major hit with four of the tracks becoming hit singles: "The Boxer," "Cecilia," "Bridge Over Troubled Waters," and "El Condor Pasa." See what I mean?

No doubt that the works of Simon & Garfunkel are well represented among quality American folk-style music and as members of the Vocal Group Hall of Fame Foundation.

The Temptations

There is a lot to write about those vocal groups whose career has lasted over five decades with a varied repertoire, but our job here is simply to feature the highlights of some of America's great singing groups. A full story of each would command a book of their own.

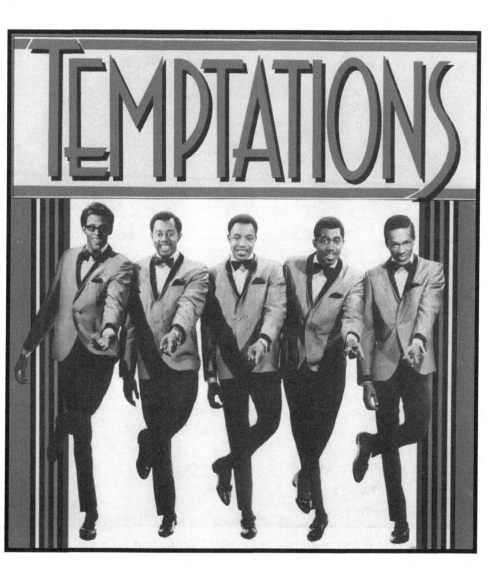

This group was born in Detroit, Michigan in the early sixties. The Temptations began as the Elgins, with five vocalists. The group became very influential on similar, future groups.

The one living member is Otis Williams, and he's still with the group. The original members were Otis Williams, Al Bryant, Melvin Franklin, Eddie Kendricks and Paul Williams. Future members were David Ruffin and Dennis Edwards, Richard Street, Damon Harris, Glenn Leonard, Ron Tyson, Ali-Ollie Woodson, Theo Peoples, and G.C. Cameron. Like all the groups we have showcased here, many lineups have drastically changed over the many years they have existed, recorded and performed.

The Temptations great numbers are "My Girl," "Papa Was a Rollin' Stone," and "Ain't Too Proud to Beg." As the Elgins, they auditioned for Motown in 1961. They were hired and had to change their name because there existed a group by the same name, so Berry Gordy had them renamed the Temptations.

It was Smokey Robinson who saw potential in member David Ruffin who had a mellow yet gruff voice, and who wrote "My Girl," with Ronnie White, which was recorded in 1964 and became the Temptations number-one hit in March of 1965. "My Girl" became their signature song.

From 1964 through 1968 the Temptations appeared frequently on *Ed Sullivan's Sunday night TV show* and regularly on *American*

The Temptations with Ed Sullivan

Bandstand, achieving international fame, as well. This is the point when the group crossed over to American standards, non-Motown tunes, and appeared, as a result, at venues like the Copacabana in New York, to increase their fame.

Ruffin became demanding in many ways and was eventually released by the rest of the Temptation members. Dennis Edwards replaced him, but Ruffin would break into live performances, jumping

Doing what they do best!

on stage to join the group.

Berry Gordy co-joined the Temptations and Diana Ross and the Supremes. And, with a new style, Gordy and his new producer, Norman Whitfield, had all five members trading lead vocals on a tune

"Cloud Nine." The performance won a Grammy, the first for Motown Records. The record achieved Top 10 position for Best R & B Vocal Group Performance of 1969. In 1972, Whitfield released "Papa Was a Rolling Stone," which won Motown's second Grammy, followed by another Top Ten hit, "Masterpiece." favored by disk jocks for its length which allowed them a break at the mike and time to leave the studio to enjoy a coffee break.

The rest of the story is contained and stretched throughout the 1990s, and enjoyed the debut of The Temptations, a 1998 four-hour television miniseries based on the life of Otis Williams. It won an Emmy for Best Direction. The Otis Williams family filed a lawsuit against the producers and NBC for various reasons.

The Temptations were inducted into the Vocal Group Hall of Fame in 1999.

The group still performs,and former members continue to perform today under names like Glenn Leonard's Temptations Revue, Richard Street's Temptations, and Legendary Lead Singers of the Temptations.

1965: "My Girl"
1966: "Get Ready"
1966: "Ain't Too Proud to Beg"
1966: "Beauty Is Only Skin Deep"
1966: "(I Know) I'm Losing You"
1967: "All I Need"
1967: "You're My Everything"
1967: "I Wish It Would Rain"
1968: "I Could Never Love Another (After Loving You)"
1968: "Cloud Nine"
1968: "I'm Gonna Make You Love Me"
(Diana Ross & the Supremes and the Temptations)
1969: "Run Away Child, Running Wild"
1969: "I Can't Get Next to You"
1970: "Psychedelic Shack"
1970: "Ball of Confusion (That's What the World Is Today"
1971: "Just My Imagination (Running Away with Me)"
1972: "Papa Was a Rollin' Stone"
1973: "Masterpiece"

1973: "Let Your Hair Down"
1974: "Happy People"
1975: "Shakey Ground"
1991: "The Motown Song"
(Rod Stewart featuring The Temptations)
1992: "My Girl" (reissue)

MY GIRL

WILLIAM (SMOKEY) ROBINSON, RONALD WHITE

I've got sunshine on a cloudy day.
When it's cold outside I've got the month of May.
I guess you'd say
What can make me feel this way?
My girl (my girl, my girl)
Talkin' 'bout my girl (my girl).
I've got so much honey the bees envy me.
I've got a sweeter song than the birds in the trees.
I guess you'd say
What can make me feel this way?
My girl (my girl, my girl)
Talkin' 'bout my girl (my girl).
Hey hey hey
Hey hey hey
Ooh
I don't need no money, fortune, or fame.
I've got all the riches baby one man can claim.
I guess you'd say
What can make me feel this way?
My girl (my girl, my girl)
Talkin' 'bout my girl (my girl).
I've got sunshine on a cloudy day
With my girl.
I've even got the month of May
With my girl

THE SUPREMES

The Supremes' string of hits has been extraordinary. I first met Diana Ross, the lead singer of the Supremes, at a group interview in her comfortable dressing room at Westbury Music Fair on Long Island. Diana was gracious and sweet and cooperated with all of us by answering questions about her career, which for over thirty years has been perched at the top of the music charts.

The SUPREMES

TOPS ON CAMPUS

College Dates Thru April '66

CORNELL UNIVERSITY

UNIVERSITY OF VERMONT

DUKE UNIVERSITY

UNIVERSITY OF ROCHESTER

DENISON UNIVERSITY

RUTGERS UNIVERSITY

NOTRE DAME UNIVERSITY

The Supremes charted twelve number-one singles, a number of gold recordings, and always enjoyed sold out live appearances, including the one we had been invited to attend, which turned out to be just fine even though they situated our seating on the highest tier of seats. In Westbury, any seat was a good seat in this theater-in-the-round with 3000 total seats.

The Supremes were the Andrews Sisters of the sixties in scope and prolific popularity, although the song list was quite different, the music quality was equal and both groups were commercially successful.

First known as the Primettes, composed of Barbara Martin, Diana Ross, Florence Ballard and Mary Wilson, the girls were teenagers so their parents had to give permission for them to travel with the tour. Ballard, Wilson and Diana could all sing lead. Ballard's voice was the best and most powerful. The girls main influence was not gospel music, but was the voices of both the Andrews Sisters and the McGuire's.

The girls auditioned for Berry Gordy, Motown Records chief. He told them to come back when they finished high school. In 1961, a year later, Gordy signed them. He had Ballard change the name of the group to the Supremes.

"The girls fared better when Gordy decided to set up Diana as lead, because her voice was young and crisp, a better commercial sound than Ballard's, which was too strong," according to Carolynn Gill of the Velvetettes.

Their first number one hit was "Where Did Our Love Go?" "It led the Supremes to appear on my show *The Dick Clark Caravan of Stars* to become the top billing act on the show," Dick Clark told me.

"Baby Love" reached number one in 1964, their second hit in a row, and even reached number one in England, the first all girl group to reach number one in the U.K.

The fourth number-one recording "Stop! In the Name of Love," reached the heights in both the U.S. and U.K.

On July 29, 1965, the Supremes were the headline act in New York's Copacabana night club. Shortly thereafter their recording "I Hear a Symphony" reached number one.

It was surmised that the relationship between Ross and Gordy spawned favoritism toward Ross which irked Florence Ballard who resisted accordingly and was replaced by Gordy, renaming the group Diana Ross & The Supremes.

Over the next twelve singles, only one reached number one. That was "Love Child."

Their remake of "I'm Going to Make You Love Me" with the Temptations was successful and their last number one recording was "Someday, We'll Be Together" one of my favorite Supremes performances. Shortly after performing the song on *Ed Sullivan's Show*, Diana Ross announced her retirement in Las Vegas and introduced the girl who would replace her, Jean Terrell.

The Supremes were fragmented due to changing personnel over and over, practically month by month, perhaps day by day? Mary Wilson formed Mary Wilson & the Supremes and even wrote a book. Sadly, Florence Ballard passed away at the age of thirty-two. In 1983, the Motown 25th Anniversary show featured the Supremes with Diana Ross, Birdsong and Mary Wilson.

In any case The Supremes were always supreme performers and have enriched American music history.

BABY LOVE

W.M. - EDDIE HOLLAND,
BRIAN HOLLAND, LAMONT DOZIER

Ooh baby love, my baby love
I need you, oh how I need you
But all you do is treat me bad
Break my heart and leave me sad
Tell me, what did I do wrong
To make you stay away so long

'Cause baby love, my baby love
Been missing ya, miss kissing ya
Instead of breaking up
Let's do some kissing and making up
Don't throw our love away
In my arms why don't you stay
Need ya, need ya
Baby love, ooh, baby love

Baby love, my baby love
Why must we seperate, my love
All of my whole life through
I never loved no one but you
Why you do me like you do
I get this need

Ooh, ooh, need to hold you
Once again, my love
Feel your warm embrace, my love
Don't throw our love away

Please don't do me this way
Not happy like I used to be
Loneliness has got the best of me
My love, my baby love

I need you, oh how I need you
Why you do me like you do
After I've been true to you
So deep in love with you

Baby, baby, ooh 'til it's hurtin' me
'Til it's hurtin' me
Ooh, baby love
Don't throw our love away
Don't throw our love away

THE PLATTERS

Although this book has omitted features on a infinite number of singing groups from the rock and roll era, we have otherwise included the Platters. This magnificent singing group crossed the bridge back into the previous musical era, including their repertoire crossover tunes from the 30s, 40s and 50s and even earlier. Numbers recorded earlier by Bing Crosby and the Andrews Sisters, Frank Sinatra, Dick Haymes and even Doris Day, among others. So they fit in here more than their counterparts who sing only rock and roll material.
Tony Williams, the most famous lead singer of the Platters was not an original member. The group was put together by manager Ralph Bass and included Alex Hodge, Cornell Gunter, David Lynch, Joe Jefferson, Gaynel Hodge and Herb Reed.

Then they added Tony Williams, lead vocalist, and Zola Taylor, outstanding female vocalist.

The group, however, lacked the ability to chart their music, but were very successful when performing on tour. Live audiences loved them. Buck Ram, songwriter and music guru, was able to effect a

contract with Mercury Records for the Platters when he simultaneously signed the Penguins, famous for "Earth Angel," and used the
Penguins deal as a trump card to have them sign the Platters, as
well.

The Platters also recorded "Earth Angel" and "Only You" with
better luck and followed up with "The Great Pretender." Legend has it
that Ram wrote the lyrics to that song in the washroom of the Flamin-
go Hotel in Las Vegas. It became a No. 1 hit for the Platters. "Only
You" and "Pretender" were performed by the Platters in the film Rock
Around the Clock.

Hit after hit followed: "I'm Sorry," "Twilight Time," the 1930s
Jerome Kern hit "Smoke Gets in Your Eyes" from the Broadway show
and later film, Roberta. The film starred Fred Astaire and Ginger Rogers. The earlier Broadway hit featured Bob Hope.

"Harbor Lights," "My Prayer," "The Magic Touch," "If I Didn't
Care," an Ink Spots favorite, and "To Each His Own," an old standard
recorded by Eddie Howard and later by The Ink Spots, the song originally from the 1946 film of the same name. So here are the Platters
singing tunes from some of what's considered songs belonging in the
Great American Songbook, and not rock and roll, or rhythm and blues
of the Platters recording era in later years.

As individual members left the group, the Platters name and
stock owned by the group's members was bought out by Ram and

his partner Jean Ben-
nett. The group's per-
sonnel changed quite
often, although the
group was steadfastly
built around Tony Wil-
liams distinctive voice.

At their produc-
tive height the public
lost interest in the
Platters due to the
publicity surrounding
their troubles with the

law that involved drug and prostitution charges, which affected play-lists on the radio, although none of the charges were ever proven or members ever convicted.

Tony Williams carried on, and Paul Robi formed his own Plat-ters group, as well as a handful of others who did the same, result-ing in a myriad of back & forth lawsuits. One of the performers not mentioned in various personnel lists is Elmer Hopper, who sang with Robi's Platters for twenty years and is now one half of the current Mills Brothers singing duo. (Read about the Mills Brothers in a chap-ter featured earlier in this book).

Because of those legal battles there are now, at last count, four Platters singing groups touring and singing the same beautiful songs in the same arrangements. I guess that can't be considered a negative thing. Imagine each group singing to audiences "The Great Pretender." (Mirror, Mirror on the wall, who's the real Platters of them all?)

Nevertheless, the Platters were all fine singers and held dear by millions over many years for their unforgettable recordings listed here.

1954
Only You/ You Made Me Cry
Hey Now/ Give Thanks
I'll Cry When You're Gone/ I Need You All The Time
Roses of Picardy/ Beer Barrell Boogie
Tell The World/ Love All Night
Shake It Up Mambo/ Voo-Vee-Ah-Bee
Take Me Back/ Maggie Doesn't Work Here Anymore
Tell The World/ I Need You All The Time
My Name Ain't Annie/ Flip w/o Platters (Linda Hayes)
Please Have Mercy/ Oochi Pachi (Linda Hayes)

1955
Only You (And You Alone)/ Bark, Battle, and Bail
The Great Pretender/ I'm Just a Dancing Partner

1956
You've Got The Magic Touch/ Winner Takes All
My Prayer/ Heaven on Earth
You'll Never Know/ It isn't Right
On My Word of Honor/ One In A Million

1957
I'm Sorry/ He's Mine
My Dream/ I Wanna
Let's Start All Over Again/ When You Return
Only Because/ The Mystery of You

1958
Helpless/ Indifferent
Twilight Time/ Out of My Mind
You're Making A Mistake/ My Old Flame
I Wish/ It's Raining Outside
Smoke Gets In Your Eyes/ No Matter What You Are

1959
Enchanted/ The Sounds And The Fury
Remember When/ Love of A Lifetime
Where/ Wish It Were Me
My Secret/ What Does It Matter

1960
Harbor Lights/ Sleepy Lagoon
Ebb Tide/ I'll Be With You In Apple Blossom Time
Red Sails In The Sunset/ Sad River
To Each His Own/ Down The River of Dreams

1961
If I Didn't Care/ True Lover
Trees/ Immortal Love
I'll Never Smile Again/ Don't You Say
Song For The Lonely/ You'll Never Know

1962-65
It's Magic/ Reaching For A Star
More Than You Know/ Every Little Movement

Memories/ Heartbreak
I'll See You In My Dreams/ Once In A While
Here Comes Heaven Again/ Strangers
Viva/Ju/Juy/Cuando Calienta El Sol
Java Jive/ Row The Boat Ashore
Sincerely/ P.S. I Love You
Love Me Tender/ Little Things Mean A Lot
I'll Be Home/ You've Got The Magic Touch

1966
I Love You 1000 Times/ Don't Hear, Speak, See No Evil
Devri/ Alone In The Night Without You

1967
With This Ring/ If I Had A Love
Washed Ashore/ What Name Shall I Give You My Love
Sweet Sweet Lovin/ Sonata
Love Must Go On/ How Beautiful Our Love Is
Thing Before You Walk Away/ So Many Tears
Hard To Get A Thing Called Love/ Why

1969
Fear of Loving You/ Sonata
Run While It's Dark/ Won't You Bee My Friend
If The World Loved/ Sunday With You

1970
Guilty/ My Ship's Coming In
Personality/ Who's Sorry Now

1973
BUCK RAM PLATTERS: A Little More (solo Monroe Powell) - Sunday
With You (solo Gene Williams)
Avalanche

1977
Here Comes The Boogie Man/ Only You (Disco)

1982
I Do It All The Time/ Shake What Your Mama Gave You

1977
Herb Reed & The Original Platters: Can't Help Falling In Love/ Showman

1978
Herb Reed of The Original Platters & Sweet River: What's Your Name, What's Your Number/ Reasons

1987
(France) Only You - Remember When
BMG RC 110

1987
Mini album (Maxi single) 45 rpm
BMG RC 120

1988
The Come Back (France) -ALBUM
BMG 900 004

1989
The Magic Platters (CD) (France)
Lazer Plus 90 007

1994
The Best of The Magic Platters (CD) (FRANCE) - ALBUM
Pomme 950 972

ONLY YOU
BUCK RAM AND ANDRE RAND

Only you can make this world seem right
Only you can make the darkness bright
Only you and you alone
Can thrill me like you do
And fill my heart with love for only you

Only you can make this change in me
For it's true, you are my destiny
When you hold my hand
I understand the magic that you do
You're my dream come true
My one and only you

Only you can make this change in me
For it's true, you are my destiny
When you hold my hand
I understand the magic that you do
You're my dream come true
My one and only you

(One and only you)

THE WEAVERS

There was a time back in the early 1950s when I simply loved the folk singing group named the Weavers. I was teaching guitar at the Flushing Music Center, a small music store on 46th Avenue. The "hot" songs to try and play were "Goodnight Irene," and "Tzena,Tzena,Tzena," and these were the two Weaver favorites that I taught my students to sing as part of their training to play and sing folk songs. The most popular member of the Weavers was, without question, Pete Seeger, who sang lead on most of the songs.

Ronnie Gilbert, Lee Hays, Fred Hellerman and Pete Seeger made up the Weavers which was first formed by Ronnie Gilbert, who was a lady. I recall watching and listening to them when I attended high school and worked after school in Greenwich Village in the late forties and early fifties when the Weavers were singing at the Village Vanguard jazz club.

Clockwise: Pete Seeger, Fred Hellerman, Ronnie Gilbert, Lee Hays

They were soon discovered by songwriter, arranger, and orchestra leader Gordon Jenkins, who arranged for them to record for Decca Records. They led off with a super-hit in "Goodnight Irene," and on the flip side an Israeli tune "Tzena, Tzena, Tzena," both which became a hit for the group and "Tzena" remained Number 1 for an amazing *thirteen* weeks.

The group sang and recorded mostly folk music and traditional tunes from around the world. They also performed children's songs, protest songs, labor songs, and gospel music. Their works inspired groups like the Kingston Trio and Peter, Paul and Mary, to form and gain popularity behind the Weavers success.

Some of their recordings were "On Top of Old Smoky," "Kisses Sweeter Than Wine," "The Wreck of the John B.," "So Long, It's Been Good to Know You," and "The Rock Island Line."

Unfortunately, the Weavers became unjustly branded Communist party Members during the McCarthy hearings era, and it effectively ruined their career as Decca canceled their contract and deleted their works from its catalog in 1953.

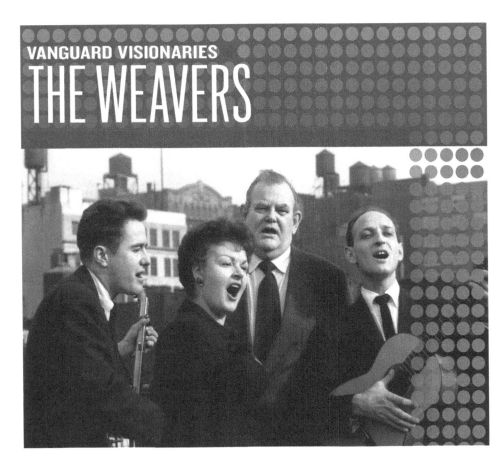

VANGUARD VISIONARIES

THE WEAVERS

Eventually exonerated, although by now the group had disbanded, and in December 1955, reunited and performed to a sold-out

concert at Carnegie Hall which was a great success.

Pete Seeger quit the group when they had signed to sing TV cigarette commercials. He knew the dangers of smoking and its results. Erik Darling of the Tarriers replaced Seeger. Darling left shortly thereafter and formed the Rooftop Singers. Frank Hamilton replaced Darling for nine months, just before a slated concert at Carnegie Hall in 1963.

Bernie Krause, who was a folk singer, quickly replaced Hamilton. The Weavers once again disbanded in 1964

Lee Hays passed away in 1981. Ronnie Gilbert toured America as a single, and Fred Hellerman became a recording engineer. Erik Darling passed away in 2008.

Pete Seeger

Pete Seeger was also a songwriter having composed/ co-authored "Where Have All the Flowers Gone?," "If I had a Hammer," composed with Lee Hays, and "Turn, Turn, Turn," which has been recorded by many other artists. He helped popularize the civil rights anthem "We

Shall Overcome," during the civil rights era. Seeger changed the song title to have it become more inspirational. He changed it from "We will Overcome," to "We Shall Overcome."

Pete Seeger is now 92 and still active now and then performing last in January of 2009 with Bruce Springsteen at the President Obama Inaugural, and at the Clearwater Concert in Madison Square Garden to celebrate his 90th birthday on May 3rd, the same birthday as Bing Crosby, tv movie host Robert Osborne, and myself.

The Weavers produced 22 albums.

In 2006 the Lifetime Achievement Award was bestowed on the Weavers by the Grammy Award committee. Typically, Pete Seeger wasn't present, just Ronnie Gilbert and Fred Hellerman accepted the award.

I'll always remember the Weavers and their brand of exciting singing in the days when for me music was most impressionable.

GOODNIGHT IRENE

AFTER LEAD BELLY VERSION
TRADITIONAL

Irene goodnight, Irene goodnight
Goodnight Irene, goodnight Irene
I'll see you in my dreams

Last Saturday night I got married
Me and my wife settled down
Now me and my wife are parted
I'm gonna take another stroll
downtown

Irene goodnight, Irene goodnight
Goodnight Irene, goodnight Irene
I'll see you in my dreams

Sometimes I live in the country

Sometimes I live in town
Sometimes I take a great notion
To jump into the river and drown

Irene goodnight, Irene goodnight
Goodnight Irene, goodnight Irene
I'll see you in my dreams

Stop ramblin', stop your gamblin'
Stop stayin' out late at night
Go home to your wife and family
Stay there by your fire side bright

Irene goodnight, Irene goodnight
Goodnight Irene, goodnight Irene
I'll see you in my dreams
Goodnight Irene, goodnight Irene
I'll see you in my dreams

PETER, PAUL & MARY

I've always been a Peter, Paul & Mary fan, but a late comer was I. Back in 1996, I attended one of their concerts in a vast outdoor tent on a very hot night at one of the Jazz Festivals they used to hold at the Planting Fields Arboretum in Oyster Bay, New York.

The heat and humidity so adversely affected an overweight Mary, that she had to excuse herself halfway into the concert and left the stage, leaving Peter and Paul to carry on. At the closing performance she reappeared for the final number, "Puff, the Magic Dragon." A true trouper.

Mary Travers, Paul Stookey and Peter Yarrow first got together back in 1961, and after 50 years their only number one charted hit was John Denver's "Leaving on a Jet Plane."

It was their manager, Albert Grossman, who got them together at an open audition and had them booked into The Bitter End in New York's Greenwich Village. They were happy performing there, as Greenwich Village is where their idols, The Weavers, also began their illustrious career. Their first album included two of Pete Seeger's tunes for the Weaver's: "If I Had a Hammer" and "Where Have All the Flowers Gone?"

This group sang the songs both young and old loved to hear: "Lemon Tree," "Blowin" in the Wind," a Bob Dylan song, "500 Miles," and the kids in special audiences always enjoyed "Puff the Magic Dragon," which they sang with much feeling and animation.

After eight years of success the trio went their separate ways. Mary produced some recordings and performed all over the country; Paul formed a band called the Body Works Band, a Christian music group; and Peter produced Mary MacGregor's "Torn Between Two Lovers," which he also co-wrote.

By 1972 they reunited, like all these groups seem to do at one time or another, and performed at Madison Square Garden to support George McGovern's bid for the Presidential election. In and about 1978 they worked concerts for political and protest causes, which rebuilt their own cause and so they wound up recording albums and performing a limited amount of concerts a year.

After a bout with leukemia that began in 2004, Mary passed in 2009. She was seventy-two. That year the trio was inducted into the Hit Parade Hall of Fame.

Peter, Paul and Mary carried on a wholesome musical legacy of always trying to include at least one song on each album for children.

Here are the list of albums recorded from 1962 through 2010.

Albums
1962: Peter, Paul and Mary
1963: Moving
1963: In the Wind
1965: A Song Will Rise
1965: See What Tomorrow Brings
1966: The Peter, Paul and Mary Album
1967: Album 1700
1968: Late Again
1969: Peter, Paul and Mommy
1978: Reunion
1983: Such Is Love

The Mamas & the Papas

I have to admit that the voice of Cass Elliot, within the vocal group the Mamas & the Papas, has always intrigued me. The group was organized by John Phillips, the manager and arranger, and included Canadian singer Denny Doherty and Michelle Phillips (Johns wife), and, of course, Cass Elliot.

The handful of hits the group produced and recorded were simply iconic beginning with their first single "Go Where You Wanna Go," followed by "Monday, Monday," with "If You Can Believe Your Eyes and Ears" nestled between. "Monday" was the only number one hit single the group ever produced. In the UK, the song fared almost as well.

Denny Doherty, Cass Elliot, Michelle Phillips and John Phillips

Cass' strong and rich intonations punctuate every phrase on the songs "California Dreaming,' "Dancing in the Street," and "Words of Love."

Unfortunately the group was partially disbanded when it was discovered that Michelle was having an affair with Denny Doherty, causing Michelle to be replaced by Jill Gibson, who sounded much like her predecessor.

The group recorded its third album, *Deliver*, but personal appearances were dismal due to Doherty's obvious drinking problem, some surmised over his feelings for Michelle.

On the group's final television appearance on the *Ed Sullivan Show*, they revealed their public demise. Their longtime recording company, Dunhill, released their first greatest hits album.

Cass Elliot quit the group when John Phillips, who always disliked her, made a humiliating comment about her at a party in London, while she was engaged in conversation with Mick Jagger, famed lead singer of the Rolling Stones,

The record company released Cass' single "Dream a Little Dream of Me," which I believe was her best single. Cass decided to begin a solo career and scored with "Make Your Own Kind of Music," and "It's Getting Better." Cass released three albums for RCA, but to little success.

After she appeared in London at the Palladium for two weeks, Cass Elliot passed away suddenly of a heart attack. She had received standing ovations at the Palladium and was vocally very happy the night before.

John Phillips was busy at this time composing music, and his collaboration with the Beach Boys produced a number one hit, "Kokomo." John reorganized the Mamas & the Papas and it included his daughter Mackenzie, and Elaine McFarlane. The group didn't last long due to John's alleged drug abuse.

THE EVERLY BROTHERS

Their great tunes became forever entrenched in your psyche. "Bye, Bye Love," "Wake Up Little Susie," "All I Have to do is Dream," "Bird Dog," and "Cathy's Clown," a neat little series of blockbuster recordings, most reaching number one on the charts. A phenomenal achievement by two very young and talented kids, Don and Phil Everly.

Phil and Don

The boys became one of the favorite and most successful acts in music group/duo history. The boys were taught guitar at an early age and sang with their parents right through high school, honing their skills non-stop.

It was country guitar-playing star Chet Atkins who met and

liked the boys and was able to secure them a contract with Columbia Records, but it didn't work out and Columbia released them after six months. The song selections were too weak.

On the Cadence Label their success surfaced and grew swiftly when they recorded "Bye, Bye Love" which practically rejuvenated the music business in Nashville, where Elvis, Chuck Berry and Little Richard were already dominating Nashville with their acts.

Songwriters Felice and Boudleaux had written three of the songs: "Wake Up Little Susie," All I Have to Do is Dream," and "Bird Dog." However, it was "Cathy's Clown" that turned out to be their best-selling recording.

The Everly's had their personal ups and downs over the years which eventually diminished their popularity. In 1983, the boys reunited. In England the duo performed at Royal Albert Hall, retaining their popularity and leading them to release a few albums together.

SPECIALTY GROUPS

THE NEW CHRISTY MINSTRELS

In the 1960s Randy Sparks organized a group of singers he called the New Christy Minstrels, fashioned after the original Christy Minstrels of old vaudeville days before and during the realm of the greatest performer of them all, Al Jolson.

Jolson wore blackface well after performers known as Minstrel Singers did during the nineteenth century. Both white and black performers wore blackface in the 1840s. They would apply black burned cork to their face. That was the tradition. The Minstrel singing and performing groups toured the country for many years.

A fellow named Edwin Christy, who authored the song "Good Night Ladies" formed the original Christy Minstrels, a tradition that lasted into the 1950s, winding up with the bio-film *The Jolson Story* which was released in 1947 to tremendous success. It brought back Al Jolson himself who sang the songs in the picture behind the acting and lip-syncing of Larry Parks. Jolson was the first actor/singer whose voice was the first to perform and sing in a talking picture, The *Jazz Singer*.

There were ten original New Christy Minstrels who performed mostly songs and lyrics written by Randy and members Art Podell and Nick Woods. Their first great success was "Green, Green," with the lead going to Barry McGuire, who co-wrote the song. From 1962 thru 1965 the group released nine albums, including *Ramblin', Merry Christmas* and *Today*.

In 1964, the group sang before the President, and had their own short-lived television show. Many new faces were born from the New Christy Minstrels including Kim Carnes, Gene Clark of the Byrds, Kenny Rogers, Christine Andreas and others.

Today the New Christy Minstrels still perform, and perform sellout shows where ever they appear. Randy Sparks remains at the helm as owner and performer

THE HOOSIER HOTSHOTS

"Well, well, welcome to your alka-seltzer national barn dance," genial greetings from your host Joe Kelly.

Here is an act with four players/singers who introduced mid-western jazz to radio on NBC's National Barn Dance show lasting from 1933 through 1946 with songs like "I Like Bananas Because They Have No Bones."

The group provided their own music. Paul Trietsch, Frank Kettering, Otto 'Gabe' Ward and Ken Trietsch were the infamous four.

At the time they were radio's highest paid musicians/singers. Paul was the "virtuoso of the washboard," (he wore out a dozen or more during his career), Gabe Ward played a hot clarinet, Frank Kettering played bass and Ken Trietsch guitar.

Comedic music was also achieved with bulb horns and a hand-pushed klaxon.

In 1980 Paul passed on and was replaced by Gil Taylor who had replaced Frank Kettering earlier.

THE SONS OF THE PIONEERS

When I was very young, I vividly recall hearing the songs of the Sons of the Pioneers played on juxeboxes and everywhere else, especially the most recognized wavering, haunting voice of Bob Nolan singing his own "Tumbling Tumbleweeds," with his and the group's signature sound.

Besides Nolan, there was another special voice and instrumentalist within the Western songs singing group, who later graduated to stardom. His name was Leonard Slye. Leonard changed his name when he began acting in films, achieving iconic fame as a singing, yodeling cowboy known to all America and to the world as Roy Rogers.

Unlike most singing groups, the sons of the Pioneers are also musicians. But, let's first get to the birth and subsequent career of this splendid singing group of Western songs.

Some seventy-odd years ago, during the great Depression, a young man from Cincinnati by the name of Leonard Slye headed out for California by working his way west as a gravel truck driver and fruit picker, and because he sang and played guitar so well, he entered a singing competition when he arrived on a Los Angeles radio station which led to an invitation to sing with an established group called the Rocky Mountaineers. Slye sang and played with the group for a while when it was decided the members wanted to extend the group with an additional singer that would expand their range and depth for their Western tunes repertoire.

Enter Bob Nolan (whose real name is Robert Nobles) a voice of experience from Tucson, Arizona, who added to the voice of the Mountaineers. Slye and Nolan developed a worthy, musical relationship, but Nolan soon resigned, stating the group was simply going nowhere. Tim Spencer replaced him. The duo wove in and out of group after group with no better success.

In 1933, Slye rounded up Nolan and Spencer, convinced them to give up their regular job to form a hardworking professional trio. They named their group the Pioneer Trio. The group debuted on

KFWB radio with their singing, playing and great personalities that listeners enjoyed hearing.

With Nolan playing string bass and Slye playing rhythm guitar, they added a violinist named Hugh Farr, a bass voice as well, who sometimes performed as lead singer. The group's name was accidentally renamed The Sons of the Pioneers when the announcer introduced them, and later explaining they were too young to be Pioneers.

The group's fame over the radio spread across the country. Decca records, a newly formed company, who also signed Bing Crosby the same day, hired the Sons of the Pioneers who recorded thirty-two sides over two years,one of which was a tune written by Bob Nolan called "Tumbling Tumbleweeds," thus promoting the group's Western image and, at the same time, establishing their theme song. The group picked up Karl Farr, who played lead guitar. Along came roles in films including The Old Homestead and The Gallant Defender, followed by Song of the Saddle in 1936, then the Mysterious Avenger, and with Bing Crosby, Rhythm on the Range, and with Gene Autry, The Big Show. They were in big time company now and well on the way to everlasting success.

Lloyd Perryman joined the Pioneers and managed the business affairs, sang with them and remained for over 40 years, longer than any other member. In 1937 the group was signed by Columbia Pictures and worked steadily with Charles Starrett's Western films. The first was *The Old Wyoming Trail*.

Now, here's where Leonard Slye takes to the movies as a star actor and entertainer. Apparently the studio was in a contractual dispute with Gene Autry so they hired Slye to replace Autry, forcing him to leave the Pioneers. The studio gave him a new name: Roy Rogers. He was to star in *Under Western Stars*.

Pat Brady replaced Slye.

Roy Rogers, Dale Evans

After some years and great success in films, Roy Rogers asked the Pioneers to appear in his films, and the billing was "featuring Bob Nolan and The Sons of the Pioneers." At the same time the group joined Decca Records. There were a number of personnel changes during World War II, and over the ensuing years.

Some of the hits at the end of the war were "Stars and Stripes on Iwo Jima," "No One to Cry To," "Baby Doll," "Cool Water," and "Tear Drops in My Heart." They were followed with revivals of "Tumbling Tumbleweeds" and "Cool Water," but the songs soon became passé, although well loved over many years.

Ken Curtis, Marshal Dillon's future assistant, Festus, featured in the television series *Gunsmoke*, sang for a while and remained with the television show. Historically and over the years the Spencer - Dolan sound was the most acceptable and recognizable Sons of the Pioneers sound by record executives. RCA had released 21 albums of the singing group over a twelve year period.

In 1971, Bob Nolan and Tim Spencer were inducted into the Nashville Songwriters Hall of Fame. In 1976, the Sons of the Pioneers were inducted into the Country Music Hall of Fame.

The last of the Sons of the Pioneers were still active into the 1990s. Featured were Rusty Richards on vocals, Doye O'Dell on guitar and vocals, Billy Armstrong on the fiddle, Billy Liebert on accordion, and Rome Johnson on vocals.

A note: The great director John Ford had the Pioneers singing their songs in four of his epic western films: *Wagon Master, Wagons West, Rio Grande,* and *The Searchers,* the latter with John Wayne.

Spencer passed away in 1976 and Nolan died in 1980. They left a legacy of an appealing sound representing America's Best Western-style music that spawned a large number of members that kept it going throughout those years.

Members over the years were:

Leonard Slye (Roy Rogers) *
Bob Nolan *
Tim Spencer *
Slumber Nichols
Hugh Farr *
Karl Farr *
Lloyd Perryman *
Pat Brady *
Shug Fisher
Ken Carson
Ken Curtis
Tommy Doss
Dale Warren
Deuce Spriggens,
Roy Lanham
Luther Nallie
Rusty Richards
Doye O'Dell
Billy Armstrong
Billy Liebert
Rome Johnson.
* MEMBERS OF THE CLASSIC PIONEERS LINEUP

Cool Water
Bob Nolan

All day I face the barren waste
Without the taste of water, cool water
Old Dan and I with throats burned dry
And souls that cry for water, cool, clear, water

Keep a-movin' Dan don't ya listen to him Dan

He's a devil of a man and he spreads the burning sand with water
Dan can you see that big green tree
Where the water's running free
And it's waiting there for you and me?
The nights are cool and I'm a fool
Each star's a pool of water, cool water
But with the dawn I'll wake and yawn
And carry on to water, cool, clear, water
The shadows sway and seem to say
Tonight we pray for water, cool, water
And way up there He'll hear our prayer
And show us where there's water, cool, clear, water

Dan's feet are sore he's yearning for
Just one thing more than water, cool, water
Like me I guess he'd like to rest
Where there's no quest for water, cool, clear, water

SPECIALTY FEATURE
VOICES FROM EUROPE

SÄMI ZÜND

LEAD SINGER AND ARRANGER OF SWITZERLAND'S BEST KNOWN SINGING GROUPS
"THE SAM SINGERS"
"SWING4YOU"
"THE VOICES"

BY MAX WIRZ

Sämi (Samuel) Zünd was borne on April 1, 1968 in Altstätten, Switzerland, a small town in the Rhine valley on the border to Austria. Sämi is married to Theresia, a piano teacher. They have two sons, Johannes age 7 and Clemens age 10.

Sämi's interest in swingy popular music came during his High School years when his Grandmother presented him a Swiss "Tell-Record" entitled "Rendezvous with Lothar Loeffler", during the 40s and 50s Switzerland's best known bar pianist, who was also regularly heard on Swiss National Radio.

Supported by his dad, a high school teacher and music instructor, Sämi took up piano lessons and became quite an expert at it. During College he realized however, that other students showed equal if not more talent. An aunt who sang opera suggested that he develop his voice. So, in 1988 he took up voice lessons and after only 15 sessions was admitted to the Musikhochschule Zurich. He studied opera, oratories, and Lied-Recitals. During the ensuing years, he worked hard and developed a smooth baritone voice, intense and full of emotion. His diligence and discipline won him the "Paula-Lindberg-Salomon-Wettbewerb" Contest in Berlin and assured him access to the world of classics. His career as classical baritone was launched and brought him thus far to the European capitals of classical music, Vienna, Berlin, Amsterdam, London, Paris as well as recitals at Tufts University in Boston. Sämi sings compositions by Bach, Schubert, Wolf, Britten as well as other classical literature in German, Italian, Spanish, English and French.

The world of SWING and JAZZ however did not pass him by. *"During my earlier musical training I played piano for The Big Band Rheintal and even French horn in the trumpet section of the Old Town Swing Band, both local amateur bands. We would play for local dances and had great fun doing so, of course, trying to follow those world known American Big Bands. Later when I sang with the college choir, and as we traveled to concerts by bus or train we would pass the time by singing and improvising popular songs by Frank Sinatra, Dean Martin and well known groups, The Four Freshmen, The Ames Brothers, The Pied Pipers, The Andrews Sisters to name a few, and of course The Smeed Trio of Switzerland which successfully toured the USA from 1954 until 1962. The "Smeed Trio* appeared in Clubs from Coast to Coast, in Radio City Music Hall, and on TV Specials, including on Liberace's evening programs.*

"One day it hit me:" 'Why don't we form our own group?'
"Therefore in 1990, I formed The Sam Singers with Vera Ehrensperg-

er, Eva Oltivany and Barbara Meszaros. We were one of only a few Swiss vocal groups doing harmony."

Again time passed. Sämi spent three years in Amsterdam, perfecting his classical training and returned to Switzerland in 1996. Shortly after his return he set up the second generation of Sam Singers with Vera Ehrensperger, Lilian Salah Eddine, Sandra Nickl and Reto Hofstetter, all of them classic singers as well. The Sam Singers performed at student parties, proms, corporate and private events through out Switzerland. All the while, Sämi Zünd's classical baritone career flourished as well.

Sämi continued:

"In 1998 came our chance for national recognition. Swiss Television produced a one time, evening filling program called "Waisch no?", "Do you remember?" It was a nostalgia talk and music show with prominent Swiss entertainers and celebrities present, including Pepe Lienhard, then already a well known Swiss band leader. We sang a medley of songs which were popular during the "Landi" (National Exposition of 1939). Some were compositions by Swiss composer Arthur Beul and played by Teddy Stauffer and his Original Teddies and the young Geschwister Schmid, later known as the Smeed Trio.

"At the end of that concert, while the audience was still applauding our performance, Pepe came up to me and told me, that we were just what he had been looking for. This was a turning point in our career, as from that time on the Sam Singers were often featured on different national TV shows.

"Pepe invited me to submit our charts. Shortly thereafter we met and The Sam Singers were contracted to accompany the 1999 tour of the Swiss Army Big Band which ran under the title "Swing for Kids". We sang: "On the Sunny Side Of The Street" a medley with "Goody, Goody - "Whistle While You Work" - "A Tisket, A Tasket" and "The Flat Foot Floogee" as well as "I'll Never Smile Again" of Pied Pipers fame. All of the songs were made popular in Switzerland and Germany already during the late 30s and early 40s by Teddy Stauffer and his Original Teddies.

As a result of this tour through Switzerland, which included also a rare gala performance at the Swiss Embassy in Berlin, and due to thousands of CDs sold, The Sam Singers were now established in Switzerland."

Another positive development came up in 2002. In preparation for concerts at the "Swiss Expo" (Swiss National Exposition) which was held in various cities in the French part: Biel, Murten and Neuenburg. The Swiss Army Big Band hosted a US Army Big Band and the Big Band of the Bundeswehr (German Army) at the open air arena in Biel.

*"I approached Pepe Lienhard with the idea of forming an all male group made up of professional singers, who, like the musician of the Army Big Band, would perform their annual camp tour with the band. Pepe agreed and I came up with the **swing4you** - Christof Breitenmoser, Tobias Pestalozzi, Michael Raschle and myself. While we keep previous material in the repertoire, we also feature many hits by The Four Freshmen and covers in German by the Jochen Brauer Sextet. By the way, I own practically all records ever produced by the Four Freshmen and maintain good contacts with Jochen Brauer.*

MAX: "It was during 1999 when I met Sämi Zünd at a concert by the Swiss Army Big Band. As I have a weakness for bass and baritone voices, I took an immediate liking to Sämi and his group. They brought back memories of the years after 1954 when I was a young immigrant in New York and listened to all those beautiful songs of the 30s and 40s on local radio stations.

SAM: "I wondered out loud: "Why did you not enter a solo career as "crooner" as well, parallel to the classical career?"

"Of course I would be interested in a career as crooner, I would love that. I have already produced an 80 minute DVD Tribute to Sinatra with the successful Big Band Kanti Wattwil, which is directed by Martin Winiger. (The Big Band of the State College of the Canton of St. Gallen, Wattwil.) The DVD has sold very well. I have also done solo concerts of popular songs of the 30s, accompanied by the Kammerphilharmonie Graubünden, a very active and known orchestra in the north eastern part of Switzerland. I am fascinated

by the arrangements and by the high quality of the recordings made seventy to eighty years ago and most of them done in one cut. They were good songs with good texts and swingy melodies. It was musical entertainment of the finest and music, people wanted to hear and still like to hear, when they can.

"But times have changed and I have to be practical. There is no big demand for "crooners" in the style of the 30s and 40s, where as I am very happy with the demand for Lied recitals and for concerts by my vocal groups."

MAX: "It is exactly this quality, Sämi talked about, that makes the recordings of Sämi's groups outstanding. Add to it, that these tunes are still in vivid memory of listeners and concert audiences today. European wide known hits, made popular by Teddy Stauffer and his Original Teddies between 1935 and 1942, or Swiss popular songs like "S'Margritli" (Margarita), "I Han En Schatz Am Schöne Zürisee" (I have a sweetheart on beautiful Lake Zurich) which were standards of the Smeed Trio during their concerts, radio and TV appearances in the USA and hits by the Hazy Osterwald Sextet, a Swiss show band that was touring Europe during the 50s and 60s and was featured on

SWING 4 YOU

many USO tours.

SAM: "To stay ahead of the game, we need be flexible, innovative and bear in mind the different kinds of audiences for which we perform. We use material that was originally done by the Comedian Harmonists" which is also part of the repertoire of Max Raabe and his Palast Orchestra. These songs call up memories in older audiences and songs out of the hit list of the Manhattan Transfer are welcome with the younger sets. All in all we have 200 pieces in the repertoire of the Sam Singers, 20 for The Voices and 50 for swing4you."

Based on interviews with other Swiss musicians and entertainers such as Hazy Osterwald, Pepe Lienhard, Willy Schmid, Dani Felber, all of whom have been featured in other books by Richard Grudens, I learned that to lead a Big Band or to prevail as entertainer in Switzerland is a tough undertaking and not really possible without exposure to neighbouring German speaking countries. With a population of 7 million, Switzerland is just too small to provide enough income to survive. Expansion into Germany and Austria is a must. That is a fact for all who seek a place in the world of entertainment.

I wanted to know which activities keep him busy during a "average" week.

SAMI: "As I said, Max, I have to be versatile and it cannot work without the active support by Theresia, who is a professional musician and piano teacher. Up front are the education of our two sons and the sharing of household chores. I write arrangements exclusively for my own groups, have a part-time job teaching voice at the Musikhochschule Zurich and the Musikschule and Conservatory of Zurich, covering oratories, opera, Lied, Swing, Chansons, popular songs, and lead vocal ensembles. It takes quite a bit of planning. I.E this week:

Monday: Morning - practice Lied Recital; Afternoon - spend time with our sons; Evening - Meeting with School board.
Tuesday: Morning - Rehearsal with Sam Singers; Afternoon - household chores, homework and play with sons; Evening - free (!)
Wednesday: All day - Teaching; Evening - Private event, Chansons at Zunfthaus zur Waage.

Thursday: *All day - Teaching; Evening - Rehearsal with Orchestra and Choir.*

Friday: *Morning - Office work, I am my own agent and work with a manager ;Afternoon - household chores, spend time with sons, rehears for evening concert at Berner Münster (Cathedral of Berne).*
Satuday: *Morning - Private lesson - Afternoon and evening prepare for and perform an oratory in the Cathedral of St. Gallen.*

Sunday: *Matinee with Swiss Army Big Band and swing4you in the KKL - Kultur und Kongresszentrum Luzern.*

"You see, I am constantly on the move. That requires discipline and concentration, like learning text by heart while riding the train to work. I have to stay fit. There's no room for alcohol, late nights or excessive sports. Instead it's exercising my breathing technique and my vocal cords in order to be able to sing the different singing styles.

I am fortunate to receive enough requests and have enough engagements. The fact, that group members too need pursue their own careers is sometimes a handicap which results in turning down requests. This is also a reason, why we have not tried to expand into the cruise entertainment business.

With my schedule as it is, there is hardly room for expansion into neighbouring countries, not to mention to the United States. Although the interest is there.
Just call me … !"

Prospects for more international activities have opened up, though. During the 2011 Swiss Tour of Pepe Lienhard's Big Band (not to be mistaken with the Swiss Army Big Band, which is *directed* by Pepe) Sämi, came up with a new formation - The Voices with Stephanie Suhner, Brigitte Wullimann, Micha Dettwyler and Sämi himself. They do more recent nostalgic material. For instance: songs by the Manhattan Transfer or the New York Voices. Pepe brought Udo Jürgens, best known singer-composer in German language popular music, to on of the concerts and Sämi relates with fire in his eyes …

"…both Pepe and Udo were excited. As a result, we will be

joining Udo Jürgens with the Pepe Lienhard Orchestra on a 34 concert tour throughout German speaking Europe. The Tour will last from January through March 2012. We will perform before crowds of up to 8'000 to 10'000 persons a night. Many concerts are already close to being sold out!"

The conversation with Sämi confirmed that the development of the singing groups has a great deal of similarities with the development of popular music during the swing era. The Zenith was reached toward the end of the 50s, beginning 60s. The audiences of The Mills Brothers, The Modernaires, The Pied Pipers, The Andrews Sisters, The Ames Brothers, The McGuire Sisters, The Four Freshmen, The Hi-Lo's, The King Sisters, he Ray Conniff Singers have aged along with their favoured singers, or even passed away. The younger crowds need to be introduced to those melodies and harmonies and recent successes by groups like The Sam Singers, swing4you and The Voices, supported by renowned entertainers such as Udo Jürgens and Bands like the Pepe Lienhard Orchestra, the Pepe Lienhard Big Band and the Swiss Army Big Band, directed by Pepe indicate that just like big band music of the swing era, groups which

THE VOICES

perform close harmony with a swingy and jazzy sound will prevail as well.

For details on Sämi Zünd and related orchestras look up: www.samuelzuend.ch, www.samsingers.ch, www.swing4you.ch, www.thevoices.ch, www.pepelienhard.ch, www.udojuergens.de.

PEPE LIENHARD

Pepe started his career as bandleader at the young age of 17, at the Zurich Jazz Festival in 1963 leading a big band of 28 musicians, an event he won in 1965 and 1969 with his Sextet. At the European Song contest in 1977, The Pepe Lienhard Band was a finalist with Pepe's innovative Swiss Lady, including an alphorn solo. The same year The Pepe Lienhard Sextet became associated with Udo Jürgens and as of 1982, Udo is being accompanied by the Pepe Lienhard Big Band. (*4) See insert on Udo Jürgens below.

TEDDY STAUFFER

Teddy was borne in Berne, Switzerland in 1909 and died in Acapulco in 1991. He played saxophone and violin and in 1928 formed the first internationally known Swiss Dance Orchestra bearing his name: *Teddy Stauffer and The Original Teddies*. After several years of engagements on ocean liners, he came to Berlin on April 1, 1936 and soon thereafter produced the first "Telefunken Record". During the Olympic Games of 1936 in Berlin, the "Teddies" became known to a large public by playing well known American standards of that time, such as: "September in the Rain," "Never in a Million Years," "Pop Corn," "Boo Hoo," "Limehouse Blues," "Ski Yodel," and of course German songs of that period. In 1939, at the outbreak of World War II he moved his Orchestra to Zurich, established himself and the Teddies as the band which introduced Miller and Goodman music to a ever growing number of people, thirsting for American Swing and Jazz . Teddy Stauffer understood to make popular Swiss songs into swingy ditties. He left the Teddies and Switzerland in 1941 to move via Canada and the United States to Acapulco in Mexico, where he was active in the hotel business, played music, got a few movie roles and was married at times to Hollywood movie stars Hedy Lamarr and had a love affair with Barbara Hutton.

Hazy Osterwald

Hazy and his Sextet is featured in Richard Grudens' The Music Men.

Udo Jürgens

Udo was born in Austria in 1934 and became Austrian-Swiss dual citizen in 2007. He is one of the most significant entertainers in the German speaking world. His repertoire stretches from hit songs, to chansons and pop music. Up to date over 100 million records and albums have been sold and during his career he has composed more than 900 songs, many of them endurable hits (wikipedia).

Jochen Brauer Sextet

Joachim "Jochen" Brauer, borne in 1929 in Görlitz, Germany is a German Jazz musician, playing alto, tenor, baritone saxophones, flute, clarinet, accordion and is an accomplished arranger and bandleader. As so many other young musicians, he too took to jazz and popular music after World War II and played in jazz and dance combos through out Germany. Despite his love for jazz music, he turned towards popular entertainment and in 1958, Willy Berk-

THE SAM SINGERS

ing leader of his own dance as well as TV orchestra enabled Brauer to appear with his quartet on nationwide television. Following this first success he enlarged his combo to sextet and was seen and heard in many German television quiz shows as well as evening filling music programs.

To enrich the musical programs, four of the six musicians doubled as the Jochen Brauer Quartet. They followed arrangements of known American male groups and set German texts to them. The Quartet sang also original German pop songs, which Brauer arranged similar to the Four Freshmen sound. That FF-Swing brought much success in sales of records as well as in live concerts. The Jochen Brauer Quartet was one of the popular "close harmony" groups in Germany and the first Quartet in Europe that performed in the "Four Freshmen" manner. As time passed, the taste of the public, or shall we say, the strategy of the recording industry changed, and the call for Brauer's Sextet diminished similar to what The Hazy Osterwald Sextet experience after their huge successes during the 50s and 60s.

Don Kennedy of Big Band Jump and Swiss Radio's Max Wirz

Over a period of 40 years Jochen Brauer produced 15 albums and about 70 singles. For the 40th anniversary of his first appearance on German TV, The Jochen Brauer Sextet issued a jubilee CD *Sing + Swing*, Brauer as a musician and his Jochen Brauer Quartet were seen on stage and TV with internationally known stars such as Gerry Mulligan, Kenny Rogers, Tony Christie as well as best known European singers and entertainers Harald Juhnke, Peter Alexander, Katja Ebstein und Udo Jürgens. The Smeed Trio is featured in Richard Grudens STARDUST - The Bible of the Big Bands.

Thanks to Don Kennedy and Max Wirz for helping keep our kind of music alive. Richard Grudens

THE PUPPINI SISTERS

So far, we have examined the lives of a fair number of singing groups and if we're fortunate enough the girl and boy singing groups shall continue to sing til' the end of time.

We can begin the future with the beautiful and talented voices of today with The Puppini Sisters.

The Puppini Sisters deliver the songs we all love from the 1920s to the present, emulating the famed Andrews Sisters of the swing era. The girls admit they have also been influenced by the earlier Boswell Sisters, and Fred Astaire and Ginger Rogers.

The trio began in 2004 with Marcella Puppini (from Italy) and Stephanie O'Brien and Kate Mullins (from England). They are currently supported by a musical trio directed by guitarist Blake Wilner and Henrik Jensen on double bass. Their debut recording was, naturally, a copy of the Andrews Sisters landmark "Boogie Woogie Bugle Boy," although they sing it a trifle faster than the original.

I remember Bette Midler singing that tune ala the Andrews' version and there was a possibility of Midler being cast as Patty Andrews in a proposed film about the lives of the Andrews girls. Patty said it never came to fruition. Too bad!

But we now have the Puppini Sisters and who knows? Also check out our Three Belles, another Andrews Sisters trio!

On their second album the Puppini girls are writing original songs. The girls have also appeared on the sound track of the television series *Grey's Anatomy* and *Chuck*. They have appeared in London on many shows of every kind.

So now we have another Andrews Sisters style trio who can sing a capella, close harmony, swing, pop and jazz.

Welcome Puppini Sisters. We need your voices.

Lisa Vemco at Shepherds Bush Empire: " The Puppini Sisters

may look to the past, but they sound swell in the here and now."

SINGLES
"Boogie Woogie Bugle Boy" (2006)
"Jingle Bells/Silent Night (Little Match Seller)" (December 2006)
"Spooky" (2007)
"Crazy in Love" (2007)
"Jilted" (2008)
"Apart of Me" with The Real Tuesday Weld (2008)

Acknowledgments

My heart goes out to many in the preparation of this work. Besides the groups listed and covered here, there had to be hundreds more to be considered for inclusion, but then the book would have exceeded one thousand pages and maybe one more thousand days of preparation. We apologize to them all.

I have interviewed many individual members of many groups, or those associated with them, over many years for other projects including the fourteen books I have put together that feature the singers, musicians, and arrangers from the 1930s to the 1990s, and even beyond.

Many have been interviewed by others and have shared their files. For many others I have relied upon autobiographies and biographies, and individuals who have known some subjects first hand, as well as endless magazine and newspaper articles and even some internet sources.

First I must thank those I have personally interviewed over the years with respect to our subject of group singing: Patty Andrews, Kathryn Crosby, Frankie Laine, John Mills,Sr., Dan Clemson, Anthony DiFlorio III, Jerry Vale, Red Norvo, Jo Stafford, Maxene Andrews, Nancy Knorr, Warren Covington, Larry O'Brien, all the Lennon Sisters, Julia Rich, Alan Brown, Frankie Dee, Prof. Richard Grudzinski, Connie Haines, Beryl Davis, Rhonda Fleming, Jane Russell, Mel Tormé, Bob Hope, John Primerano, Brian Wilson, Diana Ross, Max Wirz, the Three Belles, Pete Seeger, Lee Hale, Sybil Jason, Van Alexander, Rosemary Clooney, Lynn Roberts, Jack Ellsworth, Tex Beneke, Joe Franklin, Ervin Drake, Ray Eberle, Margaret Whiting, Helen O'Connell, and William B. Williams.

Sure, I put the text together, but my wife Madeline formatted and edited the contents, set the photos, designed the cover and kept me going until the last word of this work was complete. She gets the Nobel.

Richard Grudens
Stonybrook, New York - February 2012

We are grateful to:

Kathryn Crosby

Frank E. Dee

Al Petrone

Ben Grisafi

Jack Ellsworth

Max Wirz

Alan Brown

Al Monroe

Jack Lebo

Bob Incagliato

Robert Grudens

Madeline Grudens

BIBLIOGRAPHY

Alberts, Al. Al's Song: The Words and Music of my World, Port Charlotte, Florida. Harmony House (2004)

Clooney, Rosemary with Raymond Strait. This for Remembrance. Chicago, Illinois: Playboy Press. (1977)

Eder, Bruce. All Music.com. Vocal Group Hall of Fame Foundation. Sharon, Pa. January 1997 to Present. Bob Crosby President/CEO; Tony Butala, Chairman/Founder

Grime, Kitty. Jazz Voices. London, England. Quartet Books Limited (1983)

Grudens, Richard and Various sources. The Beach Boys-Playing Timeless Music-Sacramento, California. California Highway Patrol Magazine, July (1993)

Lax, Roger and Frederick Smith. The Great Song Thesaurus. New York, NY, Oxford University Press, (1984)

Murrells, Joseph. Million Selling Records. New York, NY., Arco Publishing Co. (1978)

Palmer, Tony. All You Need is Love. New York, NY, Gross Publishers (1976)

Slide, Anthony. Great Radio Personalities. New York, N.Y. Vestal Press (1982)

Tormé, Mel. It Wasn't All Velvet. An Autobiography. New York, NY Viking Penquin (1988)

Welk, Lawrence. With Bernice McGeehan. Wunnerful, Wunnerful. Englewood Cliffs, NJ. Prentice-Hall, Inc. (1971)

Wikipedia.org. Available general and various collectible information and recording data and dates where required and where listed. (2011-2012)

Wiener, Allen J. The Beatles-The Ultimate Recording Guide, Holbrook, Mass. Bob Adams Inc. (1986)

Additional Titles by Richard Grudens
www.RichardGrudens.com
Explore the Golden Age of Music when the Big Bands and their vocalists reigned on the radio and all the great stages of America.

Sinatra Singing

This is a book about SINATRA SINGING. Inside you will meet his arrangers, conductors, musicians, songwriters, the songs, and all of the singers who were influenced by him, over many years, from Bennett to Damone and many others, technical notes on bel canto, breathing, vocal cord problems, conquering stage fright, song polls taken over the years, singing instructions, the albums, and more.

Mr. Rhythm - A Tribute to Frankie Laine

This book celebrates the life and times of Frankie Laine: the trials, the rejections, the heartbreak, the hard work, and eventual victory punctuated by all the complexities that make up the ubiquitous profession called show business. The foreword is written by one of America's greatest films stars, five time Academy Award actor and director, Clint Eastwood, an admirer and true friend of Frankie Laine.

Star*Dust - The Bible of the Big Bands

Star*Dust is America's best and biggest book of the Big Bands with 700 pages and 650 photos that cover the glorious years of the best music ever played and featuring the musical giants of the twentieth century: Glenn Miller, Artie Shaw, Les Brown, Stan Kenton, the Dorsey's, Woody Herman, Duke Ellington, Count Basie, Harry James, and every band, musician, vocalist that ever played or recorded.

The Italian Crooners Bedside Companion

The Italian Crooners is a compendium of your favorite Italian male singers, presented in a shower of photos, stories, favorite recipes and selected discographies, with a foreword by Jerry Vale.

Chattanooga Choo Choo - The Life and Times of the World Famous Glenn Miller Orchestra

Commemorating the 100th Anniversary of Glenn Miller's life and the 60th Anniversary of his disappearance over the English Channel in late 1944, we present the tribute book Glenn Miller fans all over the world have been waiting for.

Bing Crosby - Crooner of the Century

Here is the quintessential Bing Crosby tribute, documenting the story of Crosby's colorful life, family, recordings, radio and television shows, and films; the amazing success story of a wondrous career that pioneered popular music spanning generations and inspiring countless followers.

The Spirit of Bob Hope:

Tracing Bob's charmed life from his early days in Cleveland to his worldwide fame earned in vaudeville, radio, television and films and his famous wartime travels for the USO unselfishly entertaining our troops. The best Bob Hope book with testimonials from his friends and a foreword by Jane Russell.

Jerry Vale - A Singer's Life

The wondrous story of Jerry's life as a kid from teeming Bronx streets of the 1940s to his legendary appearances in the great theatrical venues of America and his three triumphant Carnegie Hall concerts, with appearances at New York's Copacabana, whose magnificent voice has beautifully interpreted the 20th Century's most beautiful love songs

Snootie Little Cutie - The Connie Haines Story

The story of big band singer, Connie Haines, who sang shoulder to shoulder with Frank Sinatra in the bands of Harry James and Tommy Dorsey, and for years on the Abbott & Costello radio show, and who is still singing today.

Jukebox Saturday Night

The final book in the series; interviews with Artie Shaw, Les Brown and Doris Day, Red Norvo, Les Paul, Carmel Quinn, stories about Glenn Miller and the Dorsey Brothers, songwriters Ervin Drake ("I Believe," "It was a Very Good Year,") and Jack Lawrence ("Linda," "Tenderly,") and a special about all the European bands past and present.

Sally Bennett's Magic Moments

by RICHARD GRUDENS

This book is filled with extraordinary events in the life of Sally Bennett who established the Big Band Hall of Fame and Museum in West Palm Beach, Florida. Sally is a composer, musician, playwright, model, actress, poet, radio and TV personality and the author of the book *Sugar and Spice.*

The Music Men

A Companion to "The Song Stars," about the great men singers with foreword by Bob Hope; interviews with Tony Martin, Don Cornell, Julius LaRosa, Jerry Vale, Joe Williams, Johnny Mathis, Al Martino, Guy Mitchell, Tex Beneke and others.

The Song Stars

A neat book about all the girl singers of the Big Band Era and beyond: Doris Day, Helen Forrest, Kitty Kallen, Rosemary Clooney, Jo Stafford, Connie Haines, Teresa Brewer, Patti Page and Helen O'Connell and many more.

The Best Damn Trumpet Player

Memories of the Big Band Era, interviews with Benny Goodman, Harry James, Woody Herman, Tony Bennett, Buddy Rich, Sarah Vaughan, Lionel Hampton, Frankie Laine, Patty Andrews and others.

Visit Richard on Facebook and follow him on his blog: RichardGrudensBlog.blogspot.com.

Order Books On-line at:
www.RichardGrudens.com
Or Fax or Call Your Order in:
Celebrity Profiles Publishing - Div. Edison & Kellogg
Box 344, Stonybrook, New York 11790
Phone: (631) 862-8555 — Fax: (631) 862-0139
Email: celebpro4@aol.com

Title	Price	Qty:
The Best Damn Trumpet Player	$15.95	
The Song Stars	$17.95	
The Music Men	$17.95	
Jukebox Saturday Night	$17.95	
Magic Moments - The Sally Bennett Story	$17.95	
Snootie Little Cutie - Connie Haines Story	$17.95	
Jerry Vale - A Singer's Life - *SOLD OUT*	$19.95	
The Spirit of Bob Hope - One Hundred Years - One Million Laughs	$19.95	
Bing Crosby - Crooner of the Century	$19.95	
Chattanooga Choo Choo The Life and Times of the World Famous Glenn Miller Orchestra	$21.95	
The Italian Crooners Bedside Companion	$21.95	
Star*Dust - The Bible of the Big Bands	$39.95	
Mr. Rhythm - A Tribute to Frankie Laine	$29.95	
Sinatra Singing	$29.95	
Perfect Harmony	$29.95	
TOTALS		

Name:

Address:

City:	State:	Zip:

Include $4.00 for Priority Mail (2 days arrival time) for up to 2 books. Enclose check or money order.

FOR CREDIT CARDS, Please fill out below form completely:

Card No.:   Security Code:

Name on Card:

Exp. Date:

Signature:

Card Type (Please Circle): Visa — Amex — Discover — Master Card

Phone number in case of a problem with your card:_____